LISTENING WITH THE FOURTH EAR

D1598707

NEW INTERNATIONAL LIBRARY OF GROUP ANALYSIS

Series Editor: Earl Hopper

Other titles in the Series

LISTENING WITH THE FOURTH EAR
Unconscious Dynamics in Analytic Group Psychotherapy

Leonard Horwitz

KARNAC

First published in 2014 by
Karnac Books Ltd
118 Finchley Road
London NW3 5HT

British Library Cataloguing in Publication Data

A C.I.P. for this book is available from the British Library

ISBN-13: 978-1-78220-017-8

Typeset by V Publishing Solutions Pvt Ltd., Chennai, India

Printed in Great Britain

www.karnacbooks.com

For June
beloved life partner
and
Marj, Lynne, and Robert

CONTENTS

ACKNOWLEDGEMENTS

A number of colleagues and friends were of help in improving the quality of the final version of the book. Throughout the writing, Howard Kibel, close friend and colleague dating back to his Topeka days, served as reader and sounding board on much of the content. Priscilla Kauff, long an associate and friend in AGPA, read the theoretical section and offered wise suggestions for improving the clarity of the ideas as well as encouragement to persevere with this project. I am indebted to Vic Schermer, also a colleague of AGPA, for his detailed critique of areas of his expertise, especially the chapters on group-as-a-whole. Don Colson, a loyal friend who worked closely with me at the Menninger Clinic in Topeka for several decades, contributed his knowledge of psycho-therapy, both individual and group, to improving the text. My friend Walter Stone helped to strengthen the section on the contribution of self psychology. And both Molyn Leszcz and John Schlapobersky offered critiques on my last chapter comparing interpersonal and group-as-a-whole models. My daughter Marjorie cheerfully used her librarian skills in finding needed articles and tracking down obscure references. Finally, I wish to extend my thanks to Earl Hopper whose wisdom and critical eye were invaluable in improving the overall quality of the final product.

ABOUT THE AUTHOR

Leonard Horwitz is a Training and Supervising Analyst with the Greater Kansas City Psychoanalytic Institute. He has served as president of the American Group Psychotherapy Association and was a frequent presenter at workshops and panels.

He was a major figure in pioneering the introduction of group psychotherapy at the Menninger Clinic in Topeka and served as director of that program for several years. He initiated the Menninger group psychotherapy, continuing education workshops offered to a national audience. The author of many articles on group treatment, Dr. Horwitz served for many years on the editorial boards of the International Journal of Group Psychotherapy as well as the International Journal of Applied Psychoanalysis. His article on the inductive, group centered approach won a place in the AGPA publication, *Classics in Group Psychotherapy*. He earned a B.S. degree from Queens College in New York City and a Ph.D. from New York University. Following his graduate training he moved to Topeka, Kansas, joined the staff of the Menninger Clinic, and shortly thereafter began his psychoanalytic training at the Topeka Institute for Psychoanalysis, eventually being appointed training analyst. He participated with several Menninger colleagues in working on the Psychotherapy Research Project out of which grew his book *Clinical Prediction in Psychotherapy*. He directed a research project on the treatment of borderline patients which resulted in the book which he co-authored with his colleagues, *Borderline Personality Disorder: Tailoring the Treatment to the Patient*.

NEW INTERNATIONAL LIBRARY OF GROUP ANALYSIS FOREWORD

Earl Hopper

Psychoanalytical group psychotherapy and group analysis live within a broad, complex church containing many models of theory and practice. This gives vitality and creativity to the entire project. However, dialogue about its central themes is often limited and superficial, characterised by projective and introjective identification and myth making. Clearly, there is considerable scope for synthesis, integration, and development. In this context, I am very pleased to include *Listening with the Fourth Ear: Unconscious Dynamics in Analytic Group Psychotherapy* by Leonard Horwitz, Ph.D., one of the fathers of psychoanalytical group psychotherapy, in the New International Library of Group Analysis.

Dr Leonard Horwitz is one of the first psychoanalysts in the United States whose core training was in psychology rather than in medicine and psychiatry. Having become fascinated by the study of group dynamics, and having recognised the need for alternative kinds of psychoanalytically informed treatment, Dr Horwitz developed a theoretical orientation and set of clinical techniques based on his conviction that psychoanalytical group psychotherapy must, virtually by definition, regard the treatment of individual members of a group as paramount. However, the group and group setting offered special dynamics that must be understood and utilised in the service of therapy for individuals. In other words, for Horwitz the group is not a space and location for diluted psychoanalytical work by the therapist/leader of the group with each of the individual members of it. Hence, the group is not an obstacle or an impediment to psychoanalytical work, but a potential source of insights into the unconscious functioning of the members of it, both intra-psychically and inter-psychically (or inter-personally).

Leonard Horwitz draws on the study of group mentality and the matrix of the group, as well as the study of valence, role suction, and personification, as sources of insight into the way individuals partici-pate in the life of the group. Although deeply informed by the work of Sutherland, Bion, Ezriel, and others associated with the Tavistock Clinic, he has also been influenced by Foulkes and his colleagues within the Group Analytic Society International and the Institute of Group Analysis (London). Dr Horwitz regards many of the differences in their work to be a matter of emphasis and focus, perhaps based on the narcis-sism of small differences among our founders and their associates. For example, he gives special importance to the study and interpretation of various forms of the transference to the therapist/leader of the group, other members of the group, and to the group-as-a-whole, not to men-tion its social context. Schooled in both the Freudian and Kleinian tradi-tions, he has also been influenced by various members of the Group of Independent Psychoanalysts in Britain (Hopper, 2003; Rayner, 1991), as well as object relations thinkers (Scharff & Savege Scharff, 2005), and self-psychologists in the United States (Stone, 2009).

A frequent presenter at workshops and panels at Annual AGPA con-ferences and at meetings throughout the United States and elsewhere, Dr Horwitz is the author of many articles on group treatments. For many years he was a member of the editorial board of the *International Journal of Group Psychotherapy* and the editorial board of *The Interna-tional Journal of Applied Psychoanalysis*. He participated with several colleagues from the Menninger Clinic in their psychotherapy research project, from which grew his book *Clinical Prediction in Psychotherapy* (Horwitz, 1974). He also directed a research project on the treatment of borderline patients, which resulted in *Borderline Personality Disorder: Tailoring the Treatment to the Patient* (Horwitz et al., 1996).

Several of his professional articles have received special recogni-tion in being chosen as chapters in professional books edited by oth-ers. His article (Horwitz, 1977) on what he has termed his "inductive, group centered approach" as a form of psychoanalytical group therapy was selected for publication in AGPA's *Classics in Group Psychotherapy* (McKenzie, 1992). His article on projective identification (Horwitz, 1983) was the product of his struggle to discover the differences between projective identification and more straightforward projection. It was written when the concept was barely known in the field of group analysis in the United States, but it is still greatly appreciated.

Horwitz earned a BSc degree from Queens College in New York City, and a PhD from New York University. In 1954 he joined the staff of the Menninger Clinic in Topeka, Kansas. Shortly thereafter, he began his psychoanalytic training at the Topeka Institute for Psychoanalysis, eventually becoming a training and supervising analyst. He was a major figure in pioneering the introduction of psychoanalytic group therapy at the Menninger Clinic, and served as Director of that programme from 1970–1978. He initiated the Menninger Group Psychotherapy Continuing Education workshops, which in turn were offered to a national audience. He served as the Chairman of the Program Committee of the Annual Conference of the American Group Psychotherapy Association, and then as its President from 1984–1986.

As a result of his participation in human relations conferences, both at Bethel and at the Tavistock, Horwitz became interested in the dynamics of organizations. His forty-seven years at the Menninger Clinic gave him an opportunity to observe how different styles of leadership affected an organisation. When, during a period of crisis at the Menninger Clinic, Dr Karl Menninger was forced to resign as Chief of Staff, a vacuum of leadership occurred, and the staff became active in asserting their wishes. Horwitz was elected President of the Professional Staff Organization. Together, they were successful in democratising the organisation, primarily by getting the administration to adopt a policy of using search committees before appointing applicants to key administrative positions. For Horwitz, group therapy is a major vehicle for producing adaptive behavioural change, particularly in neutralising the pervasive narcissism that he regards as part of the human condition, which is as true of psychotherapists as it is of their patients, In fact, he is particularly sensitive to the clinical problems caused by the narcissism of psychotherapists.

Dr Horwitz is pleased to acknowledge the importance of his close association with Dr Jock Sutherland, the Medical Director of the Tavistock Clinic. For more than twenty-five years, Sutherland, who was a regular consultant to the Menninger Clinic, was his teacher, mentor, and friend. He also acknowledges his indebtedness to his colleague the late Dr Ramon Ganzarain for stimulating his interest in object relations theory and practice. For Horwitz, object relations thinking is associated with the shift from a one-person to a two-person psychology, which is embodied in the theory and clinical practice of group analysis and in relational psychology and psychoanalysis more generally (Hopper & Weinberg, 2011; Tubert-Oklander, 2014).

More personally, Leonard Horwitz holds liberal political values that can be described in the United States as "left of centre", which is perhaps typical of group analysts in the United States. He and his late wife June were avid supporters of the Civil Rights Movement. They supported President Barack Obama and his various policies, especially those connected with "Obamacare". He believes that the government has the responsibility for providing its citizens adequate healthcare, sufficient food and nutrition, and the opportunity to pursue a decent education through which they are most likely to able to fulfil their potential.

Although Dr Horwitz has been influenced more by the work of colleagues who were at the Tavistock Clinic than by that of Foulkes and his associates, he has been especially interested in many of the preoccupations of Foulkesian group analysis. For example, he appreciates the importance of analysing vertical and horizontal transferences. He understands processes of "equivalence", that is, the unconscious recreation of the dynamic matrix of large organisations and the foundation matrix of the wider society within the dynamic matrix of smaller groups, including those who meet for the purpose of therapy. Thus, he is sensitive to the ways in which the dynamics of a hospital influence the dynamics of group therapy within it. He is particularly interested in the "social unconscious", although he does not use the term. Most notably, he recognises that it is inevitable that a group leader/therapist/conductor will change in the course of the meetings of a group. He also recognises the importance of continuing training, supervision, and consultation, and when necessary further personal psychotherapy for each of us.

This book is not only a textbook in psychoanalytical group therapy and group analysis, it is also a historical document. The work of Leonard Horwitz, Ph.D., has shaped the contours of our discipline. This book warrants study by both students and colleagues alike.

Earl Hopper
Editor of the New International Library of Group Analysis

References

Hopper, E. (2003). *The Social Unconscious: Selected Papers*. London: Jessica Kingsley Publishers.

Hopper, E. & Weinberg, H. (Eds) (2011). *The Social Unconscious in Persons, Groups, and Societies: Volume I: Mainly Theory*. London: Karnac.

Horwitz, L. (1974). *Clinical Prediction in Psychotherapy*. New York: Jason Aronson.

Horwitz, L. (1977). A group-centered approach to group psychotherapy. *International Journal of Group Psychotherapy, 27*: 423–439.

Horwitz, L. (1983). Projective identification in dyads and groups. *International Journal of Group Psychotherapy, 33*: 259–279.

Horwitz, L. (1992). A group-centered approach to group psychotherapy. In: McKenzie, R. (Ed.) *Classics in Group Psychotherapy*. New York: Guilford Press.

Horwitz, L., Gabbard, G. O., Allen, J. G., Frieswyk, S. F., Colson, D. C., Newsom, G. E., & Coyne, L. (1996). *Borderline Personality Disorder: Tailoring the Therapy to the Patient*. Washington, D.C: American Psychiatric Press.

McKenzie, I. (Ed.) (1992). *Classics in Group Psychotherapy*. New York: The Guilford Press.

Rayner, E. (1991). *The Independent Mind in British Psychoanalysis*. London: Free Association Books.

Scharff, J. S. & Scharff, D. E. (2005). *The Primer of Object Relations: Second Edition*. Lanham, MD: Jason Aronson.

Stone, W. N. (2009). *Contributions of Self Psychology to Group Psychotherapy: Selected Papers*. London: Karnac.

Tubert-Oklander, J. (2014). *The One and the Many*. London: Karnac.

PREFACE

I have had an abiding interest in group psychotherapy since my first year in graduate school when I was a trainee in a Veterans Administration hospital and heard several introductory lectures by a charismatic and inspired teacher, Dr. Wilfred Hulse. He was a prominent figure on the New York scene and served as the first president of the Eastern Group Psychotherapy Association.

His enthusiasm for group treatment stimulated me to do a Master's degree dissertation on group therapy with chronic schizophrenic patients. My research involved a highly structured series of group sessions which today would be called a psycho-educational group. (When beginners take a group for the first time, especially without much guidance, they usually tend to introduce excessive structure.) That I undertook this project with little or no supervision speaks more to blissful ignorance than to confidence in my skills. Thankfully this work is now buried deep in the archives of the Graduate School of New York University and will never see the light of day.

But I suspect that my enthusiasm for Dr. Hulse's inspirational teaching also had earlier roots that surfaced during my preadolescence indicating an appreciation of the power of the group. As a sixth grader, I was offended by my teacher's daily bible reading to the class which began each school day. This occurred long before the Supreme Court ruling outlawed prayer in the schools. But I deemed the practice inappropriate and I drew up a petition to the school principal requesting that the ritual be stopped and circulated it quietly among my classmates. Unfortunately my effort did not succeed since my fellow students recognized that they might suffer some untoward consequences and they declined to sign, probably also rescuing me from unnecessary trouble with the school authorities.

Another instance of my appreciation of the influence of peer pressure occurred when I attended summer camp at the age of eleven. I was in a bunk with three other boys, one of whom was a bed-wetter. He was unkindly ridiculed by the two other boys and I made several unsuccessful efforts to get them to cease their harassment. One afternoon siesta period when the counselors were away attending a staff meeting, I rounded up the boys from a few surrounding bunks and conducted a kangaroo court in which I publicly accused the offenders of unacceptable conduct. The group consensus was that the culprits should be censured and the meeting had its desired effect, strengthening my conviction about the persuasive effect of groups.

Following graduate school, I made a move to Topeka and the Menninger Clinic. My interest in group work became dormant for several years as I became involved in learning other aspects of my craft as a clinical psychologist. Group psychotherapy as a developing modality was largely ignored during the 1950s in Topeka. Partly it was the geographical separation from the East Coast where most group psychotherapy activity was focused at that time and partly it was the bias in that era of psychoanalysis against any form of treatment that was not one-on-one. However, in 1958 a group of Menninger Young Turks who had been exposed to group treatment in other locales organized a study group in group psychotherapy and began writing position statements addressed to the clinical decision makers, mainly Dr. Karl Menninger, proposing the initiation of a group therapy program. Despite considerable delay and resistance, both active and passive, our program was authorized and launched in 1960. At that point three of us began psychotherapy groups. A detailed story of that development comprises Chapter Four of this book.

None of us was fully trained in this modality and it became a situation of the blind leading the blind. Roy Menninger was newly arrived from Boston where he had done group work under supervision in his residency. Otto Kemberg joined the staff from Santiago, Chile, bringing some group psychotherapy experience and knowledge of Bion's writings. While this pooling of ideas from a variety of backgrounds was helpful and created a support system and learning environment that enabled work to proceed, it was something of a Tower of Babel experience. We lacked a single unifying model that would permit us to critically evaluate the thinking and interventions that were being used.

The enterprise was changed forever when the Medical Director of the Tavistock Clinic in London, John Sutherland, arrived in the Spring of 1963 to offer a month long seminar in the Tavistock model of group psychotherapy. Along with Henry Ezriel he had pioneered a method based on the seminal thinking of Wilfred Bion whose highly original contributions are still regarded by many as a strong underpinning to the theory of group functioning.

Sutherland's teaching not only provided us with a much needed compass but put the Menninger Clinic in a unique position in this country. The Clinic group therapists were exposed to an orientation that emphasized how to identify the shared group theme that was dominating the group and how it affected each individual's participation. The post-war English therapists became considerably more sophisticated about group dynamics than did their counterparts in the U.S. American group therapy at that time was largely pioneered by Sam Slavson who emphasized a model that might best be described as individual psychotherapy in a group setting. Although there were a number of writers who were cognizant of and interested in the effect of group dynamics on group treatment, such ideas did not gain much ascendancy in the U.S. until the 1980s.

I believe that the Tavistock model that took root at the Menninger Clinic helped to further a movement in the States towards incorporating some form of group centered thinking. Even though the original Tavistock model was modified considerably at Menninger (and at the current Tavistock Clinic), the basic idea of the effect of an underlying group theme had been preserved. In some form, many American group therapists have moved from the individualized treatment of the early years and have come to appreciate the profound influence of group-wide emotions, comparable to the concept of common group tension of the original Tavistock model.

Chapter Six is the core theoretical anchor in this book and reflects my central thinking about the influence of the group-as-a-whole on the way individuals participate. Despite its emphasis on the so-called common group tension, there is never any question in my mind that the goal always remains the treatment of the individual. The thesis is that the individual's treatment in a group is best accomplished not only by understanding the patient's unique issues, but also by identifying and harnessing the powerful group currents that develop in group treatment. This is the viewpoint and perspective that has been the guiding theme of my group work over many years and hopefully makes for a clearly articulated and integrated volume on the subject.

Although I have a strong conviction that an understanding of group dynamics contributes immeasurably to the effectiveness of a group therapist's work, I do not believe that the model I espouse is the only way of treating patients. I fully recognize that therapists who embrace other approaches can also be helpful to their patients. In the concluding Chapter of the book I elaborate on this view and hope to highlight the special advantages of a group centered approach while recognizing the usefulness of a method like the popular peer interaction model.

Pressure on the mental health community to find more cost effective treatments has resulted in increasing use of group psychotherapy by treatment centers and mental health clinicians. The model presented in this book should contribute an important additional dimension to the thinking of practitioners, and hopefully, to the quality of the group treatment offered by mental health professionals.

INTRODUCTION

In the opinion of most group therapists, the professional qualification for doing group treatment is specific training in the theory and practice of this modality, preferably in an accredited training program. The rationale for this position is that in addition to the general knowledge of how to treat patients in individual psychotherapy, there are specific characteristics of groups that require knowledge and skills that are over and above what is required to practice individual therapy. I believe that there is consensus in the field that qualifications for the group therapist consist of training in both individual and group treatment. This book is addressed primarily to both practitioners and students of group psychotherapy. But also among the potential readership, I hope that those professionals who are engaging in group work without specific training would be stimulated to pursue training in this specialty.

Dynamics of small groups

The theme of this book is that a group therapist who understands and uses an understanding of group dynamics in conducting his or her group is able to add a dimension which enhances the understanding and treatment of individual patients in the group. There are a variety of dynamics that typically occur in groups and awareness of them can help the therapist better understand how the group process is impacting each individual patient and vice versa. Possibly the most well-known mechanism in this field is the phenomenon of scapegoating in which affects that are experienced toward one or more individual (such as the therapist) are displaced toward another group member because the latter is a less anxiety-laden target. Scheidlinger (1982), in his AGPA presidential address made it clear that in addition to displacement there is a second mechanism, projection, or possibly projective identification, that often leads to the phenomenon of scapegoating. Thus, when group members are defending against their own unacceptable wishes, they project such feelings onto, and sometimes into, a receptive target and may even attempt to encourage that individual to express these disavowed wishes and affects for them In many cases these targeted persons then become scapegoated by the group.

In the text I have offered a dramatic example of such an event in an experiential group in which I was a participant. Without going into detail, the group was unhappy with the group consultant's unwillingness to countenance any negative feelings toward himself and therefore they "found" a member who was encouraged to express such feelings. Immediately after his criticism of the consultant, and without full awareness of their motives, most members attacked him for his unacceptable behavior and eventually extruded him from the group.

The above vignette was a dramatic demonstration to me of a number of other mechanisms that occur in a group. In the early days of group psychotherapy, Fritz Redl (1949) coined the graphic phrase "role suction" to indicate the power of a group to entice vulnerable individuals into taking the leadership in certain roles that may seem difficult for the other members. This behavior is also referred to as the group seeking a spokesperson to express their unacceptable wishes. The importance of these mechanisms cannot be overstated since they present a distinct trap for both therapist and patient in believing that the susceptible targeted individual is speaking solely for him or herself. Certainly the man who accepted his "assigned" role was not blameless and was demonstrating a propensity for rebelliousness against authority figures. But ignoring the role of the group's projection would be a major error. When the therapist colludes with the group's reaction, he or she also becomes guilty of scapegoating behavior.

Another powerful force in groups is that of "contagion" in which affects resonate around the room with several patients, contributing to the increasing volume and intensity of the emotion. We are all familiar with the unruly mob behavior that occurs when a large group has been provoked by someone's offensive behavior and erupts into a unified, often violent, reaction. These events are often precipitated by such things as police brutality which can fuel a large group's latent anger at being treated abusively. On a smaller scale, contagious reactions in which affects concerning commonly shared issues also occur in a therapy group. An important early contributor to explaining this phenomenon is Bion (1961) who used the mechanism of projective identification to describe how members influence every other member by projecting their affects into the group and attempting to induce the others to think and act in a manner consonant with their personal wishes.

The most common occurrence of such contagion may be seen whenever the boundaries of the group are altered, often for very legitimate reasons. For example, it is quite common for groups to react with mixed emotions when a new member is introduced. On the one hand the newcomer is welcomed, like the new baby in a family, with hope and anticipation that this person will become a valuable contributor to the group. But at the same time there is apprehension about the extent to which the new member might become the therapist's favorite, or might take up too much of the group's time, or turn out to be a misfit who should not have been admitted in the first place. These fantasies are quite common even in well-functioning groups and typically show themselves in subtle and sometimes overt attacks upon the newcomer or the therapist or both. Such reactions become increasingly intense as a result of a contagion effect.

The above mentioned group-specific factors are only a few of the group dynamic mechanisms that group therapists should understand and use in their work. I have omitted a host of other important mechanisms that need attention as well. For example, there is the dynamic of subgrouping Agazarian (1997), anti-therapeutic norms Yalom and Leszcz (2005), as welll as mirroring (Pines, 1982) just to name a few. Individual therapists may intuitively grasp the presence of these dynamics but there is no substitute for systematically learning how they operate in a group setting.

In my view a major dimension in the functioning of groups is the phenomenon of the group-as-a-whole (GAW) which describes a variety of unitary or shared reactions which occur as a result of the contributions of the entire group. Bion's seminal work (1961) on basic assumptions was largely responsible for therapists noticing these reactions and has influenced generations of group therapists in understanding such vicissitudes of groups. These ideas will be explicated at length in the text and form the basis for many group therapy models which come under the umbrella of GAW.

Psychodynamic and psychoanalytic

Critics of psychoanalysis characterize it as antiquated, old fashioned, and a veritable dinosaur. They typically refer to the theory and practice of a century ago when Freud was fashioning what was then a revolutionary new talking treatment. The critics take issue with his biological, drive oriented, and mechanistic developmental theory as well as his great emphasis on the anonymity and "sterile field" concept which the analyst must maintain—all of which have been discarded or modified as the theory and practice of dynamic treatment have evolved. The most recent innovative views in the analytic world are now being expressed by the intersubjective and relational analysts as represented by such writers as Paul Wachtel (2008), Jon Allen (2012), Owen Renik (2006), Morris Eagle (2011) and Irwin Hoffman (1998).

Often overlooked is that classical psychoanalysis is constantly being updated by the contributions of thoughtful therapists who see opportunities to make psychotherapy more user friendly and effective. The underlying precepts of analysis have not been entirely forsaken such as the importance of a dynamic unconscious that helps to understand much behavior as well as the relevance of the patient's relationship to the therapist, both in its transference and therapeutic alliance dimensions. Relational theory has introduced numerous new perspectives that contribute to how therapists understand patient behavior and has proposed interventions that are likely to be more effective in helping the patient deal with themselves and others.

As a result of these new ideas, many analysts and analytically oriented therapists are beginning to refer to their work as psychodynamic rather than psychoanalytic. This change appears to be an effort by many analytic therapists to emphasize that they are not tied to the outmoded views of classical psychoanalysis and to indicate that they are open to the newer, more modern perspectives of psychodynamic treatment.

Some of the major changes that have begun to appear in the past few decades are as follows:

Relational *vs*. Drive theory. The emphasis in classical drive theory represented something of a disconnect between theory and practice insofar as the so-called metapsychology portrayed the developing individual as struggling with instinctual id forces, mainly sexual and aggressive, which needed to be tamed by a maturing ego. The modern theory puts a much greater focus on the child's attachment styles that emerge out of his or her earliest mode of dealing with parental behavior and expectations. These early developmental patterns have been shown to remain rather consistent from childhood to adulthood.

One Person *vs*. Two Person Psychology. A major contribution of the relationalists is their recognition that relationships cannot be understood solely in terms of the intrapsychic structures of the isolated individual. There is now a much greater recognition that people also respond to the stimulation that they receive from others. In fact there is a cyclical give-and-take and an inter-stimulation that typically occurs between individuals which plays a major role in determining behavior. A major change in the field is that the personality of the therapist has now become a major dimension in understanding what transpires in psychotherapy in contrast to the "sterile field" concept of yesteryear.

Intrapsychic *vs*. Interpersonal. The old view that the therapist need only "analyze" and the patient's behavior will automatically change has now been displaced by the necessity to supplement the patient's internal psychology with a greater appreciation of his or her interpersonal patterns. We now are much more cognizant of the patient's role in eliciting, however unconsciously, certain responses from others that are frequently unwanted and maladaptive. Group therapists have long been aware of this fact and individual therapists of a psychodynamic persuasion have now recognized its importance.

Anonymity *vs*. Self disclosure. The shibboleth long observed by analysts with classical background was that the analyst should remain anonymous and under no circumstances reveal details of his personal life. This policy has been modified by a number of relational theorists in the direction of careful, well considered revelations of both the analyst's personal reactions to his work with the patient as well revealing facts about his or her personal life when such revelations are likely to be helpful in moving the therapy forward. No one is calling for an end to a general policy of restraint in the therapist sharing such material but there is a growing consensus about the desirability of offering well chosen, sometimes spontaneous, reactions.

These are some of the theoretical and treatment advances that have taken place over the past few decades that have helped to update and modernize psychoanalysis and psychodynamic psychotherapy, both group and individual. Many, if not most, analysts have welcomed these developments and they bode well for the future of our field.

Bion and beyond

As mentioned earlier, the theme of the book is the advantage of the group therapist thinking about and listening to the group-as-a-whole. I have referred to this view as "listening with the fourth ear". The individual therapist must listen to his patient with the third ear in the sense that he is trying to tune in to the patient's unconscious communications, the latent content versus the manifest content. The group therapist must not only listen for the latent material of the individual but must also be attuned to what Bion referred to as the "group mentality", the commonly shared conflicts, wishes *vs.* fears, the group's basic assumptions. The field long ago moved beyond Bion's view that the group therapist must confine his interpretations to GAW interpretations but many GAW therapists like myself still believe there is an advantage to identifying the theme shared by the whole group even if each individual deals with it in his own idiosyncratic way.

After using the Sutherland and Ezriel approach for several years, I decided to make some modifications which still appear to be more patient friendly without throwing the baby out with the bathwater. Interestingly enough, a recent publication by the current group therapists at the Tavistock Clinic (Garland, 2010) seemed to have moved in the same direction. They describe their method as a combination of the contributions of Bion and Foulkes where Bion's basic assumption thinking still persists but the model has become more flexible in moving freely between individual and group-wide interventions. My particular modification is called the inductive group centered model and is presented in Chapter Six.

The book is divided into four sections: historical, theoretical, clinical, and training. The red thread running through all of this work is the usefulness of a group-as-a-whole (GAW) perspective and the inductive group centered model in particular. The historical section emphasizes the contributions of the pioneers both in Britain and America as well as their stark differences. Then the varieties of GAW thinking are presented along with the critiques of this approach.

The theoretical section deals with a variety of theoretical matters: the similarities and differences between therapy and training groups, the complexities of projective identification, the intensification and dilution characteristics of the transference in groups, and my inductive group centered model.

The clinical section consists of two chapters devoted to case illustrations of the group centered method, one of them dealing with a narcissistic patient who used the group to good advantage. Also I present a Chapter on the promises and cautions of treating borderlines in groups followed by another chapter on the special features of group that make it especially useful in the treatment of many narcissistic patients. My interest in narcissistic pathology has lead me to write about the self in group psychotherapy followed by a chapter on the effect of narcissistic leadership in groups, a topic which is receiving increasing attention.

Training is of vital importance, not only for the student but also for the journeyman professional. Three chapters are devoted to issues regarding intramural training, the importance of experiential groups and typical processes, as well as a model of a continuing education workshop for students and practitioners. Finally I included a keynote address I presented to a group of participants about to start an experiential group at an AGPA conference.

The book ends with a summary of my views about the comparison of a GAW approach with the interpersonal model.

PART I

HISTORICAL

The first four chapters summarize the background and main thesis of the book to the effect that an especially useful model for the group treatment of individuals is not only to respond to each individual's life issues and conflicts but therapists should also strive to integrate dynamics of the group with the struggles of the individual. One model for doing this is an inductive, group centered approach derived, but different from, the early Tavistock model. This section will present the historical context in which the inductive group centered model developed and will also attempt to describe a variety of group-as-a-whole models.

Chapter One is devoted to the contrast between the early British and American approaches to group treatment depicting how the American method has gradually moved in the direction of incorporating some of the group-as-a-whole thinking that had originated in Britain in the 1940s. Chapter Two presents an historical survey of a variety of group centered theories and methods, both the early pioneering contributions as well as the more recent developments. In Chapter Three, the main critiques of group centered thinking are presented and evaluated. Finally Chapter Four consists of the forty year history of the group psychotherapy program at the Menninger Clinic which includes the story in some detail of how the resistance to group psychotherapy was gradually overcome in a psychoanalytic institution which at first was not receptive to this modality. Also I relate how my thinking developed from my initial exposure to the early Tavistock model and my reasons for modifying it in an effort to make it more patient friendly and helpful.

This historical section constitutes both the history of how the field of group psychotherapy moved gradually to accepting some form of group-as-a-whole thinking and intervening. In the United States, in particular, an individualistic approach took root early and was gradually replaced by a variety of models in which individual and group dynamics became integrated.

CHAPTER ONE

The American and British perspectives

Ever since psychotherapists began treating patients in groups, they have had to face the issue of understanding the dynamic forces that are set in motion, as well as the challenging problem of how to use those forces to therapeutic advantage. The controversy in this field has not been whether group dynamics exist in psychotherapy groups but rather to what extent they can be exploited therapeutically. Attitudes have varied from Bion's contention that the group therapist's major task is to attend to the group's basic assumptions as opposed to Slavson's (1957) quite different view that any effort to work with the dynamics of the group-as-a-whole will lead to a variety of anti-therapeutic effects. This debate was waged rather heatedly in the late 1950s and early 1960s. Now, however, the debate has shifted to how best to integrate the dynamics of the group with strategies of individual intervention. In order to appreciate the evolution from the individualistic to the group centered approach, one must contrast the philosophies of the two groups, the American and the British, separated by an ocean and a common language, as G. B. Shaw once quipped.

The American scene

Beginning in the 1940s which marked the first organized steps of group psychotherapy internationally, there have been two major loci of activity, the United States and Great Britain. The indisputably dominant American figure for over a quarter of a century was S. R. Slavson, founder of the American Group Psychotherapy Association. The mentor of many who later became leaders on the American scene, he was quite forceful, if not dogmatic, in asserting an individualistic point of view as the proper model of group psychotherapy. He addressed the issue in a 1957 article entitled "Are There Group Dynamics in Therapy Groups?" and answered this question with a resounding "No!" He differentiated therapy groups from a wide variety of other groups, contending that the former do not have a "common group goal". Groups other than therapy groups show a "synergy" in which individuals give up a portion of their egos to encourage a group ego, while therapy groups avoid doing this. Although there may be a group-wide reaction or a contagion effect in a group, said Slavson, the therapist is always focused on individual differences in these reactions, the individual character patterns, the quantity and kind of affect, as well as the source of the reaction.

Thus, even though Slavson acknowledged a number of dynamic forces in all groups, including mutual induction, intensification, and identification, he believed that the pivotal difference between psychotherapy groups and ordinary groups is that the former seek to uncover intrapsychic determinants within each member; hence, any emphasis on the similarities among members based on group dynamic considerations is anti-therapeutic. In fact, says Slavson, group dynamics should be nipped in the bud, analyzed, and explored before a group pattern or group effect begins to set in. He equates these dynamics with homogenization, artificial uniformity and submersion of individual differences, with the result that individual problems cannot be thoroughly communicated—and worked through. Slavson (1964) decried any evidence of the group acting as a unit: "The therapist has to deal here with a mass reaction rather than with an individual, a situation fraught with difficulties and even danger. The therapist must always be on the alert against unanimity of any sort in the therapy group, for unanimity in groups is derived from hostility against the therapist" (p. 386).

Equally vehement in their attack on group dynamics were Wolf and Schwartz (1962) who crusaded forcefully to eliminate the heresy of thinking about the group as a unified entity. Because much of the work on the study of the dynamics of groups at that time was conducted by social psychologists under the leadership of Kurt Lewin and his students, the above writers were concerned with the wholesale transfer to psychotherapy groups of concepts derived from the study of non-clinical groups, thus engendering superficial thinking and a neglect of unconscious motivations. Like Slavson, they were afraid that conceptualizing the group as operating in a unitary fashion would lead to a neglect of individual differences, to a demand for conformity on the part of the members, and to an expectation that the patients would become submissive to the leader's wish for homogeneity. In general, Schwartz and Wolf established a dichotomy between treating the group and treating the individual, and believed that the two modes of thinking were incompatible.

These anti-group centered points of view were extremely influential on the American scene in the 1950s and the 1960s, but they were by no means representative of all American group psychotherapists. In fact, several leading writers of that period expressed views considerably different from those of Slayson and his followers. Thus Redl (1949) emphasized both the phenomena group contagion and role suction and Semrad and Arsenian (1951) proposed the similar concept of billet. They believed that an individual's behavior in a group setting cannot be understood fully by reference only to individual dynamics, and that the emotional currents within a group often pressed patients into relatively atypical roles. Durkin (1964) joined this debate and displayed an unusual degree of openness to group dynamic concepts, in particular the view that the cohesiveness or the attractiveness of a group to its members should be an essential part of every group therapist's thinking. Whitaker and Lieberman (1964) produced the first systematic theory in the United States which recognized the unitary functioning of the group in what they termed the "group focal conflict" or the commonly held wish or motive countered by a defense.

Saul Sheidlinger (1968) attempted to steer a middle course between the anti-group dynamicists and those writers such as Bion (1961), whom he believed were exclusively preoccupied with group phenomena at the expense of individual personality factors. Scheidlinger has consistently been interested in various group dynamic elements, such as group climate, group structure, and norms, but he has equally been opposed to any characterization of the group that smacks of "group mind":

> Group members can maintain shared or common fantasies; they can even act in unison in response to group occurrences, such as the entry of a new member or the absence of the leader. And yet, this need not mean that the group as a group now has a certain fantasy or acts in a certain manner ... Shared fantasies are far from being the same in each individual ... A group can possess observable characteristics, can be perceived and related to as a whole, but this makes it a social and psychological reality, not a physical reality; it does not indicate a "group mind". (1968, p. 8)

Although the major early contributors, Bion, Ezriel, and Foulkes, had different technical perspectives, they were all definitely in a group centered camp which emphasized the importance of group dynamic properties and, to a greater or lesser extent, used the concept of unitary functioning. Depending on one's perspective, these British writers were either too enamored about group commonalities or had an important insight into how groups function, as I believe. Although most writers would agree that shared fantasies are not the same as identical fantasies, Scheidlinger appears to believe that Bion's "group mentality" opens the possibility of a belief in the fallacy of each patient marching in lock-step. The challenge the American raises is how to utilize the observed commonalities for therapeutic purposes while at the same time respecting the individual differences of each member.

The British scene

In contrast to the Amercan emphasis on an intra-individual approach, some have described the British as "caught up in a group illusion" or, as I prefer to believe, they were influential in facilitating a significant shift toward integrating individual and group dynamics. It appears that American group psychotherapy has gradually begun to incorporate some of the significant contributions of our British colleagues as we have moved from Slavson's individual emphasis to incorporating a group dynamic or group centered approach. How and why the British adopted a group centered stance so much earlier than the Americans is an interesting phenomenon. An important development was that many leading British psychiatrists and psychoanalysts were assembled during World War II at the Northfield Hospital (Trist, 1985) where they collaborated on applying group methods. In the treatment of psychiatric casualties of the war, this unique collaboration undoubtedly contributed to their thinking about group methods.

The contrast between the British and American contributions will be briefly outlined here and a more detailed description as well as my evaluative comments will be given in the next chapter. The single most important contributor to group psychology theory, whose influence has been felt universally by all group scholars, is Wilfred R. Bion. Social psychologists associated with Kurt Lewin's Survey Research Center studied Bion's writings for insights into the more regressed levels of group functioning. To a greater or lesser extent, the work of the Tavistock Institute of Human Relations, the group relations conferences sponsored by the A. K. Rice Institute, and the sensitivity training programs sponsored by the National Training Laboratories used Bion's views regarding the basic assumption life in groups and the way these forces obstruct or facilitate the primary task of a work group. Although Bion interrupted his work with groups prematurely and did not write extensively about the application of his ideas to psychotherapy groups following the publication of his major work in 1959, many of his theoretical notions were adopted by the group psychotherapists at the Tavistock Clinic where his ideas were translated into a specific model of group psychotherapy.

Following World War II, Bion was invited by the Tavistock Clinic to begin "taking groups", and he pursued an intensive study of work with patient groups as well as study groups of professionals for the next few years. His series of articles on his experiences and formulations were published first in the journal Human Relations between 1949 and 1951 and were assembled subsequently in the book, Experiences in Groups (1961).

According to Bion, groups operate at two levels of functioning, the work group and the basic assumption group. The former consists mainly of conscious, rational, goal-directed activities dictated by the task of the group, while the latter consists of less conscious, more regressed emotional currents that express a primitive "group mentality" and often tend to interfere with the primary task. He believed that the group develops "basic assumptions" as a defense against primitive regressive forces that threaten the group. Bion described the mechanism by which the group becomes caught up in one of the three basic assumptions (dependency, fight-flight, pairing) as the Kleinian concept of projective identification in which members attempt to put parts of their psyches into each of the other members and attempt to influence and manipulate the others into certain desired roles. The therapist's main tool for perceiving and understanding the group mentality is the "numbing" feeling of being manipulated by the group into certain behavioral responses. This description is not unlike the phenomenon of counter-transference reactions within the analyst that illuminate the patient's conscious or unconscious attitudes. Bion's important contribution, however, was his detailed description of the unitary functioning of groups with some suggestions about how to turn these understandings into therapeutic benefit.

Using Bion's notions of the group mentality, Ezriel (1950) proposed that the group therapist's interpretive task is to ferret out the underlying common group tension, a conflicting fantasy shared by all group members but experienced in idiosyncratic ways by each member. The conflict consists of a commonly held wish that cannot be openly expressed because it would create excessive anxiety. Ezriel described this conflicted situation as a three-tiered relationship: a wished-for or "desired" relationship, defended against by a "required" relationship, lest a "catastrophic" situation ensue. The therapist's role is to diagnose both the common group tension as well as the three-tiered relations manifested by each member (a somewhat formidable task!). The general structure of the interpretation offered by the therapist to the group is essentially an explanation of the prevailing common group tension and how each individual is responding to this conflicted situation in his or her own unique, personal way. Here we have the first effort to integrate the commonly shared dynamic force within the group with each individual's characteristic patterns of dealing with this conflict, that is, an integration of individual and group dynamics.

Foulkes (1975) also endorsed the view that there is a unitary quality to the functioning of a therapeutic group. This idea is embodied in his concept of matrix, which he described as "the common ground of operational relationships, comprising all the interactions of individual group members" (p. 110). He believed that all individual reactions must be understood as a "figure" in relationship to the "ground" of the group-as-a-whole. He also used the metaphor of the individual as a single neuron embedded in the total nervous system which is analogous to the total network of communication within the group. His view of the group functioning holistically is concretized by his recommendation that the group's productions should be regarded as equivalent to the free associations of a single individual, and that the latent meaning of the communication within a group can best be ascertained by means of this free associative approach.

All three British writers share a common perspective on the functioning of the group-as-a-whole. Bion's group mentality, Ezriel's common group tension, and Foulkes's communicative matrix may differ in detail and specificity, but they share the notion of an all-important group affect—whether it be a commonly shared fantasy, conflict, or simply a shared background—that produces a significant effect on the behavior of each member. These writers also agree that, to intervene accurately and usefully, the group therapist must at some point define and integrate the influence of the group upon the individual. Their contributions will be described in greater detail and then critiqued in the next Chapter.

The current scene

Slowly and imperceptibly the theory and practice of group psychotherapy have increasingly incorporated some kind of group centered thinking. Very early Parloff (1968) predicted a gradual move away from a strictly individualistic and interpersonal approach toward an "integralist" or group centered approach. Evidence of such a transition may be seen in the work of Rutan, Stone, and Shay (2007) and Agazarian (1997), both preceded by the report of the AGPA Task Force on General Systems Theory chaired by Helen Durkin (1982). The present writer has also been an early, active proponent of the group centered approach (Horwitz, 1977).

Group centered thinking is represented by a broad spectrum of theoretical approaches ranging from a circumscribed application to specific developments in a group to a view that group dynamic forces are omnipresent and need to be uncovered by the group therapist. I shall delineate three main points of this spectrum.

The most limited view of group-wide phenomena and their interpretation is that espoused by Yalom and Leszcz (2005). Although recognizing that a group has important system properties, they are opposed in general to what they describe as "mass interpretations". The pejorative connotation of the term seems to convey their attitude that such interventions unduly emphasize patient–therapist relationships as opposed to peer interactions, and, furthermore, that one may fall into the error of artificially squeezing into the mass interpretation individuals who may not belong there. Therefore, Yalom and Leszcz would restrict their group-wide interpretations mainly to situations wherein the therapist finds it necessary to remove obstacles to the progress of the entire group. Thus, when the entire group is under the influence of some anxiety-laden issue that members are unable to address, or when an anti-therapeutic group norm is beginning to develop, such as the collusion among members to begin taking turns.

A second, more expanded view of group-wide functioning is one in which individual and group issues alternate or where group-wide issues surface only intermittently. According to Whitaker and Lieberman (1964), the group focal conflict consists essentially of a shared wish countered by a commonly held fear, and only through interpretation can the group begin to resolve the conflict and find an "enabling solution", thus progressing in its task of dealing with personal conflicts of its individual members. This perspective contrasts sharply with the Ezriel notion that personal issues become integrated with group issues, and that it is best to work on the two simultaneously rather than discretely.

Day (1981) gradually became disillusioned with the Tavistock method of emphasizing the common group tension and organizing individual interventions around group-wide themes. His observation from his clinical experience was that if the therapist continues to address primarily the group, the patients will eventually leave and find their satisfactions elsewhere. He currently uses group-wide interventions only when certain events clearly affect the entire group (such as the therapist's absence, a member's success or failure, an entry or departure of a member), particularly events that alter the group "envelope". On the other hand, when the group is working cohesively and there are no group-wide disturbances in the alliance, individual transferences become prominent. Day agrees that there are times when individual transferences may have some similarities and may be explored in parallel. His point of view regarding the alternation between group and individual issues seems close to that of Whitaker and Lieberman.

Scheidlinger's views on this issue are not readily categorized, mainly because he does not believe that our field has yet achieved a good theoretical or practical integration of group and individual elements. As mentioned earlier, even though he recognized the presence of certain shared or common fantasies in reaction to group occurrences, he asserted that phenomena such as regressions, identifications, and fantasizing operate in individuals only. Furthermore, he believed that individual personalities in a group, with their genetic and dynamic properties, are involved in a complex interaction with group dynamic elements, such as group climate, goals, and structure, and that this dual interaction is embedded in two main levels of group functioning: (1) the dynamic contemporaneous level that is more readily observed and includes the expression of conscious needs and adaptive patterns, and (2) the genetic-regressive level which primarily consists of unconscious and preconscious motivations, defenses, and conflicts.

Although Scheidlinger believed that we are not ready to formulate a method of integrating these varied and complex forces, one gains the impression that he leaned toward Whitaker and Lieberman's alternation hypothesis. In referring to focal group conflict theory he wrote approvingly of the idea that a common theme tends to alternate with the surfacing of individual conflicts and issues.

The third and broadest conceptualization of the group centered approach views the common group tension as a constant presence in the group, although not always readily observable. Rutan, Stone, and Shay (2006) adhere to this point of view and state that at times group-as-a-whole factors are quite significant, while at other times these processes may fade into the background, but never disappear. According to these writers, group-wide phenomena become most significant when boundaries are changed, such as when a new member enters the group, because the change affects the entire group.

Kibel and Stein (1981) have also moved close to a constant presence point of view, but not in technique. Their major thesis is that the transference to the therapist is a basic "major dynamic force" (p. 421) behind all group interactions and that, at any given moment, it determines the direction and nature of the group process. But they caution against interpreting such transference before dealing with and interpreting the peer interaction. They believe that peer transference is comparable to transference resistance, while the therapist transference is the major transference content, and argue that resistance should be addressed before content. In recent years Kibel (2005) has shifted his point of view to a Foulkesian model which is more receptive to using GAW interventions.

Like Kibel and Stein, Scheidlinger explicitly addresses the dilemma of recognizing that there is a certain unity in a group's functioning (e.g., group-wide themes, reactions, and resistances) but that the group also manifests diversity based on differences among individual members. But he cautions against extending shared group reactions into an unwarranted uniformity of reaction which he refers to as the fallacy of the "group mind".

The system of group psychotherapy that I have proposed (Chapter Six) clearly embraces the idea of a common group tension as a constant presence and shares the Bion and Ezriel theoretical base that associates the unity of the group with projective identification (Chapter Eight). But this inductive group centered model modifies the original Tavistock approach sufficiently to overcome some of its weaknesses.

John Sutherland, Medical Director of the Tavistock Clinic and a collaborator with Ezriel, became a consultant in 1963 to the newly formed Menninger Group Psychotherapy Service after a professional encounter with Dr. Karl Menninger in London. After Sutherland's first month-long consultation with a few Menninger staff, the Tavistock model that he taught became the modus operandi at the Menninger Clinic for the next decade. Gradually, however, we found that the method exerted undue constraints on the role of the therapist insofar as individual work with patients could be done only after the group theme or group conflict had been uncovered and interpreted. As noted earlier, the weakness of this deductive method was also described in the research report by Malan. Balfour, Hood, and Shooter (1976). The modification I proposed was to use an inductive rather than deductive method in which the individual work with several patients precedes the interpretation of the group theme; that is, group-wide phenomena are gradually defined only after sufficient work has occurred with a number of individual patients.

The inductive method is a model or paradigm, not a rigid system, and it needs to be adapted to particular circumstances. In some instances, a group-wide theme may extend over several sessions, and the therapist may wish to move back and forth between individual and group interventions. Also, the method represents a way of thinking rather than a specific technique and superficially may appear quite similar to an individualistic approach. The difference from other models, however, lies in the therapist's special perspective toward the material, and in his or her way of listening to it, processing it, and occasionally bringing these observations to the attention of the group. The therapist "listens with the fourth ear": The third ear listens for the unconscious communication of each individual member, while the fourth ear attends to the group's common theme.

Among all of these perspectives using the group-as-a-whole in some form, the inductive group centered approach, in my view, has the following advantages:

1. It enhances group cohesiveness by consistently emphasizing shared anxieties, defenses and conflicts.
2. It contributes to a deepening of the material insofar as one usually uncovers a more regressed level associated with commonly shared transference reactions.
3. It leads to discerning such defenses as the spokesperson, scapegoating, or role suction—usually indications of a shared conflict.

Using an inductive method, one can accrue these advantages while not suffering from the disadvantage of submerging individual needs.

Summary

American and British group psychotherapy developed from widely divergent beginnings, but they now are showing a greater degree of convergence. The American approach, mainly under the dominance of Slavson, emphasized the uncovering of each individual group member's conflicts and defenses and regarded group dynamics as anti-therapeutic as well as homogenizing. Conversely, the British contributors, such as Bion, Ezriel, and Foulkes, held that a common group tension was omnipresent and required attention, if not interpretation, to fully elucidate the completeness of individual reactions. American group psychotherapy seems to have moved steadily toward some adaptation of the British theoretical base, although many variations in its application exist. One of these variations is a so-called inductive group centered approach proposed by this author that modifies the Tavistock model by giving greater emphasis to the needs of individual members.

CHAPTER TWO

Varieties of group centered models

Morris Parloff (1968) did a comprehensive survey of the analytic therapies in which he described and contrasted three models: the individualistic, the interpersonal, and the integralist. The last term referred to those group treatments which attempted to integrate the personality dynamics of the individual with the dynamics of the whole group. This term never took hold in the literature, but rather has been referred to as the group-as-a-whole approach and occasionally as the group centered approach. Parloff predicted that in the coming years these integrative models, then very much in the minority, would begin to gain increasing prominence among group psychotherapists because they held the promise of providing an integration of group and individual dynamics.

Parloff's prediction has indeed been validated. The early individualistic approach in which group dynamics were minimized, even "stamped out", and conceptions of the group functioning as an entity were vigorously attacked, has lost its former influence. In its place has arisen the increasingly prominent idea, expressed in numerous publications, that the behavior of every individual in a therapy group is influenced and modified by the tensions and conflicts that pervade the entire group. Evidence for this shift toward emphasizing a group-as-a-whole or group centered approach may be found in the major publications that have appeared during the past two to three decades. Most of the authors who have described their theoretical and technical views in recent years have embraced some kind of group-as-a-whole approach, even though they are far from being unanimous or uniform in their perspectives.

Many, if not most, recent writers subscribe in some form or other to the principles of a group centered theory. First, they believe that the group-as-a-whole (GAW), perceived consciously and unconsciously by each individual in his or her unique way, has a significant impact on each member of the group. It is one of the triad of transferences, the other two being the transference to the therapist and the peer transferences. These transferences are interdependent and interact with each other to influence the behavior of each patient. Furthermore, none should be given priority over the other and usually they work in tandem.

Second, the more recent viewpoints endorse the idea that psychotherapy groups, either intermittently or on a constant basis, manifest some form of unitary functioning evidenced by a theme or conflict that is shared by the entire group. However, each individual patient reacts to this theme in his or her own idiosyncratic way. Third, the group centered therapists believe that the group-wide theme or conflict needs to be interpreted to the group as a way of providing the most complete explanation of what is transpiring in the group. The particular mode of making such interpretations differs among the various group centered therapists.

Theories of unitary functioning in psychotherapy groups have proliferated over the years, and in this chapter I propose to review a range of these theories, comment on their implications for technique, and offer a personal perspective on their strengths and weaknesses. I shall first describe the theories of the early contributors in greater detail and then describe the more recent views.

The pioneering contributions: Bion's basic assumptions

Without doubt, the earliest pioneer in this area was Wilfred Bion, whose Experiences in Groups (1961) was the seminal, ground-breaking contribution to a theory of unitary functioning. He proposed the conception of small, unstructured groups coming under the sway of basic assumptions (dependency, fight/flight, pairing) and that this form of shared group emotionality serves as a defense against more primitive regressive tendencies such as fusion experiences and loss of identity. The group moves spontaneously from one basic assumption to the other and its influence upon each individual depends upon his or her "valence" or predisposition to being affected by the particular emotional current prevailing at any given time. Furthermore, he believed that the mechanism that explained the development of the basic assumptions was the accumulation of projective identifications by each group member upon every other group member, and these affective impacts give rise to a commonly shared basic assumption.

On a more conscious level, a group may function as a "work group" in which reality prevails, time boundaries are observed, and rationality is emphasized. All groups are subject to the conflict between rationality of the work group and the emotionality of the basic assumption group. Which group mentality prevails is dependent on the degree of structuring of the group's procedures, the kind of leadership that is implemented, and the degree of pathology of the members.

In assessing Bion's contributions, I believe that his views produced a sea change in beginning to move the field of group therapy from a simple transfer of a mainly individual psychology of psychoanalysis, to a beginning of an understanding of the role of group dynamics in the functioning of groups. He stimulated a number of other theorists to incorporate his notion of the influence of group wide processes on the behavior of the group-as-a-whole as well as individual reactions.

However, he did not pursue his study of groups beyond his initial contributions, presumably because his analyst, Melanie Klein, discouraged this work (Ganzarain, 1989) and preferred that he devote his talents and attention to dyadic treatment. His technical recommendations of restricting one's interventions only to group-wide interpretations never was accepted by other practitioners and one wonders if he would have modified these ideas if he had continued beyond his initial forays. There is a consensus among theorists that his insistence upon only group-wide interventions with no comments to individuals as well as his personal style of being relatively opaque caused his patients to feel unduly frustrated. Furthermore, even though his theory of basic assumptions embodies the most basic human drives (dependency, aggression, and sexuality), his view of basic assumption defenses is probably excessively restrictive. For example, Hopper (2003) has introduced a fourth basic assumption, the Incohesion: Aggregation/Massification or

I/A/M, which encompasses earlier primitive defenses than mentioned in Bion's three basic assumptions.

Ezriel's common group tension

Henry Ezriel, in collaboration with J. D. Sutherland (1952), was the author of the Tavistock model which applied Bion's conceptualizations but not his precise technical recommendations. In contrast to Bion's belief that group therapists should confine their interventions to the group-as-a-whole and interpret only the basic assumptions, Ezriel proposed a model whereby it would be possible to integrate both the dynamics of the group-as-a-whole with the personality conflicts of each individual member. Like Bion, he believed that the group would be caught up at any given time in a commonly shared, unconscious conflict, wishes countered by fears and defenses that he referred to as the common group tension.

Borrowing from Bion, he saw this shared emotional current developing out of efforts on the part of each individual to manipulate every other individual in the direction of a desired response, that is, projective identification. Although Ezriel shared Bion's view of the unitary functioning of groups, his technical recommendations were considerably more complex. He believed that the common group tension impinges upon each individual in a unique and idiosyncratic way, depending upon the individual's personality structure. Thus, when the group is in a struggle with its hostility toward the therapist, one person might react with an ego-syntonic expression of anger and rebellion, another with reaction formation and compliance, while still others could resort to somatic reactions, depression, withdrawal, or other defensive postures consonant with their own personal repertoire. In fact, Ezriel believed that the therapist needed to diagnose three elements of each individual's personal reaction to the common group tension: the relationship that the individual felt required to assume, his secretly desired relationship, and the catastrophe that he feared would ensue if he expressed his desires openly.

Ezriel prescribed the formidable task for the therapist of not only diagnosing the common group tension, but the three relationship elements for each individual before rendering a comprehensive interpretation in which all of these facets were spelled out. Although this effort at integrating both the group and individual dynamics seemed theoretically sound, there were practical difficulties inherent in it. First, consonant with views of psychoanalytic technique of his era, Ezriel restricted his comments to very sparing interventions, eschewed supportive interventions, and only spoke when he was able to diagnose the common group tension as well as the particular reactions of each individual. His long silences were bound to engender iatrogenic responses and excessive frustrations by members. Second his minimalist technique promoted a transference reaction toward the omniscient therapist. And finally, as revealed in the important research conducted by Malan at the Tavistock Clinic (1976), the technique gave patients the impression that the therapist was more interested in the group-as-a-whole than in the needs of his individual patient.

Foulkes' communication matrix

Even though he was very much concerned about the functioning of the group-as-a-whole and its impact on each individual, Foulkes and Anthony (1973) chose to be more impressionistic and metaphoric in viewing the relationship between the group and the individual. His concept of matrix is that it is "an interactional communication network, a series of interacting mental processes and usually serves as the background or context for each individual's reactions. We analyze in the interest of each individual but in the group context" (1973, p. 215). An individual's psychopathology is revealed in his or her becoming a deviant within the group's norms and expectations.

Thus, he does not seem to go as far as either Bion or Ezriel in promoting the idea of the unitary functioning of a group, of shared fantasies or shared conflicts necessarily taking place, although he would not rule out such phenomena. Rather, he prefers to view the group situation as one in which individuals influence the group and the group in turn affects the individuals, and all of the evolving affects and meanings become the matrix. One would address the group-as-a-whole when the therapist wishes to point out a shared response in relation to himself or to some other member, but one might equally well address an individual or a subgroup because every intervention by the therapist addressed to an individual impacts other members as well.

Despite the fact that the members of the group are subject to the same input from the same communicative network, Foulkes did not take the next step, as did Bion and Ezriel, in formulating a theory of a commonly shared conflict, basic assumptions, or group tension. Rather, he emphasized that the matrix needed to be considered as a background factor that influenced each individual in the group. His matrix or communicative network appears to this writer as quite impressionistic and vaguely defined and hence does not systematically attempt to integrate the individual and group dynamics to the same degree as Ezriel.

Hinshelwood (2008) compares the views of Bion and Foulkes with regard to group-as-a-whole and although they both recognized the influence of the whole group on each individual, Foulkes gave primacy to the individual's needs while Bion believed that there was a group neurosis that his members were coping with and therefore his emphasis was on intervening on a group level. Bion's ideas about a model of group treatment never caught hold while Foulkes' model has flourished in many training centers in Europe.

Whitaker and Lieberman's group focal conflict

Whitaker and Lieberman (1964) associate themselves in very significant ways with Bion and Ezriel in subscribing to the general notion that groups develop affective forces, group tensions, and group conflicts which impinge strongly upon the individual members. They contend that the particular way in which these group forces operate is via the conflicts that develop within the group that are conceptualized by a "disturbing motive" being countered by a "reactive motive".

This group-wide conflict eventually becomes resolved by either an enabling solution or a restrictive solution. The therapeutic effect on the individual patient is his or her experience of a series or accumulation of enabling solutions which will eventually lead to a decrease in the individual's defensiveness and a willingness to give up maladaptive behaviors. However similar their thinking was to their predecessors, there were some fundamental differences that also set them apart. They were reluctant to formulate their focal group conflicts in terms either of transference or of object relations, and as a result, their theory tended to lack the depth of unconscious conflict and primitive defenses that characterized the avowedly psychodynamic contributors. Furthermore, they viewed the focal group conflict as intermittent rather than ever-present. Thus, once a solution for the ongoing conflict is found, the group can deal with individual issues until a group wide conflict surfaces once again.

Recent group centered theories

A variety of efforts have been made in recent years to incorporate new modes of thinking to the problem of integrating individual and group dynamics. More than most others, Agazarian (1997, 2008) has incorporated general systems theory into her model. On the other hand, Ganzarain (1989, 1992) has relied both upon Bion's basic ideas as well as the object relations theory of Melanie Klein to formulate and integrate group and individual psychology.

Agazarian's system centered therapy

Following the tenets of general systems theory, groups are conceptualized in terms of a hierarchical and isomorphic set of systems, including a group-as-a-whole system, a subgroup system, and an individual member system (1989). The three modes are visualized as concentric circles with permeable boundaries. Pathology is formulated in terms of difficulties and conflicts in communication, and the task explicitly assigned to each member is to join a subgroup and thus experience similarities and differences with other members of his subgroup. This process contributes to the development of permeability in the boundaries between conflicting subgroups and helps in developing some degree of resolution of differences. The more the antagonistic subgroups are able to communicate across boundaries and ultimately become better integrated, the greater the positive change both for the group and for the individuals.

Agazarian differentiates her approach from other group-as-a-whole approaches in that the system-centered leader attends to the communication process across subgroups rather than to the content conveyed in the individual member communications. She believes that the weakness of the usual group centered approach is its potential to fail in undoing the projective identification and consequent scapegoating that is often permitted to occur. She believes that her method avoids this pitfall by encouraging the development of "functional subgrouping" in which the therapist clearly structures the task for the group. Although obviously concerned with the functioning of individual members, she adheres to a strong conviction that personality change and repair within a group can best occur through attending to the process of communication.

The method involves a considerable departure from analyzing individual dynamics using the group process, characteristic of most prevailing group centered approaches. The method seems to have considerable similarity to certain family therapy approaches which emphasize treating the family as a malfunctioning system where the therapist encourages each member of the family to find his or her voice.

Its main difference from most analytic group therapy approaches is that it is highly structured and directive and thus does not encourage the emergence of pathological personality patterns which can then be scrutinized by both the individual, the group, and the therapist and become the subject for therapeutic work. For example, she explicitly conveys to the group that they should make an effort to be "good citizens" and thus encourages more compliance and conformity than one usually sees in analytic groups. In a recent critique, Aledort (2008) makes the important point that patients must have room to exhibit and act in his or her own personal dramas that they usually seek to change, whether it is scapegoating, power plays, masochism, seduction, or narcissism. He believes that Agazarian tends to discourage such behavior rather than let it happen.

Ganzarain's object relations model

This model is a type of group centered approach characterized by a heavy reliance upon the contributions of both Wilfred Bion and Melanie Klein with its emphasis upon early "psychotic-like" anxieties (1989, 1992). He emphasizes such primitive defense mechanisms as splitting, projective identification, omnipotent denial, projection, and introjection as the "full resources to protect the endangered self and the threatened objects from fantasied imminent destruction" (1992, p. 205). He also relies heavily on Bion's conception of basic assumption life and sees the group as operating as an entity that is largely influenced by the pressures of primitive anxieties and defenses. Consistent with Kleinian theory, the conflicts and defenses mainly revolve around primitive aggression, the fear of one's own destructiveness as well as the potential threat from others, and the patient's efforts to steer a safe course in a world fraught with dangerous anger. Ganzarain's object relations group psychotherapy focuses mostly on the vicissitudes of the group entity but, in contrast to Bion, does not exclude intrapsychic or interpersonal components of group life. Like Ezriel, Ganzarain addresses each member's intrapsychic struggles as a conflict that the patient shares in varying degrees with the other members. However, Ganzarain differentiates his particular group centered approach from that of others, like Ezriel, in his emphasis on primitive defense mechanisms against psychotic-like anxieties. Ganzarain's method illustrates the usefulness of an object relations approach with its emphasis on the patient's internal world and its relationship to external reality in attempting to bridge individual and group psychology.

In summary, Ganzarain's view was that "object relations group psychotherapy technique is centered at the core of group psychology, which is formed by shared fantasies about a common internal object: the group entity situated in the 'area of illusion' in the members' minds, as a mother surrogate" (1995, p. 69). Ganzarain hews closely to the thinking of Melanie Klein and Bion and subscribes to basic assumption thinking. On the other hand he does not precisely spell out his ideas about how he deals with individual issues, within or outside, the context of the prevailing group conflict. Judging from his illustrative material, he works at both the group and the individual level and he views the individual contributions within the context of the group-as-a-whole.

Earl Hopper's fourth basic assumption

Earl Hopper has assumed an important leadership position in the school of Group Analysis founded by S. H. Foulkes. In his book on the fourth basic assumption (2003), an addition to Bion's original three, Hopper implies a move away from Foulkes' more simplified view of the group matrix which is the overall emotional network that influences all of the individual contributions. Bion's basic assumption theory is an attempt to define the specific impulse-defense configurations that get mobilized in a group to ward off intense primitive anxiety. Thus, Hopper is at the very least adopting a major addition to Foulkes' theory and asserting that groups react in a unitary fashion to the emotional currents that develop. He further believes that the group therapist's role is to decide which member personifies the group's main emotional struggles and presumably begins by interpreting the individual's conflicts and defenses before generalizing to the group.

Hopper's (2004) addition to Bion's three original basic assumptions is a fourth basic assumption, Incohesion: Aggregation/Massification (I:A/M). When a group is traumatized, usually by a significant loss, the group members tend to move towards a state of incohesion: they become less openly communicative, less unified, and more subject to a fear of annihilation. This incohesion may take either one of two forms, aggregation or massification, and often oscillates between the two. Aggregation indicates a move toward isolation and "me-ness" as a defense against a feeling of at one with a disintegrating group. Massification, on the other hand, consists of a homgenization, a fusion or submergence of the self within the group in an effort to avoid annihilation. This conceptualization is a well developed formulation that is persuasively argued and is a significant contribution to the literature on primitive defenses both by individuals and groups. It encompasses the primitive and archaic defenses that individuals resort to under the threat of severe trauma.

In terms of technique, he remains true to his Foulkesian roots in emphasizing that ideally therapists should deemphasize their own influence in favor of shifting responsibility to the group members, reasoning that if the group members sense that the group belongs more to them, they are not only assuming more initiative, but also the leader's failure to respond appropriately would be less damaging.

Although Hopper's approach has some differences from the present writer's inductive approach, I am struck by the basic similarity in the two methods; that is, working with individuals first before generalizing to the group's basic assumption or common group tension. The one caveat I would insert is that consistent with giving the group more responsibility, I would prefer to let the group make the decision as to which member(s) become the spokespersons, rather than give that decision to the therapist as Hopper seems to suggest.

Ettin's group-as-a-whole theories

Mark Ettin has devoted much of his extensive writings on group psychotherapy and group process to a study of the group-as-a-whole. His own synthesis of these views is best captured in his scholarly and clinically-oriented book, *Foundations and Applications of Group Psychotherapy* (1992). He begins with the premise of "group as a trinity", referring to its intrapsychic, interpersonal, and group-as-a-whole levels. He believes that an "informed leader" must be sensitive to each of these levels and focus his interventions on each of them as the process changes. He states that the whole group usually needs special attention during early group meetings, members coming and going, confidentiality concerns, and outside group contacts: "At other junctures, group level processes, while always operating, may form a backdrop for individual and inter-personal exploration" (p. 129).

Interestingly enough, he describes both the inductive and deductive processes that give rise to the therapist's formulation of what is tran-spiring at the group-as-a-whole level.

He describes induction as occurring in the head of the therapist, and something that is reached by a bottom-up, empirical-additive process. Here he is describing the common clinical task, whether in a group or with an individual, of finding the "red thread" that underlies the series of free associations in a given session. The deductive aspect is captured by the therapist's awareness of the background events that may be influ-encing the wishes and fears that bind the whole membership, such as the addition of a new member, the termination of a member, cancellations of sessions, etc. which the therapist may listen for during a group session.

Ettin very aptly observes that individual problems transform into group wide dilemmas and the latter spur individuals to work on their individual issues. Thus there is a reciprocal influence of individuals on the group-as-a-whole and vice versa. An important difference from the Tavistock method is that there is no attempt in his technical approach to specifically integrate the group-wide issue with the individual's idi-osyncratic way of dealing with the common wishes and fears that bind the whole membership. But like this author's inductive model, Ettin implies that working with individuals first and only later introducing the commonly held emotional themes is his preferred method.

Walter Stone's self psychological approach

Walter Stone has joined his co-authors Scott Rutan and Joseph Shay (Rutan, Stone, & Shay, 2007) in taking a position on the issue of group-as-a-whole in relation to individual and interpersonal interventions. First they express skepticism about the possibility of providing an easy road map to integrate individual and group dynamics. Next, they observe that there are times when the whole group is in the ascendancy, such as when a new member enters the group, because whenever the group boundaries are changed or endangered, the entire group reacts and individuals are best helped by careful attention to the group-as-a-whole process. On the other hand, the latter often fades into the back-ground, though it never disappears. They conclude by stating that the group therapist must learn how to move effectively across boundaries from group-as-a-whole to the interpersonal and the intrapsychic.

Stone has further refined these views in his thoughtful treatise (2005) on group centered theory from a self psychological perspective. First, he correctly asserts that group-as-a-whole has multiple meanings. From his orientation as a self psychologist, for example, he mentions that (a) the group may be perceived as a gratifying or alternatively as a threatening self-object; (b) the identification of the patient with the group results in either an enhanced or diminished sense of self, a structure called the group self; and (c) the group may be perceived as a subject or agent capable of initiating action expressed in such statements as "the group is resisting". Next, he applies the distinction between empathic understanding and interpretive explaining to the relationship between individual and group-wide interventions, stressing the need to convey to the individual patient the sense that the therapist is empathically attuned to the patient's special issues, before he can introduce interpretations that apply to the group-as-a-whole. He also emphasizes the importance, whether intervening to the individual or to the group, of offering observations that are sufficiently tentative and inviting of the patient's perspective in order to avoid the impression of therapeutic omniscience.

Stone adheres to the view that the dynamics of the group is at least an intermittent factor in shaping the life of the group and the reactions of each patient. He also quotes the present writer in his conclusion that first working with individual issues is the key to conveying to the patient that he or she is not subordinate to the needs of the group. But like many clinicians he does not try to take the next step and explicate how the whole group influences each patient depending on the character structure of the individual. This would be the basis for integrating individual and group dynamics, a model that would complete the circle or connect the dots of group behavior.

Hinshelwood's container as integrater

Hinshelwood (2008) has made an important contribution toward the integration of individual and group dynamics through the use of Bion's concept of the container. He set out to "form a conceptual bridge such that group dynamics are not simplistically reduced to individual dynamics, nor that the individual is lost in the group-as-a-whole concept". (2008, p. 283) Both Bion and Foulkes attempted to find bridging concepts but he believed neither was entirely successful. He characterized Bion's concepts of group mentality, valency, and basic assumption as "rather stale and intellectual" (p. 285). Furthermore, he thought Foulkes' concept of the communication matrix lacked sufficient interest in analyzing group dynamics and was focused more on guiding the group toward a particular kind of communication culture.

Hinshelwood's thesis is that the individual externalizes her internal conflicts into the group which serves as a container, and after the group interaction has processed the various contributions, the individual re-internalizes her conflict in some modified form, transformed by group or social dynamics. Depending on whether the group is a fragile, rigid, or flexible container, the content is adaptively or maladaptively altered. He further states that individuals experience both intrapersonal and interpersonal containment when a linkage occurs between group members and simultaneously a comparable linkage occurs within the minds of each individual. The group patient is both an individual member and "a representative of an element of a mind that is the whole group" (p. 295). He emphasizes such group dynamic processes as spokesperson and scapegoating as integrating forces producing a group mentality.

Although he believes that his formulation is closer to Foulkes than it is to Bion, I view his conceptualization and his technique as moving in the direction of a common group tension idea. That is, he seeks out the group's shared mentality which he interprets and this process provides each individual greater freedom to explore their social roles in the group. It sounds quite similar to the approach in which the common group tension, once it is identified, provides each individual with the opportunity to explore his shared affects and conflicts with his peers as well as his unique way of dealing with these issues.

Summary

Considerable progress has occurred since the various pioneers introduced their views about the role of the group-as-a-whole in group psychotherapy. Unfortunately Bion failed to persevere in his group psychotherapy work and if he had, it is conceivable that he would have supplemented his basic assumption interpretations with personalized, individual comments to his patients. Ezriel's now defunct Tavistock model has been found wanting both in a research study and by clinicians using his method and a modified model will be presented in detail by this writer in a subsequent chapter (Chapter Six). Foulkes' communication matrix appears to be less of an integrative tool for individual and group dynamics and more of a general conception, agreed by most, that the group-as-a-whole influences the behavior of the individual and at least occasionally needs to be interpreted. While still adhering to many of Foulkesian ideas, Whitaker and Lieberman gave impetus to group centered thinking but they seemed to differ from Bion and Ezriel in taking the position that the group focal conflict surfaces only at particular points and then disappears for another period of time.

Turning to the modern theorists, Agazarian appears to be the sole contributor who has clearly departed from a psychodynamic method and has focused her theory almost entirely on the work of the general systems theorists. She deserves credit for her effort to push her theory and technique in this direction but most psychodynamic therapists would probably take issue with the active structuring that she uses with her groups. The other five authors in this chapter all embrace the view that there is a reciprocal influence between the group and the individual and emphasize that members develop shared themes and conflicts although each patient handles such issues in her own characterologically determined way. If there is a dividing line between the cited theoreticians, it probably consists of the difference between those who view the basic assumption or common group tension as a constant, though sometimes obscure, presence as opposed to those who believe that the group wide emotion is intermittent and phasic, disappearing and appearing depending upon the particular process occurring within the group at any given time. Thus, Ganzarain, Hinshelwood, and possibly Hopper would be in the constant category while Stone and Ettin are more likely in the intermittent group.

On the other hand, none of the above writers subscribes to the Ezriel framework of systematically relating the group-wide conflict to each of the individuals in the group. I believe that he made the most ambitious attempt to integrate individual and group dynamics. Even though his method was eventually found to be lacking by most writers, it seems to me that his general conception has merit and could be incorporated into a more effective technique once his original model has been modified.

CHAPTER THREE

Critiques of group centered theories

A number of theoreticians subscribe to the idea of the therapy group being characterized by some form of unitary functioning that influences each member's behavior, but they are loathe to accept the proposition that an interpretive focus of the therapist, his or her technique, ought to be concerned with systematically clarifying the patients' conflicts in relation to a group theme or group conflict.

Interpersonal model of Yalom and Leszcz

Irvin Yalom has the distinction of being the author of the most widely used group psychotherapy textbook in the field, a book that is now in its fifth edition since its original publication in the 1970s. The author of a number of novels and short stories, Yalom's most recent edition (2005), written in collaboration with Molyn Leszcz, is comprehensive, scholarly, and highly readable. They make quite clear that their model is one that is based on the underlying assumption that interpersonal interaction in the here-and-now is crucial to effective group psychotherapy. Their thesis is that freely interacting patients in a therapy group can be helped to identify and understand what goes wrong in their interactions and ultimately they are enabled to change maladaptive patterns.

31

On the other hand, they are also cognizant of the fact that there are "common group tensions" that are always present in every group such as the struggle for dominance, the conflict between seeking support *vs.* rivalries, as well as the conflict between dependency *vs.* the fear of one's individuality being submerged by the group. They describe these tensions as providing the "hidden motors of group interaction" (p. 169). While recognizing the importance of group-as-a-whole reactions, they believe that explicit comments about such reactions should be made rarely and only in two instances: first, when the group is clearly avoiding an important issue due to anxiety and second, when an anti-therapeutic group norm is being established. With regard to the timing of group-wide interventions, they state that "an issue which is critical to the existence or function of the entire group always takes precedence over narrower interpersonal issues" (p. 198).

While recognizing the importance of the group's transference to the therapist, they recommend that one should attach equal importance to the "interpersonal learning that ensues from relationships between members and from other therapeutic factors" (p. 203). At another point, they convey that given a choice between therapist transference and transference between group members, one should opt for dealing with the latter. And finally, they recommend that transference to the therapist should typically be dealt with either by consensual validation by the group members or by increased therapist transparency.

First, I would like to call attention to the common error made by numerous writers, including Yalom and Leszcz, who conflate Bion with the old Tavistock model. While Ezriel (1973), author of the original Tavistock method, used much of Bion's basic assumption thinking, he revised Bion's method of offering only group-wide interventions in favor of incorporating individualized interventions within the context of interpreting the common group tension. The Malan study (1976) was quite critical of the Ezriel approach but in my view, did not necessarily detract from the usefulness of the concept of the common group tension in formulating interventions (see Chapter Six). Furthermore, the current, contemporary Tavistock model has evolved considerably and is characterized by Garland (2010) as having much similarity to the technique described by Foulkes and his followers.

Next, while the Yalom and Leszcz view of how to handle therapist transference using both consensual validation and therapist transparency is certainly useful and may contribute to a therapeutic benefit, these methods are not always sufficient in providing the patient with the help she needs. The glaring omission in their discussion of technique is the failure to mention the use of interpretation, either to the individual or to the group, of the transference distortions of the therapist. They correctly note that sometimes the parental transference is enacted vis-à-vis another patient but frequently one sees it directed toward the figure of the therapist; but their attitude is that interpretations of transference to the therapist tend to detract from the all-important peer interactions. Whether the transference be idealization, dependency, erotization, anger, rebelliousness, mistrust, etc.—my view is that these significant issues in relation to parental authority figures call out for being addressed since they are so frequently the cause of difficulties in living.

There is a growing consensus among many psychodynamic group therapists that there are three kinds of transference: to the therapist, to one's peers, and to the group-as-a-whole. Neither deserves precedence over any other and, where some combination is being manifested, the clinician must use his judgment as to the "point of urgency" that requires his attention. Finally, I believe that while their method of focusing on the peer interaction can undoubtedly yield rich learning for their patients, their failure to systematically interpret the commonly shared group tension, which they describe as the motor of the interaction, tends to overlook another strong source of patient material. In the epilogue of this book, the final chapter, I shall deal in greater detail with the contrast between what I consider to be the two major approaches to group psychotherapy, the interpersonal *vs.* the group-as-a-whole.

Aaron Stein's peer interaction

Aaron Stein, in collaboration with Howard Kibel (Kibel & Stein, 1981), believed that group-as-a-whole interpretations, particularly as they apply to transference to the therapist, can be anti-therapeutic. Their reasoning is particularly noteworthy because, like Yalom and Leszcz, they definitely subscribe to the view that the motive force behind much of the group interaction is based upon commonly shared group transference to the leader. But they take a firm position that the traditional Tavistock approach of focusing upon the therapist transference fosters an undue preoccupation with the leader, tends to induce excessive dependency on him or her, and forces patients to neglect important peer transferences. Thus, they analogize peer transferences to a resistance to dealing with the therapist transference, and they cite the analytic aphorism that resistance must be interpreted before content. Their view is that therapist transferences should only be interpreted after the defensive peer transferences have been dealt with.

The authors are correct in pointing up one of the defects of a rigid adherence to the group centered, therapist-centered approach exemplified by both Bion and Ezriel. Indeed, one must not overlook that most group centered therapists believe there are tripartite transferences (therapist, peer, and group-as-a-whole). But the suggestion of avoiding therapist transference until peer transference has been dealt with may, in my view, lead to avoidance of important therapeutic material. Conflicts about dependence on authority, trust in parental figures, fear of losing parental love, struggles with aggressive feelings toward maternal and paternal figures, etc. are common human struggles that are best dealt with in terms of the main parental figure in the room, the therapist, although obviously not confined to him. And I doubt that such issues need to be dealt with first, in every case, in terms of peer transference. Their recommendation is based upon an underlying view that the major vehicle for therapeutic influence is group interaction: they state that the Ezriel-Bion approach "did not allow the members to develop the necessary interaction with each other that is the essence of group therapy" (p. 425). While peer group interaction is certainly a significant element of a therapeutic group, I believe that interaction with the therapist needs at least equal attention.

Interactional theorists, like Aaron Stein, criticize group centered thinking, and especially technical approaches that emphasize interpretations to the group-as-a whole, on the grounds that it tends to diminish peer interaction. Their critique is based mainly upon their examination of the work of Bion and Ezriel, and their reservations about these writers seem quite valid since Bion's iatrogenic personal style and Ezriel's long silences combined with oracular interventions made from a position of high authority indeed lent themselves to a preoccupation with the leader.

However, group centered technique is not monolithic and group centered therapists also differ, both in personal style and in their technical approaches. A group-as-a-whole approach does not preclude a focus on peer interactions. As mentioned earlier, peer interaction both contributes to and is affected by the shared group theme.

Kibel's later view

In an article on this topic written a quarter of a century later, Kibel (2005) modifies his earlier position and uses object relations theory and the concept of the social unconscious to bolster his view. First, he makes clear that he has no quarrel with the concept of group-as-a-whole as a major determinant of group behavior, and only objects to incorporating it into one's technical interventions. In fact, he emphasizes that "group-level processes were seen as always operative ..." and at another point he states "ultimately, shared fantasies become intrinsic to the group's organization, even if any particular fantasy varies from member to member and is not shared by all" (p. 143).

But he reiterates his earlier objection that group centered interventions inevitably involve emphasizing the therapist transference and this approach bypasses the major resistance which is the peer transference. Furthermore, states Kibel, the main vehicle for change involves effecting behavioral change in peer relationships and therapist transference would tend to minimize work with peers. Despite his avowed belief in the significance of group-as-a-whole and shared fantasies, he expresses general discomfort with the concept of a unifying theme in a group when he characterizes Ezriel's term as the "alleged common group tension" (p. 141).

He also offers a criticism of the present writer's modified Tavistock model on the grounds of "constructing the group in a particular way" (p. 142). He continues that it unwittingly intrudes into the group process to suit a preconceived view of its dynamics and thus usurps the freedom of the patient to behave authentically. I would argue that all clinicians conceptualize the treatment process as proceeding in a certain optimal way and we all have an influence on the process through our interventions. It is only a distorting influence when the therapist either structures the session excessively or behaves too passively, thereby engendering undue anxiety.

In an extended clinical vignette, one can gain a window into his reluctance to offering group centered interventions. He reports two sessions which occurred following four cancellations within a period of less than two months. The first session was characterized by considerable reports of depression as well as an escalation of anger between two patients that the therapist had to interrupt with the request that they remain silent for a period of time. Parenthetically, the therapist notes: "Although he recognized that the disruption in the treatment schedule could be contributory, if not causal, he judged that the members were too resistant to examine this" (p. 152).

In my view, there were clear signs that the group was attempting to express criticism of the therapist for the disruptions. One patient spoke openly of her fear as well as anger that the therapist would eject her from the group because of her lack of compliance with her treatment plan. Several patients talked about how anxious the open hostility in the group had made them.

The second session was further evidence that the group was indeed sitting on their hostility toward the therapist for his absences. The group was dramatically different, more conciliatory toward each other, and an infectious laughter erupted in the group that included the therapist. He correctly observed that the group seemed to be in flight from the tension of the previous session. What was remarkable was the group's spontaneous comments that the depressions of the previous week reflected a shared feeling of missing the group during the therapist's absences. "All agreed the therapist's absences were ill-timed. Some considered that the anger between members to have been in response to the breaks in the treatment schedule" (p. 153). The therapist, however, favored an interpretation based on the group's social unconscious: the notorious "Beltway sniper" had just been caught that very morning and both he and the group were expressing relief that the murder spree in the Washington D.C. area (some 250 miles away) was now over.

In his discussion, he pondered the relative influence of the treatment interruptions as opposed to the social context (the sniper) and came down on the side of the latter. He weighed whether social conditions had a greater effect on the patients than did the therapist's absences. He concluded that in times of social stress, the social context trumps within-treatment events. My reaction was that perhaps philosophically as well as counter-transferentially, Kibel was averse to dealing with therapist transference. He is quite aware, as any experienced therapist would be that the group might be dealing with feelings of anger about abandonment and he even seems to entertain the notion of interpreting this. But despite the patient's allusions in both sessions to their feelings of anger toward the therapist and their unhappiness about his "ill-timed absences", he tended to minimize their anger for his abandonment of them.

Scheidlinger's contributions

Throughout his long career as a major contributor to the group psychotherapy and group dynamics literature, Saul Scheidlinger (1980) has focused on the issue of integrating group dynamic forces with individual psychology. He has consistently called attention to the regressive forces in groups, to the process of identification among group members, to the varieties of scapegoating, and to the shared perception of the so-called "mother group". While criticizing those writers like Slavson who dominated the scene a few decades ago and who attempted to exclude the influence of group dynamics, he was also critical of Bion's idea of a group mentality. He agreed with the view that groups may sometimes experience shared common fantasies and be in the grip of a common group tension at certain times; that is, the entry of a new member or the cancellation of a session, but he believed that group centered thinking had to be modulated in three ways.

First, he has been extremely critical of any notion of a "group mind" and stressed that the process of fantasizing occurs only in individuals, not in groups. Second, he does not agree with the Bion/Ezriel notion that conflicts are omnipresent in a group setting; rather, he subscribes to the view that fluctuations occur between conflict-determined and conflict-free behavior in groups, implying a view of group wide emotional reactions as intermittent rather than constant. And third, he is critical of Bion for his excessive emphasis on the unconscious and primitive aspects of group functioning, contending that there are adaptive, conscious aspects of group functioning that require equal, if not greater, attention. Thus, he questions the concept of group regression, stating that regression only occurs in individuals and that a common occurrence in groups is regression in the service of the ego. He also emphasizes the supportive aspects of group participation such as sense of belonging, identification with the healthy aspects of the group and its members, and the gratification of being nurtured by the "mother group".

His emphasis is on the good mother aspects of the group rather than the view expressed by several theorists that groups are characterized by the potential of both good and bad mother fantasies. In general he believes that Bion in particular attributed excessive importance to disorganizing forces in the group and did not recognize the positive and adaptive aspects. Scheidlinger's objection to Bion's idea of group mentality appears to be based upon the idea that Bion's basic assumptions involve a sameness of thinking among all group members. However, Bion's concept of valence recognizes the existence of individual differences among group members in relation to their shared fantasies. In fact, Ezriel (1973) built the original Tavistock method specifically around differences among individuals in how they deal with the common group tension.

Scheidlinger's view of group theory as still in the realm of "limited domain" is frequently cited by other writers in agreement that the issue of the integration of individual and group is far from settled. He says that the question of what interacts, how the interaction occurs, and why it occurs is still not fully answered. These observations are well taken but I believe he would agree that one should push theory as far as one reasonably can with the caveat that there is always more to be learned in the future.

Even though he recognizes the presence of-certain shared or common fantasies in a group in reaction to group occurrences, he asserts that phenomena such as identifications and fantasizing operate in individuals only. Furthermore, he believes that individual personalities in a group, with their genetic and dynamic properties, are involved in a complex interaction with group dynamic elements, such as group climate, goals, and structure. And that this dual interaction is embedded in two main levels of group functioning: (1) the dynamic contemporaneous level that is more readily observed and includes the expression of conscious needs and adaptive patterns, and (2) the genetic-regressive level which primarily consists of unconscious and pre-conscious motivations, defenses, and conflicts.

Although Scheidlinger believes that we are not ready to formulate a method of integrating these varied and complex forces, one gains the impression that he leans toward Whitaker and Lieberman's alternation hypothesis. In referring to focal group conflict theory he wrote: "Conflictual phases were found to be interspersed with periods of group interaction which were devoid of conflict. This last observation, together with a greater allowance for individual group member differences and varying degrees of repression, is more consistent with current notions of ego psychology than the concepts of Bion and Ezriel" (1980, pp. 277–278).

Malcolm Pines and group analysis

Turning now to Pines and his colleagues (Pines & Schlapobersky, 2010; Kennard, Roberts, & Winter, 2000), they appear to remain close to their Foulkesian roots in emphasizing that the group is not constantly under the influence of a group-wide transference. They believe that the therapist ought to shift frequently between individual and group-wide interventions without giving priority to either one. "Theories which confine the role of the therapist to dealing entirely with the group process or which insist that all work has to be done in the transference to the therapist are artificial limits on that necessary freedom and have been shown not to be effective as therapy" (Kennard, Roberts, & Winter, p.140).

Without stating explicitly the basis for their last statement, they are apparently referring to the well-known Malan study of 1976 in which outcome results of the Tavistock method were found to be less than encouraging. In my view this may be a case of throwing the baby out with the bathwater. As we will see in greater detail later, it is possible to maintain a theory of group-as-a-whole functioning, a la the now-defunct Ezriel model, and still not convey to the patients that the group takes precedence over the individual.

In contrast to Hopper who has subscribed to the usefulness of some of Bion's views, most group analysts have criticized Bion's basic assumption theory and by extension, group centered thinking. Like Aaron Stein and Irvin Yalom, Dennis Brown (2006) focuses on peer interaction and tries to de-emphasize transference to the therapist. Brown's view is that Bion tended to induce basic assumptions by his personal style which tended to be distant and oracular. The inability of patients in his groups to experience a sense of intimacy with him as the therapist and the difficulty of the patients to begin working out their relationships with each other, presumably because of a preoccupation with the un-giving leader, leads to regressive reactions and a real difficulty in becoming a work group. Malcolm Pines (1993), agrees that Bion's method tended to be centered around a depriving leader, and thus common group themes were iatrogenically induced. While not denying the universality of basic assumption conflicts and affects, or the importance of dependency, aggression and sexuality in groups, both Brown and Pines question the conception of their dominance in group life.

Other writers, even those more sympathetic with Bion's approach (Sutherland, 1982), have also noted the possible iatrogenic effects of Bion's personal style. But aside from these personality influences, what might we conclude from the Foulkesian critique about group centered thinking? As stated earlier, my belief is that the therapist's focus upon transference to the therapist, as exemplified by Bion and Ezriel, does indeed lead to a preoccupation with the group's conflicting feelings about the therapist and a de-emphasis on peer transference.

On the other hand, if one adopts an approach of systematically minimizing attention to therapist transference, as seen in the approach of certain writers in the group analytic tradition, one would tend to push the group in the direction of denying and avoiding important universal conflicts surrounding parental figures, usually personified by the therapist, the central person in the group. Furthermore, one need not equate commonly shared themes with transference to the therapist alone. Indeed, peer transferences and transference to the group-as-a-whole, as well as transference to the leader, most commonly interact and it is the task of the therapist to integrate them in his interpretations when appropriate.

Ashbach and Schermer's tri-systemic model

These writers have attempted a comprehensive and bold paradigmatic shift in conceptualizing the complexities of group psychotherapy (1987). They postulate the existence of three systems: the individual in depth, an interactive system characterized by the processes of communication, and the group qua group characterized mainly by common unconscious themes. They regard the interactive system as the link between the intrapsychic structure of the individual and the dynamics of the group field. They speak of a continuous tension and interchange among the three dynamic systems and the regulatory boundaries between them.

They do not offer a specific modus operandi or therapeutic model for conducting a therapy group. Rather, they imply that the therapist needs to attend to each of the systems and the boundaries between them more or less simultaneously, and should intervene at the level which seems to require most attention at any given moment. They emphasize that the field of group psychotherapy must emphasize the study of the types of interactive processes used by group members to build bridges between their deep inner experiences and the group reality: "The role of symbol, metaphor, and myth as regulatory mechanisms cannot be overemphasized" (p. 160).

Their contribution has been to call attention to the reciprocal influences of the individual upon the group and the group upon the individual, and the importance of attending simultaneously to the three interrelated systems within a group. In a broadly comprehensive way, they bring together object relations theory, self psychology, and general systems theory. They stop short of proposing a specific strategy for working with the interconnections. In his most recent work on this topic, Schermer edited a two volume series in the journal *Group* (2005), in which he assembled some of the major recent contributors on the topic of group-as-a-whole to describe their current views. He wrote two extensive critiques of the articles and then summarized his own views. His first main point was that the field of psychotherapy has advanced considerably since the time of Bion and Ezriel in the direction of intersubjectivity, dialectical constructivism, and co-creationism. Group therapists are still observer-participants, but they are more open in their participation and in sharing their own feelings. They are no longer simply the expert, omniscient interpreters of the group process, and they emphasize that each member is capable of making valid and useful observations about the group process, including critiques of the leader's style and perspective.

His second criticism, directed more specifically at group centered theory, is that group-wide interventions have tended to be too rigidly conceived and he argues in behalf of a more flexible approach in which the therapist should have the freedom to address the individual, the subgroup, or the group-as-a-whole depending on where the major affect happens to be. He presents a vignette from a training group (pp. 230–231) in which the therapist deals with one member's complaints as a spokesman for a group-wide feeling. The intervention fell flat and could not be used by either the individual or the group until he explored more fully the individual's feelings of low self-esteem and issues concerning his marriage. It was only after the individual's personal needs were dealt with empathically that the therapist could effectively broach the group's ambivalent feelings toward the therapist.

The first issue regarding the shift toward intersubjectivity and co-creationism is, in my view, not strictly relevant to group centered theory since it deals with psychotherapy as an evolving discipline and one would expect that all group therapists, whether of the group-as-a-whole persuasion or not, are inevitably affected by the changes developing in the discipline of psychotherapy. In passing one should note that while Bion did not engage in self-disclosure as many therapists are now doing with some effectiveness, he was quite aware that his subjective responses were key to understanding the group process. In fact he contended that the main indicators of basic assumption life and the influence of the group's projective identifications were the emotional impact of these forces on the therapist's own experience.

On the second issue of the modern view that one needs to adopt a more flexible attitude toward interventions and not focus exclusively on the group-as-a-whole, he is correct that the pioneers tended to give primacy to what was occurring in the group-qua-group, which has been shown to be less than helpful.

Billow's relational psychology

Richard Billow has become a prolific and valuable contributor to the literature, incorporating the most modern thinking of relational theory while extracting, translating, and applying Bion's "metapsychology". His book on relational group psychotherapy (2003) relies heavily not only on Bion's views about the basic assumptions in groups but also on his later writings about psychic functioning, mainly derived from his work in dyads, including the human resistance to thinking about one's inner world and about learning from experience. These considerations undoubtedly enrich and add depth to Billow's understanding of his own and his patients' struggles in doing therapeutic work.

But Billow also makes clear his parting of the ways with Bion in technique. Like most others, he does not confine his interventions to group-wide interpretations nor to minimalist therapist participation. And he also does not believe, as did Ezriel as well as the more modern contemporary Tavistock therapists do, that therapy groups typically develop a common group tension that lends itself to interpretation that can affectively impact each member. In fact when Billow offers a group-wide intervention he thinks of it as applying to a number of the patients but not to all, and he typically does not search for group themes. His view is that the therapist should move flexibly between interventions to individuals, interpersonal interactions, relations among subgroups, as well as to the entire group. He is particularly averse to systems that focus on transference to the therapist.

The major value of his contribution is calling attention to the key role of the therapist at all stages of the group's development, how his or her psychology and interpersonal behavior impinge on the group, for better or for worse. He clearly works towards passion in both therapist and group members, that is, "an intersubjective process of bearing and utilizing the primal affects to reach self-conscious emotional awareness" (p. 31). One wonders if this objective would not have been further enhanced by his seeking out and interpreting the shared group theme which leads to a deepening of the group's affective experience without at the same time dampening valued freedom and spontaneity of the group's interactions.

The theory of unitary group functioning

Many group therapists nowadays agree that common group themes develop in relation to significant group events, such as the entry of a new member, departure of an old member, vacation interruptions, etc. But during the interim periods between such events, some believe that group themes are either relatively weak or completely absent, and during these times the group is dealing with individual or interactional issues which are unaffected by the group-as-a-whole.

In contrast, the group centered theorists point to a number of group dynamic phenomena where common themes may not be obvious but may easily be inferred. Perhaps the most common instance is the scape-goating phenomenon in which the group disowns unwelcome characteristics which are, by projection or projective identification, put into a given individual who is then attacked and sometimes extruded (Scheidlinger, 1982). Or, as Agazarian (1997, 2008) illustrates, struggles and polarities between subgroups may often represent the externalization of a group's commonly shared conflict, such as a wish for intimacy countered by the fear of closeness.

But even more frequent would be the emergence of conflict out of the everyday mundane contributions of each member. When a patient reports on his successes, improvements in his life situation, or even triumphs, the group becomes a fertile field for such feelings as pride about one's peers, encouragement that such progress might also be in one's own future, but may also fan the flames of competitiveness and envy. By the same token, reports of failures, setbacks, or personal disasters may reverberate throughout the group in a wide variety of ways, including a sense of depressive anxiety about one's personal, as well as the group's future. Thus, the so-called interim periods between occurrences that clearly affect the group-as-a-whole may be influenced by group events that could subtly have the potential of building into a dominant group theme.

Further evidence for group theme thinking is derived from the clinical experience of understanding an individual's productions more fully and more deeply once the theme of the group-as-a-whole has been understood. In other words, there is a circular, reciprocal enhancement of individual to group and group back to individual in terms of fullness of understanding. Thus, a patient described an intense outbreak of hypochondriacal symptoms which on the surface appeared to be related to the break-up of a long-standing romantic relationship. But the group was also being influenced by the therapist's announcement of a vacation interruption, and the patient's reaction to this abandonment was also a contributing factor to his outbreak of symptoms. In other words, he was adding to the development of the abandonment theme in the group while at the same time the group theme was contributing to the intensity of his symptomatic flare-up.

A most comprehensive and masterful discussion of group centered thinking may be found in Ettin's (1992) important book. He discusses the epistemology of the group-as-a-whole approach in terms both of its inductive and deductive aspects. In other words, one may collect specific instances or specific patient contributions and find the common denominator which becomes the group-as-a-whole theme. Conversely, one could begin to understand individual contributions in terms of one's knowledge of group background factors, such as boundary issues like past or future cancellations, the entry or departure of members. In practice, both inductive and deductive mental processes occur more or less simultaneously, as typically happens in hypothetico-deductive scientific reasoning, particularly when the therapist is listening both to the specifics of an individual's reaction combined with a mental set of discovering a group-wide theme.

One consensus that has emerged among a wide variety of theorists, starting with Bion and including Durkin (1964), Scheidlinger (1980), and Ganzarain (1989), has been the view that the group-as-a-whole is unconsciously viewed by its members at a rather primitive, part-object level in terms of the attributes of mother. As mentioned earlier, Scheidlinger (1974) emphasizes the nurturant, soothing, and holding aspects of the maternal introject, while Durkin points to the critical, intrusive, demanding qualities of the pre-oedipal mother. Ganzarain takes a more integrative approach in which either side of the ambivalence may become dominant at any particular time. The latter line of thinking is consistent with a theory of unitary functioning.

As mentioned earlier, there are probably as many models among group centered therapists as there are writers. Bion's (1959), technical recommendations of only addressing the group-as-a-whole in terms of the basic assumptions with which they are struggling, has essentially been disavowed by all subsequent writers. Ezriel (1952, 1973) attempted to correct for the deficiencies of the Bion method and introduced the idea of individualized comments that were only given after the therapist had interpreted the common group tension, a model that one might describe as deductive in structure. Whitaker and Lieberman (1964) emphasized the uncovering of the focal group conflict consisting of a disturbing motive, usually some unconscious wish, that is countered by a reactive motive, the expected punishment for the wish, and this conflict eventually becomes resolved by either an enabling or restrictive group solution. Agazarian (2008) has underlined the importance of defining subgroups within the total group to express conflicting wishes and to begin working in the direction of making the boundaries between the subgroups more permeable and thus enhancing communication. Ganzarain (1989) is a group centered therapist who distinguishes his approach from others in ferreting out psychotic-like anxieties and other primitive content in the tradition of Melanie Klein.

Summary

Group centered thinking has become an increasingly prominent force in group psychotherapy writings during the past few decades. Not only is there greater acceptance of the view that the network of communications has an important impact on each member, but there appears to be increasing acceptance of the idea that psychotherapy groups give evidence of unitary functioning in the sense of developing common group themes and reactions to shared group conflicts. Such group centered thinking, however, does not lead to a single monolithic approach to group psychotherapy technique, and a variety of models of integrating individual dynamics with group dynamics has emerged.

The most common criticism of group centered approaches, based primarily on the Bion-Ezriel models, is that the primary emphasis upon the therapist tends to override the important peer relationships that develop in the group. There is no doubt that this criticism has some validity and undoubtedly was a shortcoming in the early models. However, the modifications of the Tavistock model suggested by this writer, as well as others (Garland, 2010), go a long way toward correcting this weakness. Second, there is the hazard of generalizing about a common group theme based on too little evidence and the group centered therapist must indeed be cognizant of such a possibility. Finally, there is the criticism of a tendency in the original Ezriel/ Tavistock model to convey that the fount of all wisdom lies in the omniscient therapist. There is little doubt that that approach lent itself to such a perception by the patients, insofar as the therapist waited for a considerable period of time before he intervened and when he did, his interpretation consisted of a "lecturette" that his obedient "students" were supposed to hear attentively.

In my view, these weaknesses in the Tavistock model have contributed to an aversion to interpret the transference to the therapist, much to the loss of valuable opportunities to help the patients deal with important issues concerning dependency, oedipal, parental, and authority issues. Without minimizing the importance of attending to peer interactions and peer relationships, the therapist transferences are among the most important areas of conflict for our patients and need to be accorded sufficient attention.

CHAPTER FOUR

Forty years of group psychotherapy at the Menninger Clinic

In the spring of 2001 the world renowned Menninger Clinic of Topeka, a bastion of mental health services and training, came to an unexpected and untimely demise. During its seventy-five years of existence, it had gained preeminence as an institution of last resort for patients who were proving refractory to treatment in their home communities. This outstanding institution, founded by Drs. Karl and Will Menninger, had attracted and nurtured some of the most respected names in the mental health field including Robert Knight, David Rapaport, Merton Gill, Gardner and Lois Murphy, and Otto Kernberg, to name just a few. It had been an important resource for education and training of mental health professionals where psychiatric residents, psychology post-doctoral fellows, postmaster social work students, and nursing graduates came for high quality post-graduate training or continuing education. The sudden collapse of this venerable institution with its proud tradition of quality clinical work and respected training and research programs came as distressing news to both its outside admirers and referral sources as well as to the hundreds of staff members who had expected to make Menninger their lifetime careers. A few staff members moved to Houston where the clinic joined forces with the Baylor School of Medicine.

In many ways Menninger clinical practices became the touchstone for quality psychiatric care. Menninger pioneered in the development of the analytically oriented hospital, utilizing psychodynamic thinking as a model for its treatment of hospital patients. When group methods started to be used in hospital treatment, we devised a pioneering innovation, a largely psychoanalytic group oriented model of in-patient care. In addition, we developed a day hospital treatment program, mainly used as a transitional treatment for recently discharged in-patients, which also served as a valuable model for other institutions seeking to offer continuum of care to its patients. Finally, Menninger began an out-patient group psychotherapy program that was primarily influenced by the work of John Sutherland and Henry Ezriel (1952) of the Tavistock Clinic. This represented an important innovation in the U.S. given its stress on group dynamic perspectives eschewed by such contemporary authorities on group psychotherapy as S. R. Slavson and Alexander Wolf.

The purpose of this chapter is to recount the history of group treatment at the Menninger Clinic with special emphasis on the uphill struggle that we encountered in the early days, the various programs we introduced that facilitated its growth, and the special contributions we made to the American scene.

The prevailing attitude of psychoanalysis toward group methods in the fifties and sixties

The 1940s and 1950s were the halcyon days for psychoanalysis and psychoanalytic psychotherapy. Students were flocking in the droves either to psychoanalytic institutes or to graduate schools with an analytic orientation. Being in analysis was a badge of distinction and many spoke with pride about their analysis and their analyst. Most of the chairmen of departments of psychiatry at that time were trained analysts. Many of us look back with nostalgia to that golden era.

But organized psychoanalysis and many leading analysts at that time were either indifferent or antagonistic to group psychotherapy. The prevailing attitude was a conviction, or at least a bias, that intensive analytic work was impossible in a public arena like a group and the only way a person could open up and explore the depths of his or her psyche was in the privacy of the dyadic consulting room. There was, furthermore, a widely circulated rumor in New York during the fifties that the institutes of the American Psychoanalytic Association would suspend the training of any candidate who practiced group treatment. The last fifty years have seen a considerable change in this attitude and it is somewhat difficult to conjure up the basis for this extreme bias. At that time there were two contradictory prejudices operating. First, there was the idea that group psychotherapy can only touch the surface because people cannot disclose their innermost feelings and honestly discuss their most private thoughts in a group context. Second, there was the idea was that the emotions stirred up in a group can be so intense and uncontrollable that various kinds of acting out are likely to occur both inside and outside the group.

I recall a vivid example of this bias. In 1964 Anna Freud was visiting the Menninger Clinic to launch the newly formed Academy of Child Analysis and one evening a reception was held in her honor. I happened to be passing by the area where Dr. Karl Menninger and Miss Freud were chatting and was taken by surprise when Dr. Karl beckoned to me. He seemed to be eager to leave her company and he introduced me to the honored guest, "Miss Freud, this is Dr. Horwitz. He is interested in group psychotherapy"; at which point he beat a hasty retreat. We each looked at each other awkwardly for a moment and she blurted out, "I don't believe in group psychotherapy". The conversation went downhill from there.

The negative attitude toward group methods among analysts at large was mirrored at the Menninger Clinic as well. Throughout the 1950s there was no group therapy in existence, either with in-patients or out-patients. The hospital maintained a clearly anti-group bias, manifested by the fact that there were no therapy groups on the wards and in fact, even talking with a peer about your personal problems was regarded as a form of acting out against the revered relationship with your individual therapist. A patient government with a so-called Patient Council was a structured group whose main business focused on facilitating communication between staff and patients as well as orienting new patients to the policies of the hospital.

The beginnings

The first tentative steps toward a group psychotherapy program began in the Fall of 1957 when a few young clinicians formed an informal weekly study group to learn more about this new modality with an eye toward eventually instituting this modality. There were about ten staff members out of a total of approximately 150 who participated and I served as chairman. Most had been exposed to some group therapy training or practice in other centers, although none considered themselves truly experienced. Most had some positive impression of group treatment mainly based on contact with an enthusiastic teacher or participation in an experiential training group that had impressed them with its therapeutic potential.

Practically all of the members were junior staff and none were in analytic training at that time. There was a missionary attitude in the air based on the awareness of an opposition to this method by a conservative administration, and indeed by a majority of the staff. The agenda of the meetings dealt with discussions of the current literature in addition to sharing previous experiences and beliefs regarding indications and contraindications, curative mechanisms, relationship to individual therapy, as well as specific techniques. The outcome of these meetings was a written proposal to the administration advocating the introduction of group therapy training and practice at the clinic.

The administrative group to whom this proposal was addressed was a committee of department directors, but they functioned as more of an advisory group than a decision making body. Their deliberations were sometimes heeded, but often ignored, by Dr. Karl Menninger, chief of staff and founder of the clinic. A charismatic leader, his management style was quite authoritarian and he exerted control over all matters, large and small. We all knew that he needed to give his approval to the introduction of a new modality, especially one that on its face did not seem to accord with the prevailing treatment ideology. As stated earlier, the view that psychotherapy required the privacy of a one-to-one relationship in a quiet consulting room was an ingrained belief and the idea of treatment "in public" was an alien notion. Besides, the individuals proposing this innovation were relatively junior in the organization. As one might expect, the proposal did not receive an enthusiastic response.

During this time, our self-appointed "committee" continued to discuss both scientific and strategic matters, and we began to introduce the idea of the organization sending some of its members to the American Group Psychotherapy Association annual meeting. The latter proposal resulted in my being summoned to an audience with Dr. Karl in order to justify the trip. I persuaded him that group treatment was a development worth studying and I was pleased that he gave permission for the writer to attend. However, he sent a follow-up memo in which he made clear his expectation that I would evaluate the validity of the modality, make some judgments about who would be a suitable consultant to such a program, and be prepared to offer some orientation to the staff, residents, and to him. It was clear that he did not wish to stifle the group's initiative but at the same time he was a long way from endorsing the plan.

The written report of my experience and observations at the AGPA, however intriguing and inspiring to me, left Dr. Karl less than enthusiastic. He was clearly not ready to have group psychotherapy introduced to the Clinic but temporized by recommending that we "try the method on non-paying customers" at the Topeka State Hospital. For the next year and a half, I cut my teeth as a group therapist by working with a group of young adolescent in-patients. I met this group once a week and was supervised in a control group of relative neophytes. Needless to say this was a trying experience for me since this population is notoriously action-oriented and simply getting them to remain in their seats for an hour was a significant accomplishment.

The possibility of beginning a program at the Menninger Clinic remained in limbo during this period but a breakthrough finally occurred through the confluence of two events. Dr. Hermann Van der Waals, a training analyst from Amsterdam, was appointed director of the C. F. Menninger Memorial Hospital. He was a contemporary of Dr. Karl, a quiet, dignified man, and one of the few members of the staff toward whom Dr. Karl would defer. Some time after he arrived he read a book by a Dr. Thomas Freeman, *Chronic Schizophrenia*, that described work with hospitalized schizophrenic patients in small groups in a Scottish hospital. The patients responded quite positively to this treatment, became somewhat more social, and showed remission of their most disturbing symptoms. Based on this work, Van der Waals authorized us to start a program of group treatment in the hospital. Although our intention was to conduct more expressive type groups than the ones described by Freeman, we regarded this invitation as the opening we were seeking.

The early phase

Four groups were started with hospital patients in early 1962. These were not ward groups but rather were patients who were selected by their hospital doctors as good candidates for group treatment irrespective of whether they were receiving individual therapy. Actually, a majority of the in-patients were assigned to individual therapists as a matter of course. The Menninger Hospital at that time had an average length of stay of longer than one year (unbelievable in these days of managed care) and the groups were long term and open-ended.

The " committee" not only received a boost from Dr. Van der Waals but around the same time Dr. Roy Menninger, son of Dr. Will, who had trained in psychiatry in Boston and was on the staff of Brigham and Women's Hospital, had decided to return to his native Topeka and begin a stint at the Menninger Hospital. Having been trained in group psychotherapy in Boston and having already published a paper on group therapy, Roy's visibility in the organization and prior experience gave us additional credibility.

The groups were conducted by Jerome Katz and Gunther Ammon (co-therapists), Stephen Appelbaum, Roy Menninger, and Leonard Horwitz. The original organizing committee soon became the official Group Study Group. We met once a week and became the peer supervisory body for the therapists who presented their process material on a regular basis. There were at least two theoretical orientations in the group at that time. One was derived from the New York area as personified by Wilfred Hulse who worked very much in the Slavson and Postgraduate Center tradition of individual therapy in the group. The other represented the Semrad-Max Day tradition of Boston with its emphasis on the dynamics of small groups such as the spokesman and the role suction phenomena. Allegiances developed toward one orientation or the other but despite these differing perspectives, the control group was able to carry on its work in a constructive manner.

Our messiah arrives

To some extent our group was like a ship without a rudder in that we did not have a clear model of group psychotherapy within which to operate. Through a bit of happenstance we were rescued by a consultant with considerable expertise and leadership ability. The British John D. Sutherland arrived in Topeka in early 1963 prepared to teach us the Tavistock model. He was medical director of the Tavistock Clinic in London where the primary modality of treatment was psychodynamic group therapy. He had been invited by Dr. Karl who had fortuitously met him on a trip to London and quickly surmised that he would be a valuable resource to the persistent (and pesky?) group therapists at the Menninger Clinic.

In collaboration with Henry Ezriel Sutherland (1952), developed a model of group-as-a-whole therapy which emphasized the interpretation of the underlying "common group tension" that they believed developed in all groups. Although they differed with Bion on his particular method of group therapy, their common group tension shared much in common with Bion's basic assumptions. During that first visit which lasted a month, he conducted two or three evening seminars per week for a small group of interested students and his presence served to unify our group with regard to a theoretical model. It supplied a badly needed conceptual integration by an experienced mentor that we had been seeking. Sutherland's value as a consultant soon became obvious to many others beside the group therapists and for over twenty-five years, until he died, he became a valued adviser to the organization as a whole, a counselor to the president, and a warm friend to many of us. Also, as the head of the prestigious Tavistock Clinic, his advocacy of group therapy was of immense help in establishing our legitimacy in the eyes of the Menninger Clinic leadership and staff.

Education and training

The courses that the group therapists offered to the psychiatric residents and other trainees in the Menninger School of Psychiatry and Mental Health Sciences proved to be invaluable in developing an institution-wide group program. Finding converts among the staff was considerably more difficult than among the trainees. The first venture in this direction occurred in 1961 when we began, almost accidentally, the so-called Group Dynamics Seminar, basically an experiential group using, at that time, the Bethel T-group model. It was actually introduced in Topeka by a social psychologist, Howard Perlmutter, who had been trained in that method and was on the staff of our Industrial Mental Health Department for a short time. It turned out to be well received on the part of the residents who were interested in a quasi-therapeutic experience. When Perlmutter left, he invited the group therapists to continue what he had started and two of us somewhat hesitantly took it on, since none of us had experience in conducting experiential training groups. But it turned out to be a boon for our program since the majority of residents valued the experience and many of them sought out further training in group therapy. When they graduated, and some of them joined the Menninger staff, they became the referral sources for group psychotherapy or joined the growing numbers of staff who wished to gain experience in group work.

As time went on, and particularly after our exposure to the Tavistock/A. K. Rice model in the late sixties, we began to conduct the Group Dynamics Seminars in that style. Although these groups were quite popular with the trainees, the school administrators found it a disquieting experience since it did not fit into the usual mold of other courses. First, we did not give grades or even report attendance to the school authorities since confidentiality was part of the contract with the residents. Second, to the extent that the anxiety generated in these unstructured sessions caused a very small number of the participants to become upset, further doubts by the administration were created about the value of the course.

In December 1965, a formal teaching program of group psycho-therapy was introduced. It came into being as a result of the growing prominence in the sixties of the modality nationally (Scheidlinger, 2004) combined with the conviction of its importance by several members of the Menninger staff. As mentioned above, the residents and junior staff were generally more receptive to new modalities than were the older members of the staff. And it was here that we first benefited from our association with the AGPA where we acquired knowledge about training guidelines including the content of didactic courses, hours of supervision, and qualification of supervisors. We were able to use the guidelines for training established by the AGPA, the major association for group therapy in the U.S., in devising curriculum and supervision standards. But the biggest boost to our program was the requirement by the Residency Review Committee for Psychiatry in the late sixties that all psychiatric residents be trained in group therapy. Whatever question had persisted regarding the validity of this modality among the staff and the administration was necessarily muted by this endorsement of a national accrediting body.

A further dividend of the residency review committee's action was the requirement that psychiatric residents engage in the supervised practice of group psychotherapy for at least a year. This requirement actually put us under some strain to begin finding groups for our residents but it also opened up new arenas of practice for them. For example, the residential treatment center for delinquent boys in Topeka had had a long standing program in group therapy but was lacking in trained staff to continue this work. It was accordingly bolstered by the influx of a number of our residents offering to take groups. In addition, one pair of psychiatric trainees hit on the idea of starting a group for residents of a local nursing home and both the therapists and the patients had an unexpectedly positive experience.

Growing pains of the sixties

The decade of the sixties showed slow but steady growth in our program while coping with some significant systemic problems. The Group Study Group continued to meet on a weekly basis and gradually recruited new staff members, some of them quite senior. In addition to Dr. Jerome Katz, then a graduate analyst, who joined us quite early and was one of the first therapists to take a hospital group, Dr. Francisco Gomez, another graduate analyst, joined our ranks and began an out-patient group. Dr. Povl Toussieng, a senior staff member in the Children's Department, began an adolescent group as did Dr. Bruno Magliocco, a senior staff member in the adult hospital. Other staff members who joined our ranks included Drs. Otto and Paulina Kernberg, Dr. Francis Broucek, Dr. Stuart Averill, Dr. Esther Burstein, Dr. Estela Beale, and Dr. Stephen Appelbaum, all of whom were in various stages of a psychoanalytic career. These members added to the prestige and visibility of the group.

A highly significant addition that occurred in 1967 was the arrival from Chile of Ramon Ganzarain. Not only was Ramon a Training and Supervising Analyst and former director of the Chilean Psychoanalytic Institute, but he was an experienced group therapist. He quickly became a major spokesman for group therapy and a sought after teacher and supervisor as well as leader of the Group Dynamics Seminars. His videotapes of his group therapy work were superb teaching tools and engendered considerable interest by staff and trainees alike. His presence signaled another leap forward in the recognition and acceptance of our cause.

While the addition of these staff members provided a welcome boost to establishing our standing in the clinical services, we became increasingly aware of a systemic problem with which we had to struggle throughout the life of the Menninger Clinic. The symptom of the problem was the difficulty we experienced in keeping the patient census of our groups sufficiently high to comfortably maintain their viability. The first reason was the fact that our outpatient department staff were not oriented toward group treatment and did not keep it in mind when making treatment recommendations. We attempted to correct this difficulty by attending their case conferences and making presentations on the usefulness of group, both to the outpatient service as well as to the staff as a whole. These measures were important but produced limited results. But the second reason was an enduring structural problem; namely the plethora of therapists and modalities of treatment that outweighed the relatively small patient pool. The C. F. Menninger Memorial Hospital during the sixties and into the seventies had an adult population of nearly 150 patients and the Children's Hospital had a usual census of about fifty. The Outpatient Clinic served a local population in the Topeka and surrounding area of perhaps two to three hundred thousand people. But the ratio of mental health professionals to the number of patients seeking treatment was quite high. Our professional staff of psychiatrists, psychologists, and social workers numbered 125–150 and the number of trainees in the various training programs almost equaled that number. Added to that was the fact that the modalities available consisted of psychoanalysis, individual psychotherapy, group psychotherapy, family therapy, and marital therapy, resulting in rather keen competition by the many departments and training programs to supply their constituencies with patients.

Our relationship to the AGPA

During the decade of the sixties a slowly increasing number of our group staff began to attend the annual institute and conference of the American Group Psychotherapy Association. At first the relationship was one of being students and observers of the American group therapy scene. We also began to cultivate contacts with some of the experts in the field for the purpose of bringing them to Topeka as consultants. But as time went on many attained sufficient expertise to serve as faculty, offering workshops, scientific papers, and participating on panels or symposia.

One of the first consultants who came to Topeka was Dr. Aaron Stein, director of group psychotherapy at the Mount Sinai Hospital in New York. He was valuable in helping us to conceptualize the role of group therapy in a clinic that was both psychoanalytically oriented and which emphasized the primacy of individual treatment. His orientation, suitable for that time, was that group should be regarded as an adjunct to individual treatment.

Another consultant who visited our program on several occasions was Dr. Saul Scheidlinger, a prominent theoretician and clinician associated with the Albert Einstein College of Medicine in New York. He consulted with our group therapy staff on more than one occasion and emphasized methods of increasing the cohesiveness of our ongoing groups. He also lectured to the staff as a whole on the relationship between group and individual psychology, and conducted continuing education programs.

A third consultant was Dr. Howard Kibel who held the unique position of having taken his psychiatric residency in Topeka in the early sixties and afterwards joined the staff of Mount Sinai to work with Aaron Stein and further his group interests. His experience in a Menninger group dynamic seminar led him to an abiding interest in group treatment. He eventually became director of group therapy at New York Hospital, Westchester Division, and developed an expertise in the theory and practice of in-patient group treatment.

Among the staff members who began presenting their work at AGPA conferences were Dennis Farrell, Roy Menninger, Don Colson, Tetsuro Takahashi, Karen Wakefield, Joseph Hyland, and James Kleiger. Several were elected to leadership positions. Ramon Ganzarain, Larry Kennedy, and Pearl Washington won seats on the Board of Directors and became Fellows of the association. Bonnie Buchele, along with the writer, gained the position of president and were later honored with the designation of Distinguished Fellow. Nomund Wong joined the staff in the 1980s and participated in our continuing education workshops and made scientific presentations locally and nationally.

The unique contribution that our group made to the national association and to the American scene was to explicate the usefulness of understanding how group dynamics can be integrated into a modality that nevertheless emphasizes the treatment of the individual. We had the special advantage of having been taught the Tavistock model which emphasized the role of the group-as-a-whole and that point of view was relatively absent in the U.S. for many years. During the decade after Jock Sutherland's initial consultation, we gradually began to modify this model with the idea of making it more user friendly. Our modification is described as the inductive model in a widely recognized article by this writer (Chapter Six). This revision was published around the same time that Malan, Balfour, Hood, and Shooter (1976) made known the results of his outcome research on a large number of group patients at the Tavistock Clinic. They found that many of the patients experienced the method as somewhat austere and objected to the emphasis on the dynamics of the group which gave the patients the impression that their individual needs were being slighted. I believe that the inductive model corrected these deficiencies and contributed to group centered thinking in this country.

A further contribution of the Menninger group was the insertion of an object relations perspective into group theory and practice by Ramon Ganzarain. Through his presentations at AGPA and through the publication of several articles and two books, one on object relations in group psychotherapy and the other on the treatment of incest in group (co-authored with Bonnie Buchele), he helped to introduce greater depth into the perspective of analytic group therapists. His Kleinian orientation permitted him to understand and interpret primitive, archaic fantasies that tend to be overlooked in less depth oriented psychologies. He also reinforced the Tavistock/Menninger group centered approach by his emphasis on Bion's theories of group functioning.

The group relations conferences

Dr. Roy Menninger assumed the presidency of the Menninger Clinic in 1967. The contrast between his administrative style and that of Dr. Karl could not have been more striking. Dr. Roy was interested in making the organization more democratic and less hierarchical. He attempted to encourage both the department directors and the staff to assume more responsibility and initiative in instituting changes in the organization. But he soon discovered that the culture of the institution had become quite passive and accustomed to an authoritarian leadership style.

Because of his own orientation toward group methods for producing change and in consultation with the group therapists who had been using experiential methods in teaching, he decided to invest some of the organization's resources in sending a majority of staff members over several years for group relations training. Because of our Tavistock orientation, the Tavistock Institute of Human Relations was the training site of choice and several staff members had the opportunity to attend the training sessions in Leicester, England. Subsequently the sister

American organization, the A. K. Rice Institute, was established and a number of staff attended the group relations conferences at Amherst and Mt. Holyoke and other sites.

Dr. Roy had considerable personal and financial investment in this program which took place between 1968 and 1974, during which approximately 150 staff members had attended at least one group relations conference. Following his or her attendance, each participant was asked to describe what the experience was like and to candidly detail the kind of learning, or lack thereof, which occurred. This material was initially described in an article in the International Journal of Group Psychotherapy (1972). More than ten years later, Dr. Roy once again made a similar survey of those staff members who were still at the clinic and he summarized his findings in Group Relations Reader 2 (Colman & Geller, 1985).

Both the initial response as well as the follow-up survey yielded predominantly positive reactions: "… most of the respondents remain strongly positive about their GRC (group relations conference) experience after nearly a decade, and believe that it has had a substantial, valuable, and lasting impact on the organization" (p. 297). Not only was the experience of value to the improved functioning of the organization but it alerted many staff members to the special value, indeed the power, of a group experience. We believe that many staff members who had been indifferent to the therapeutic use of groups became more favorably disposed to group treatment.

The growth of hospital groups

In the fifties and sixties the average length of stay for patients in the C. F. Menninger Memorial Hospital was between one and two years. There was a growing recognition, however, that some patients could benefit from a brief hospitalization, particularly where the focus was on dealing with a relatively acute crisis situation. In 1970 under the leadership of Dr. Dennis Farrell and with the encouragement of Dr. Otto Kernberg, hospital director, a study of several institutions similar to ours was undertaken and a new short term unit was formed with the purpose of keeping hospitalization limited to four to six weeks. (Ironically, this length under the present managed care environment is now considered long term!) In a dramatic reversal of previous policies regarding the sanctity of the individual therapy relationship, the patients were expected to discuss their problems in groups that met daily. The prevalent philosophy of the time regarding therapeutic community a la Maxwell Jones was combined with the analytic group therapy methods used in our clinic to form a predominantly group orientation to hospital treatment in the new unit.

During the next several months this development had a profound ripple effect on the entire hospital. Other hospital sections viewed the short-term unit with envy in terms of its high morale and sense of excitement engendered by pioneering a fresh new approach to the treatment of in-patients. The nursing staff was given new therapeutic responsibilities insofar as they often became therapists or co-therapists in the various groups. Clinical decision making within each treatment team became the modus operandi and many of the staff who formerly felt peripheral now experienced themselves as responsible and involved.

A contagion effect developed in the hospital at large and before long, every unit began instituting staff-patient meetings on a regular basis, both for the entire unit and for various sub-groups. There was considerable diversity in the functioning of these groups and how they defined their tasks. Sometimes the meetings were solely devoted to dealing with staff-patient tensions, sometimes with peer group issues, while other groups encouraged patients to bring in requests for changes in privileges which the entire patient group would discuss and often decide on, with the staff always holding veto power if the group decisions seemed unwise. Since there was no centralized program that controlled or coordinated the development of these groups, they very much grew like Topsy, differing in tasks, agendas, leadership methods, frequency, etc.

In 1975 Dr. Peter Hartocollis, director of the hospital, appointed the writer chairman of an ad-hoc Hospital-Wide Committee on Groups to work on the issue of the increasing diversity in philosophy and method with regard to hospital group treatment. A multidisciplinary committee, representing each of the seven sections of the hospital, was selected by each Section Council. Our task was to compare philosophies and methods of group treatment on the various hospital sections and hopefully arrive at a set of recommendations for the hospital as a whole to follow.

After one year of weekly deliberations, the committee produced a consensus report that included a set of recommendations for optimal group treatment. An important ingredient of the process consisted of two way communication between the section representatives and their section members, so that each delegate was careful to appraise his or her section of the deliberations of the committee. As a result the hospital sections were considered part of the process and the experience of having a policy, or even guidelines, suddenly imposed on them by fiat was minimized. The recommendations were submitted to the Hospital Council and hospital director and were adopted as recommended procedures for the various sections to follow.

An indication of the positive reception of the committee's recommendations was the fact that the hospital director in consultation with the Hospital Council requested the writer to organize another hospital wide committee in order to deal with a related problem that had surfaced as a result of the growth of group treatment. There was a feeling that the pendulum may have swung too far in the direction of neglecting the individual relationship between the hospital therapist and the patient, particularly those patients who find it difficult to profit from group treatment. The new committee became known as Hospital-Wide Committee on Groups and Related Treatment and once again was composed of representatives of each section as well as the disciplines working in the hospital.

The group deliberated for over a year on the ideal model and guidelines for the use of individual hospital treatment and reached a consensus on principles and recommendations. The major thrust of the report was to emphasize the importance of a central person on each team to be the individual treater or coordinator who would be recognized by the patient as his or her main staff contact in the hospital. There was a positive reception by the hospital staff as a whole and by the hospital administration for these recommendations and guidelines.

This two year process of attempting to develop the best model available for a psychoanalytically oriented hospital was largely influenced by a combination of two strong currents that existed in the organization. The first was the appreciation of small group processes that had developed among the group therapists during fifteen years of group therapy practice. It influenced our thinking about the difference between the semi-structured team meeting with its clearly defined tasks and agendas as opposed to the unstructured therapy groups where self-disclosure and regressive transference developments are encouraged. The second and possibly even more important influence were the group relations conference experiences that most of the professional staff had experienced between 1968 and 1973. Both of the Menninger hospital-wide committees were very much involved in a grand inter-group exercise, not too different from what took place at the A. K. Rice Institute, in which the committee members had to be aware that their roles were more than mere observers but less than full plenipotentiaries. There undoubtedly was a heightened awareness of the way the rivalries and identity issues among sections had to be appreciated in working toward an organization-wide consensus. The success of the process was undoubtedly related to the relatively sophisticated staff representatives who were able to recognize the emotional barriers and resistances to cooperation and to work through them.

The group psychotherapy workshops

As mentioned earlier, the struggle to keep out-patient groups filled continued throughout the life of the program. Efforts to find patients were organized by the various directors of group psychotherapy who all used an executive committee representing different segments of the organization to work at this central issue. I succeeded Francisco Gomez as director in 1969 when he left the clinic. I resigned in 1978 to devote my energies to being chief of the Psychology Service and was succeeded by Ramon Ganzarain who held the post until he departed from Topeka in 1987. Joe Hyland, assisted by Bonnie Buchele, took over the reins until his appointment as director of the Outpatient Department in 1989 when Bonnie became director. She held the position until 1995 until she left the clinic to start a private practice and was succeeded by Steve Saeks who was the last director before the Menninger Clinic in Topeka closed in 2001.

An important development in out-patient work occurred in 1973 when we instituted group therapy workshops for professionals, open to a nation-wide audience. These continuing education workshops proved quite popular both to the participants and the staff. Their design was derived partly from the AGPA Institute experiential sessions and partly from the Tavistock/A. K. Rice Group Relations Conferences. They were a combination of didactic and experiential sessions and provided the participants with an exposure to an analytic-expressive mode of conducting groups. Many participants who were relatively uninformed about a psychodynamic approach to groups were quite surprised to find that refraining from structuring and attempting to fill silences with directive interventions could actually facilitate important disclosures and work by members. They were also surprised to experience intense transference developments, mainly to the leader, and thus learned that the source of important resistances in their groups were often due to feelings about the therapist.

For the staff it was a cohesion and morale builder. These workshops lasted three to four days and involved day and evening meetings among the staff to discuss developments within the various groups as well as therapist counter-transferences. Often the entire faculty offered peer group supervision and sometimes the therapists met with a supervisor privately to get help in better understanding the process. The staff valued very highly this opportunity to work intensively with each other and by the end of the workshop there had usually developed an esprit de corps and collegiality that carried over into our everyday interactions. A summary of the method and the rationale is described in Chapter Eighteen.

As our group therapists multiplied in number, a wish to have a personal group therapy experience began to surface. Perhaps this grew out of the brief small group experiences we had in the group relations conferences or at the AGPA institutes. Perhaps it grew out of the envy of the positive experiences that the participants had in the workshops we were leading. At any rate the group decided to organize a leaderless therapy group for our active group therapists and the majority attended a weekly session which went on for more than two years. It became clear that there were certain boundaries that needed to be observed since we worked closely together, socialized with each other, and because there were supervisory and administrative relationships existing among the members. Despite these handicaps, the group was able to attain a certain degree of trust and intimacy and was only terminated when we recognized that going further would involve more self-disclosure than was desirable in our work setting.

Summary

A group psychotherapy program at the Menninger Clinic in Topeka was initiated through the efforts of a small group of clinicians with a conviction that it was an important and valid treatment. The major resistance in the organization was the belief, shared by other psychoanalytic groups in the fifties and sixties, that significant therapeutic work could only be accomplished in the privacy of the consulting room with an individual therapist. After a few years of effort to initiate group treatment, we were finally authorized to begin but found that lack of interest and ingrained resistances within the staff and the administration were not easy to overcome. On the other hand, the fellows in the various training programs were the most open and amenable to engaging in group treatment and developing group skills, aided by their exposure to the group dynamic seminars and later to the formal courses we offered in the School of Psychiatry and Mental Health Sciences. When the association that accredited the curriculum of psychiatric residencies in the late sixties declared that residents must receive training in group psychotherapy, including supervised experience in conducting groups, our position became considerably strengthened. Other factors that contributed to our acceptance included recruiting relatively senior staff members to our ranks, mainly psychoanalysts in various stages of their careers. We invited nationally and internationally known group therapists to consult and teach which lent visibility and legitimacy to our early efforts. The decision by our administration to send most of our staff in the late sixties and early seventies to the Tavistock/A. K. Rice Group Relations Conferences furthered the staff's acceptance of the validity of group methods. And finally, when the hospital in the seventies began to adopt group methods as an integral part of its treatment, the acceptance of group psychotherapy as a full partner in the treatment modalities of our organization was no longer in doubt.

PART II

THEORETICAL

The following section contains four chapters that are mainly theoretical in nature. Chapter Five compares the use of transference in short term experiential groups with transference as it is typically used in many long term psychoanalytic groups and was based on the author's experience with the human relations groups sponsored by the National Training Laboratories in Bethel, Maine. It touches on the use of feedback by peers as opposed to transference interpretation in providing insight and has relevance to the difference between the interpersonal peer interaction model compared to those models that rely on transference. Chapter Six is the cornerstone chapter of the book insofar as it presents the author's inductive group centered approach in which the now outmoded Tavistock model is revised in order to make it more patient friendly and effective The original paper, significantly updated, was honored to be included in the 1992 publication of an AGPA book *Classics in Group Psychotherapy*. Chapter Seven presents a clarification of the Kleinian concept of projective identification and resulted from my struggle to understand the meaning of this complicated process insofar as it is not only a defense mechanism but also a mode of relating to others. The original article was given special recognition as a paper used for detailed discussion on the internet by AGPA members over a period of several weeks and has been widely adopted for reading lists of various training programs. I have always thought of its popularity as due to my initial difficulty in grasping the difference between projection and projective identification, the latter having been introduced to me by my Kleinian colleague at the Menninger Clinic, the late Ramon Ganzarain. My personal struggle with this issue, I believe, resulted in a clarification that other colleagues appreciated. Finally, Chapter Eight was devoted to the issue of the depth of transference in groups compared to what transpires in individual expressive psychotherapy. The literature contained divergent views concerning the nature of transference in groups and once again I sought to clarify the reasons for the presumed difference. The chapter explicates my conclusion that groups have the potential to both dilute and intensify the transference, depending on the therapist's technique as well as the ego strength of the patients.

CHAPTER FIVE

Transference in therapy groups and experiential groups

A wide variety of experiential groups, including human relations training groups, sensitivity groups, and group dynamic seminars, began to attain increasing popularity during the 1960s both in America and abroad. They are now used with considerable frequency in a variety of training settings as diverse as psychiatric residency programs, psychology internships, and group psychotherapy workshops such as those sponsored by the American Group Psychotherapy Association. In addition these groups are used by business and professional organizations in an effort to enhance membership and leadership skills among staff members.

Under the sponsorship of the National Training Laboratories in Bethel, Maine, the technique of using the small unstructured group (referred to as sensitivity groups or training groups) was used to enhance the sensitivity of individuals to significant events in groups and especially to help individuals become better group members within their organizations. The usual method consists of studying the processes occurring within the small group as well as aiding members in the acquisition of personal insights. Yalom and Lescsz (2005) have offered a description of the parameters of experiential groups, including encounter groups, partly based on the classic research study by Yalom and others (Lieberman, Yalom, & Miles, 1973). Yalom and Leszcz describe experiential groups as face-to-face, consisting of eight to twenty participants, time limited, often compressed into hours or days, focus on the here-and-now, usually vague in their goals, although striving for individual change of some kind.

In an early groundbreaking article, Jerome Frank (1964) made an attempt to describe and conceptualize the similarities and differences between training groups and therapy groups, noting certain clear-cut differences in goals and processes between the two. He based his observations upon an experience at Bethel as a member of a training group (T-group). Frank emphasized the following major difference in objectives. Training groups attempt to help members become more sensitive to their own functioning in groups and to the important events occurring within the group so that they may become more effective as members and as leaders of other groups. A therapy group aims to help its members attain insight into their functioning in interpersonal situations of all kinds and thus aims to help relieve neurotically determined distress. Frank further describes the major difference as follows:

> Training groups are composed of individuals trying to learn new skills from the trainer. Therapy groups attempt to modify more pervasive and more central attitudes than training groups, so they put relatively more emphasis on unlearning old modes of behavior as compared to learning new ones, and take longer to achieve their aims.

A second distinction Frank makes is that teaching membership skills in the training group focuses on interpretations about the group-as-a-whole, rather than about individual motivations. Feelings of members are elucidated only insofar as they shed light upon and illustrate group process. Therapy groups, of course, focus primarily upon the individual and his or her underlying motives and conflicts. A third important difference lies in the role of the central figure. In therapy groups, the initial dependence upon the therapist is greater and is never completely resolved: "The therapist can never become fully a member of the group, though he may approximate this, whereas trainer and member of a training group can become genuinely indistinguishable" (p. 451).

More recently, Ettin (1992) has observed that patients in group psychotherapy, compared to the participants in a group relations conference, tend to have a clearer sense of their goals and objectives, their reasons for participating, and a better understanding of the expectations of the leader. Another pioneer in this field, Margaret Rioch (1970) held T-groups to at least the same standard, if not a higher one, when she stated that T-groups should be committed to "a ruthless honesty about one's self and one's group without any assumption that such honesty will necessarily lead to the resolution of conflict" (p. 8).

In the early days of NTL there was a trend toward de-emphasizing the study of group processes in T-groups in favor of enhanced personal insight. Some leaders have referred to sensitivity training as "psychotherapy for normals" although many decried this therapeutic trend in T-groups. There was an implicit recognition among many that personality traits were the product of early parental influence and this led to increased focus on individual dynamics. Group level interventions were replaced by more personally oriented interventions and the National Training Laboratories began to focus on the problem of "giving and receiving feedback" and gradually personal feedback became the most important feature of the T-group.

Although there was a shift toward personal insight among some trainers, Bethel groups do not typically aim at uncovering and resolving unconscious conflict. Rather, they attempt to help the individual perceive more clearly her own style of interaction which may impair her effectiveness. Perhaps one could say that T-groups aim to impart insights concerning the more conscious or overt levels of personality functioning.

The most recent view in NTL now emphasizes individual insight as a way of improving one's functioning in work groups, usually as members of an organization engaging in teamwork. Golumbiewski (1999) delineated the difference between training and therapy as (1) sensitivity training is for "normal people" and (2) T groups emphasize the here-and-now and refrain from psychodynamic explorations characteristic of therapy groups. In fact, nowadays there-and-then discussions are usually considered out of bounds by most trainers. Despite this point of view, there continues to be the objective in a T group to increase individual insight and heighten individual authenticity.

Since insight-giving is still an objective in training groups, a natural question is how much similarity there is between the techniques and models of training groups as opposed to the typical psychodynamic therapeutic group. More specifically, does the trainer attempt to use transference reactions to him and to other members as a vehicle for uncovering personal dynamics, as is done in many therapy groups? On the basis of the recent training group literature, and as well on my own experience in a few Bethel T-groups, I propose to examine the differences in leader roles in the two groups, particularly in the use of transference, and to explore the consequences of the differences in method.

Before describing these differences, I wish to emphasize that neither group psychotherapy nor human relations training may be adequately represented by a single method. Practitioners in each field span a wide range of models, techniques, and theories. I will confine myself to therapy groups that operate within a psychodynamic frame of reference and hence emphasize transference, although there are distinct variations even within this field in therapists' use of leader versus peer transference as well as the degree to which they engage in self-disclosure. Similarly, trainers differ widely in their "visibility" or anonymity within their groups. The modal points to be used in our comparison will be the Bethel NTL training group described recently by Golumbiewski (1999) with the therapy group described by this writer as the modified Tavistock model (1993).

First, how is transference, particularly with regard to the leader, conceptualized in the therapy group? The psychodynamic, group centered therapist clearly and explicitly views his role as a transference figure: a relatively neutral figure upon whom wishes and fears are projected, brought into awareness by interpretation, with the object of their amelioration. He or she encourages transference reactions: (1) by confining his participation as much as possible to creating a permissive atmosphere in which free expression of feelings and fantasies is received uncritically, (2) by promoting an attitude of reflection about the meaning of individual and group behaviors, and (3) by emphasizing interpretations of group themes and individual variations around them and offering supportive interventions only as needed to avoid excessive frustration and anxiety. His role has similarity to that of the psychodynamic individual therapist whose limited participation tends to induce the emergence of regressive wishes and fantasies which then become the subject of elaboration and interpretation. This model of the therapist who limits his interaction with the group varies according to the capacity of the group to tolerate the frustration induced by such a procedure.

Role of T group trainer

The central figure in the human relations training group, on the other hand, plays multiple roles. He may permit the group to struggle with its transference reactions toward him, but he does not consciously and explicitly attempt to promote transference. Little, if any, explicit reference to this cornerstone conception of psychotherapy appears in the group relations literature. Certain generic issues, like members' reactions to the trainer, the prototypes of dependency and counter-dependency, the distorted attitudes toward authority figures, are observed by all writers of the Bethel school.

The consensus is that the NTL trainer should serve other functions than simply those of observer and interpreter. First, the usual laboratory setting generally reduces transference reactions. There is an atmosphere of informality between trainer and participant, including the use of first names as well as a two week period of being together on a "cultural island", that is, trainer and participants see each other during coffee breaks, evening social hours, and other real-life situations where the trainer emerges as a real person. Second, a trainer role which tends to attenuate transference reactions is that of the person who "models" the ideal of openness and transparency in expressing one's feelings. Thus he may at times share his own feelings of perplexity, anxiety, or confusion about what is transpiring in the group, partly to encourage others to express their reactions freely and partly to help the group resolve unrealistic fantasies of the omniscient leader. Finally, the trainer sometimes is "teacher", who may deliver a "lecturette" about the group dynamics being played out or summarize some shared event which has special value as a generalization about group behavior. While none of these features of a training group eliminates transference to the leader, insofar as the trainer continues to be the central person in the group and is always a special member, they do serve to attenuate these reactions.

Perhaps the most significant factor in limiting the expression of fantasy and feelings, both about the trainer and one's fellow participants, is the extra-group contact that is a feature of a Bethel Human Relations laboratory. Staff members are encouraged to socialize freely with the participants and of course, the participants live in the same quarters, eat with each other, and everyone attends the evening social events. Thus, the permeability of boundaries between staff and members and among members of the same small groups undoubtedly contributes to a restraint upon the development and free expression of transference reactions.

While training groups attend to problems regarding group process, members of therapy groups have little, if any, interest in the dynamics of groups per se. Observing group dynamics in a therapy group is incidental to its major purpose of enhanced personal insight. Thus, while both groups seek some form of personal insight for their members, the training group in addition attempts to teach important dimensions of group functioning. Membership expectations and their vicissitudes during the life of the group, the dynamics of decision-making, and the growth of group norms are studied in the training group as they develop. Such problems may also be part of the data generated in a therapy group, but they are not a focus of learning for the patients. Both trainer and therapist, for example, must always be alert to restraining group norms which tend to interfere with free communication of feelings. The woman, for example, who emphasizes the "intellectual brilliance" of the male members, tends to freeze the men into highly restrained and competitive roles. Their attempts to fulfill her expectations result in intellectual muscle-flexing. Both therapist and trainer are likely to call attention to the inhibiting effect of such a statement, but the trainer will also attempt to show how rigidifying norms in a group may easily be established, particularly early in a group's life, and such events must be carefully scrutinized and dealt with.

Members of one T-group, for example, were asked by the trainer two days after having started, about accepting a new member. They sensed that this was the preference of the trainer and though disposed to comply, they were not enthusiastic about the idea. One member, who vehemently opposed the proposal, finally enlisted many supporters to his side. In an instance of this kind, both training and therapy groups have the opportunity to explore feelings about newcomers, the leader's power, and submission to a powerful peer. For the training group, it was an excellent illustration of an important facet of group dynamics: the numerical majority is often secondary to the "emotional" majority in the decision-making process. Such lessons are not relevant to the objectives of a therapeutic group, because patients are not encouraged to understand the dynamics of groups, but they provide the trainer with an opportunity to clarify and point up a principle of group dynamics. Such teaching also makes for some attenuation of transference to the trainer. These interventions reveal the trainer as a real person with a particular style of teaching and thus tend to make him less of a projection screen than a less active therapist. Furthermore, this kind of teaching also reduces the oral frustration within the group and contributes to the reduction of the more regressive fantasies of the members.

The trainer as a model

In addition to his role of teacher, the trainer often moves gradually in the direction of a membership role, so that toward the end of the life of the group, his style of participation approaches, but never reaches, those of a peer. This develops largely through his "modeling" behavior by which the trainer exemplifies the ideals of openness and a willingness to face uncomfortable, conflictual situations without smoothing them over. Of course, the group therapist also confronts such issues in her group, but she does so without blurring her identity as the central figure, in contrast to the trainer who moves closer to a membership role.

How the trainer moves from the position of central figure toward that of membership status may be illustrated by several examples of trainer behavior. Not infrequently during the inevitable ritual of self-introductions around the table in the first session, the trainer will be asked to introduce himself and describe his background as the other members do. Usually the trainer will introduce himself, perhaps more briefly than the others, to avoid frustrating the group. In so doing he contributes to the reduction, at least in part, of the members' preoccupation with the mysterious leader who maintains a boundary between himself and the group. A therapist would more likely explore the meaning of the request as well as the patients' reaction to his failure to introduce himself, rather than meet the request.

One kind of recommended trainer behavior is a willingness to express his own situationally induced feelings of discomfort, anger, uncertainty, and helplessness with the group. Such expressions serve two major purposes. One, they presumably help members to express more easily their own feelings which may be threatening to reveal. Two, they also help limit the regressive fantasies which inevitably develop in the unstructured group in which the central figure is seen as magically endowed with powers for both good and evil, and against which various defenses must be erected. The group therapist, on the other hand, would attempt to interpret the group's regressive and dependent wishes toward him without abdicating his special role as the central figure. Thus, the trainer presents himself as a real person, with the same kind of weakness and fallibility common to the other members. Even though self-disclosure is becoming more common among many analytic therapists, the general policy is to be sparing in such revelations and to become transparent only when such interventions are clearly deemed to be helpful to the process. Rather, he or she prefers to help the patients to modify their dependency position by making them more aware of it.

The following is an example of a membership-modeling intervention used by the trainer: A T-group came into one of its early sessions to find that the nameplates on the table had been shuffled around in a way to suggest that somebody was attempting to manipulate the seating arrangement. Resentment simmered, but the group was fearful of dealing with the issue. The trainer forthrightly said that he felt "pushed around" and his frankness permitted the group to uncork its anger. In a similar situation, the therapist would undoubtedly try to encourage and elicit feelings about such an event and try to uncover the meanings of behavior, but without necessarily imparting his own feelings to the group. A by-product of the trainer's intervention would be to enhance his image as a member and further help to strip him of his "projection screen" qualities.

Effects of trainer's membership status

The trainer never fully achieves the role co-equal or peer with the members. The powerful dependency strivings are not that easily resolved, and hence the members will not permit the trainer to become just another member. Thus, feedback from the trainer must be carefully attuned to the trainer's perceived position in the group. The therapist, on the other hand, operates in a more protected position. The group centered therapist often gives interpretations within the safety of a group theme; that is, he tends to interpret to each individual his unique reaction to the common group tension.

This movement toward increasing membership status of the trainer, with consequent attenuation of transference reactions toward him, raises the question of the effects of such an approach in contrast to what develops in the usual therapy group. In my experience in both kinds of groups, the outstanding difference between the training group and the therapy group is the reduced preoccupation of members with the trainer as compared with that of patients with the therapist. While both groups develop magical expectations toward the central figure, their intensity—as well as the elaborate fantasies concerning what "he" is thinking or planning and why he is behaving as he does—tends to be substantially reduced in the training group. The therapy group encourages the development of regressive transference reactions toward the leader; in contrast, the T-group attempts to keep them in check by having the trainer play a member-like role and focusing his comments upon peer relations rather than trainer-member relations. In this way, members of the T-group go through a relatively abbreviated period of dealing with their dependency problems toward the trainer and begin to focus upon their relationship to each other, the problems of intimacy and closeness, and learn from this emphasis upon peer relationships about their characteristic modes of interaction.

Another development in the therapeutic group, largely absent in the T-group, is an explicit termination process. Regressive developments as termination approaches in a therapeutic process are well known. Typical are the reappearances of dependency feelings characteristic of the beginning, anger at not having been magically cured, and depression over having to give up valued relationships. Training groups usually undergo a similar process but in an attenuated fashion. Since the members have been in the group for a shorter period of time and the self-disclosure is typically less extensive, the termination process is touched on but not elaborated in great detail. Aveline (1993) emphasizes the need to "end well" as one of the tasks of the leader of a brief training group.

The definite time limit and pre-determined number of sessions in a T-group (often about ten sessions or less) will in itself set limits upon the degree of dependence upon the central figure that is likely to develop. A significant self-regulation tends to occur in time-limited groups. The leader's "membership" role also will reinforce this decreased dependency upon the leader and consequent increased reliance upon peers for personal learning primarily by means of feedback.

Dorothy Stock Whitaker in a personal communication stated: "I think there is a termination process in T-groups, but it is not focused around the leader. Two things I have noted: first, mourning over the impending separation from one's peers; and second, disappointment at not having achieved all one's individual goals and for not having dealt as hoped, with all the issues which came up during the course of the group. I have seen groups which dealt with both these issues admirably and realistically, making the last few sessions very productive and satisfying. Groups which have not seem prone to reunions".

Feedback in a training group versus insight in a therapy group

The leadership of NTL has become increasingly clear that they are attempting to help members to make changes in their behavior even though they clearly attempt to differentiate their activity from therapy. "T-group interaction does have a heavy emotional tone and it is very much concerned with the development of insight and sensitivity about self and others" (Golumbiewski, 1999, p. 185). The primary technique for achieving this goal is through the feedback process, primarily from peers.

Feedback is designed primarily to enable the participant to become more aware of some of his characteristic modes of interacting, which become apparent to others in the T-group but which are typically hidden from the participant herself. It is a process of communicating one's perceptions of others in a setting where members are ideally attempting to help each other and where the observations are hopefully gauged to the level at which the member is ready to accept them. Usually, the feedback received by a member in a T-group has a special impact upon her because it generally is derived from a consensus of observations, and the sheer weight of numbers, combined with an effort to give responsible help, usually produces a significant effect upon the member. The extent to which these insights produce stable, significant behavioral change is a question still to be answered.

A dramatic instance of feedback occurred in one T-group in connection with Jim, a member who attempted to dominate and control the group. The initial comments to him concerned his drive for power and his lack of any genuine interest in others, despite his superficial solicitousness. One member said he thought Jim was contemptuous of the others in the group, of their opinions, abilities, and of what they had to offer him. Jim opened his notebook which contained a voluntarily kept personal diary and he read a paragraph describing his impressions after the initial meeting. He had written that not a single person in the group showed any leadership ability and none could hold a responsible position in industry like he did. He then acknowledged to the group that he had heard similar criticisms from others and he even admitted some explosive and sadistic behavior toward his wife. His subsequent behavior in the group became considerably less "phony" and pseudo-sympathetic and there was little doubt that the group's feedback had produced, or at least reinforced, an important growing personal insight.

How does the feedback process in a Bethel group compare with the insights which develop in a therapeutic group? The psychodynamic group therapist, particularly one who works with the group-as-a-whole, attempts to uncover an underlying conflict or defense characterizing a particular member and ideally the interpretation is made in the context of a group-wide conflict. Thus, in the group which is dealing with a dependency conflict in its initial phases and is looking toward the leader for omnipotent and magical solutions, some will ask the therapist what to discuss, or will ask for instruction about the theory of group psycho-therapy, while others may silently and expectantly await the therapist's magical words to rid them of their anxiety. The therapist must inter-pret this group theme while at the same time pointing out to individual members their own characteristic mode of expressing their wishes and fears. Although various kinds of distortions, projections, and manipula-tions occur in the behavior of members toward each other, the therapist uses these behavioral data in relation to the shared group theme, that is, the dependency wishes toward him.

A common myth which has developed about T-groups is that feed-back is nothing more than a "no-holds-barred" attack upon a fellow member. While angry outbursts may occur, the trainer takes pains to point up the difference between such retaliations and the more deliber-ate and constructive efforts involved in the feedback process. It is not a means of "tearing down defenses", as some have described it but rather, ideally a genuine effort to encourage growth and change by enhancing self-understanding.

In one therapeutic group I conducted, much of one meeting con-sisted of a heated argument over the obscene language of a young male patient. During the argument, it became increasingly clear that the "offender" (who was usually the therapist's most vocal proponent) perceived the therapist as a bourgeois and repressive individual who kept him from talking as freely as he wished. He displaced this per-ception onto persons in the group who most closely approximated his image of the therapist. One of his antagonists, a young woman who argued for more gentlemanly language, was struggling against her own introject of the evil, seductive father who had little control over his sexual and aggressive impulses. (This patient had suffered a brief psychotic episode during which she had the delusion that her father was going to rape her). The common tension which involved the group in this instance was the fear lest their sexual impulses get out of hand. The young man defended himself against these impulses by projecting a severely repressive superego onto the group, only to struggle vigorously against it. The prudish woman, on the other hand, unable to tolerate her own sexual wishes, was doing battle with the projected licentiousness which she saw ready to run rampant in the group. The therapist attempted to show that despite their polarized positions, they were struggling with transference distortions based on the same fear of sexuality, one by projecting id wishes and the other by projecting superego injunctions. When they became aware of these distortions, they were able to begin dealing with these internal, repressed conflicts. Obviously, the level of insight into unconscious motives which the therapist aims for is considerably deeper than the insight which occurs in a training group. Aveline (1993) makes a similar observation in asserting that the insights offered in a training group tend to be of the conscious and preconscious variety.

Therapeutic and training groups emphasize two different methods of insight-giving: The training group depends more upon personal feedback from one's peers, while the therapy group depends more on the therapist's interpretation of transference, either to the therapist, to peers, or to the group-as-a-whole, even though peer observations are also thrown into the mix.

One may speculate on whether or not it would be useful to employ a transference approach with a brief, time-limited group, like a T-group, to enhance the objective of personal insights. If the trainer were to confine his role to observer and interpreter and thereby encourage the development of transference reactions to him, the group would undoubtedly become more preoccupied with the central figure and develop more intense feelings toward him. In that context the group might spend a considerable portion of the limited number of sessions expressing and coming to terms with their frustrated dependency needs and their wishes to be given a few omniscient observations about themselves from the trainer, or conversely some would struggle in a counter-dependent fashion against these wishes. Efforts to learn about themselves from the observations of peers would certainly decrease inasmuch as the members would tend to defer to the transference-mediated perception of the expert professional within the group. To the extent that the group did acquire insights from the central figure, it would tend to be limited to a narrower sphere associated with the members' dependency and authority conflicts.

The feedback method, on the other hand, encourages peer observation in the form of mutual evaluations in which each member has the opportunity of hearing a consensus opinion about his role in the group. It appears to have some special advantages over the transference method as applied to a brief, time-limited group. First, feedback is in no way restricted to a group-wide transference and therefore is likely, at least in the early stages, to encompass a wide range of behaviors and observations. Rather than emphasizing individual modes of relating oneself to the authority figure in the group, the T-group permits a wider range of reactions: a person's over-readiness to rush to the defense of those who are attacked, another's habit of quickly acceding to pressure from others, or still another's tendency to stir up hostile interactions by subtly getting others to do battle. Second, the feedback method exploits the power of peer pressure. A common occurrence in a T-group is the report by a member who has just been evaluated by her group that she has heard these observations many times before, by her spouse, by her colleagues, supervisors, or friends. But the previous comments were rarely as telling in their impact as the group consensus. The power of group opinion, especially in an atmosphere of mutual care and trust, carries with it considerable persuasive force.

A final, and perhaps crucial, advantage of transference attenuation in the T-group is the trainer's wish to avoid the depth of regression which the therapist seeks to elicit. The therapist aims to promote regressive responses from the patient in order to bring into awareness the unconscious conflicts which impair his functioning. The therapist is best able to do this by refraining from excessive participation, by being relatively anonymous, and by some degree of frustration of the patient's conscious and unconscious wishes. The trainer, on the other hand, would see such behavior as creating an "artificial" authority problem and would seek to resolve the authority transference as quickly as possible by playing roles which tend to remove the aura of mystery surrounding the more neutral and less "visible" therapist. The trainer is content to work with more superficial and more conscious layers of the personality than is the therapist.

Aveline's discussion (1993) of the same issue leads him to a similar conclusion, at least in terms of the appropriate model for a training group. His personal orientation to group therapy is to use an interpersonal, or peer interaction, model similar to that prescribed by

Yalom and Leszcz (2005). He attempts to avoid "the more withdrawn, detached observer position of some group-analytic conductors" and similarly to deflect the group's focus away from group-wide transference to the leader. Aveline's emphasis on the examination of peer interactions is his preferred method of working with training groups.

My conclusion is that the use of transference is appropriate for the intensive, uncovering approach of a long term therapeutic group but is best attenuated and minimized in a training group. Where the objective is restricted to helping an individual gain insight about his major blind spots in relating himself to others, and where a time limitation exists with regard to the life of the group, the feedback technique seems to be the method of choice.

Summary

Experiential groups such as human relations training groups have the objective of understanding how groups behave and how each member tends to react in a relatively unstructured group. To the extent that T-groups also attempt to enhance individual insight, the problem is posed as to why a central vehicle of psychodynamic group psychotherapy, that is, transference, is not emphasized as a tool of the typical training group. The group therapist encourages the development of transference by confining his behavior largely to that of observer and interpreter of group and individual conflicts and resistances. He thus facilitates regressive reactions toward himself which are fundamental in uncovering unconscious conflict. The trainer, on the other hand, not only interprets but often moves in the direction of a "member" role, by "modeling" behavior and contributing his own reactions to group events as a way of helping the group to understand and learn about itself. These member-like behaviors contribute (1) to an attenuation of transference reactions and to diminished preoccupation with the central figure, (2) to a decrease in regressive reactions, and (3) to increased interaction and interdependence among the members. To achieve the goal of maximum learning about blind spots and distortions in one's personal interactions in a brief time-limited group, the "member-like" role of the trainer seems preferable to the transference role of the therapist. In sum, the preferred method is to emphasize feedback about peer interactions rather than attempting to uncover more regressive transference reactions characteristic of the long term therapy group.

CHAPTER SIX

An inductive group centered approach

A major split in the field of group psychotherapy at the present time is that between those therapists who actively embrace the use of group dynamics and, in particular, significant attention to the group-as-a-whole (GAW), as opposed to those who focus primarily on the interaction among peers. This difference in perspective has had a long history, starting with the controversy between Slavson and his followers who decried the idea of therapists using group dynamics versus Ezriel who applied a special GAW approach in his early, now outmoded Tavistock model. The field has recognized that Slavson was too extreme in his rejection of group dynamics and that some form of recognition must be paid to the operation of group-wide forces. On the other hand, most therapists have deemed the Ezriel approach of placing his common group tension in the forefront of his technique as less than productive, an opinion shared by several clinicians, including myself as well as the current, contemporary Tavistock group therapists (Garland, 2010).

This chapter will present a model which employs the use of group processes in order to further the treatment of the individual. We will argue for the therapeutic utility of incorporating a group centered method while avoiding the pitfalls of the past which we will examine in detail. A model will be presented which, it is hoped, corrects the aforementioned weaknesses without discarding the power of group centered treatment.

The group centered approaches

Group-as-a-whole approaches to group psychotherapy have been associated in the past mainly with Bion (1961), Ezriel (1973), Foulkes (1975), and Whitaker and Lieberman (1964). Each of these authors has presented a somewhat different system from the others, but they have all been consistent in their effort to use the properties, processes, and dynamics of the entire group in the service of furthering the therapy of the individuals within the group. They make explicit in their systems a variety of group dynamisms which they utilize in their interventions. They concern themselves with such phenomena as resonance, mirror reactions, scapegoating, spokesman phenomena, projective identification and cohesion.

But the group phenomena mentioned above does not constitute the essential nature of the GAW approach nor does their use necessarily differentiate the group centered therapist from those with a more individualistic orientation. The latter have been variously described as intrapersonal or interpersonal and they utilize in varying degrees certain of these group phenomena. For example, it is a rare group therapist, regardless of background, who does not recognize scapegoating as an important group phenomenon which influences his management and interventions. Irvin Yalom and Molyn Lescez (2004), who describe themselves as a cross between interpersonalist and GAW, pay considerable attention to properties of the whole group, and in fact make the phenomenon of cohesion a fundamental organizing concept in their therapeutic work. Additionally, they set forth conditions under which they will make group-wide interventions or "mass interpretations". Even Wolf and Schwartz (1962), despite their vehement polemics against the intrusion of group dynamics and the "group mystique" into group psychotherapy, seemed to move gradually toward recognition of the need to understand group-wide processes.

It would appear at first blush that the distinction between the holistic therapist and others who use varying degrees of individualistic and group orientations is hardly worth making. But my contention is that there is a fundamental difference between the group-as-a-whole (GAW) therapist and others in terms of what I shall call the "group centered hypothesis", that is, the ongoing presence of a common group theme which influences much of what transpires in a group. This unifying factor is variously described and named by the leading GAW authors: Bion calls it the basic assumption, Ezriel the common group tension, Foulkes the communication matrix, and Whitaker and Lieberman the group focal conflict. The common feature among these writers is that over and above their interest in various specific group phenomena mentioned earlier, they make the assumption of an underlying unity of theme or shared conflict which binds the members and gives coherence to the process.

The most explicitly developed GAW approach is the now outdated Tavistock method, which has been most closely identified with Henry Ezriel. It has been described in detail in the preceding chapters, and I shall offer only a most concise summary. Ezriel contends that the common group tension grows out of a commonly shared transference and resistance toward the therapist, and, furthermore, that each patient responds to these shared wishes and fears with his own unique defenses, symptoms, and behaviors. When the therapist has been able to diagnose the common group tension as well as the idiosyncratic responses of each individual to the group theme, he offers a comprehensive interpretation of the "group structure" at that time.

The present writer believes that there are several distinct advantages to using a group centered hypothesis like the common group tension. Although I differ with certain important aspects of the Ezriel method, I believe that the group centered hypothesis offers several outstanding advantages over other methods, briefly summarized here: (1) The issue of sharing group time is minimized since most contributions are a part of the group theme. (2) Since the common group tension, to a greater or lesser extent, affects each individual's reactions, each patient is better understood. (3) The universalization phenomenon gets emphasized and provides beneficial effect of knowing that others often share your anxieties. (4) The protection of the group theme helps to reduce anxieties about sharing shameful personal material.

These advantages, however, are only acquired at the expense of certain clear-cut weaknesses and these are particularly exemplified in the now defunct Tavistock/Ezriel method. But before turning to these weaknesses, let me deal with certain objections to the group-as-a-whole approach which I consider invalid.

Invalid objections to holistic approaches

Parloff (1968) characterized the holistic approaches as engaging in "treatment of the group" as opposed to treatment of the individual. He described this orientation as dealing with the "group as a unit" and as regarding the group as a "composite single patient". All of his character-izations contain a partial truth but a major, that is, group psychotherapy always had the objective of helping the individual patient achieve personal change. Even Bion, who confined himself to group-wide interventions, believed his method was directed toward helping indi-viduals believing, erroneously it now seems, that his method would permit individuals to extract whatever was applicable to their personal issues.

Ezriel, on the other hand, adopted a model which integrated group forces with individual pathology and therefore could hardly be charac-terized as treating the group as a unit. Rather, it would be more accurate to say that the group's unitary properties were used by the therapist to further the understanding and treatment of the individual. The sali-ent point is that the objective of group psychotherapy for the GAW as well as the individualistic therapist remains the treatment of each individual.

A related objection is that the GAW point of view tends to anthropo-morphize the group. Insofar as one looks upon the group as a "compos-ite single patient", one is attributing properties to the group which more properly belong to a single individual. The error of this argument lies in the confusion between analogy and identity. The group may develop certain norms which are analogous to the superego, or it may develop a common group tension which is analogous to an intrapsychic conflict, or it may even free-associate in a manner similar to a single patient on a couch. This kind of analogical thinking has a practical value in helping the therapist move from the familiar to the less familiar provided he or she is aware that the phenomena in question have important differ-ences as well as similarities. The anthropomorphizing objection incor-rectly assumes that the analogies of the group to an individual patient are a reality, rather than a convenient *façon de parler*.

Another serious reservation voiced by many against the holistic point of view comes under the category of the "tyranny of the group". Its pro-ponents argue that a method which encourages the search for under-lying commonalities leads to a variety of abuses against the patient's individuality, his autonomy, his freedom of choice and action. They say that such groups tend to breed conformity, fail to recognize individual differences, and require each patient to fit into a mold. Some writers in the past have characterized their groups as democratic in contrast to GAW groups which were described as autocratic or even fascistic.

The above characterization of the GAW point of view confounds insight into significant group forces with a prescription for certain group behavior. One might well argue that a group centered hypothesis has never adequately been proven and therefore the holistic therapist is operating on an erroneous assumption. But to argue that the application of a group centered hypothesis curbs freedom of choice is tantamount to saying that the interpretation of an unconscious motive to an individual destroys his autonomy. On the contrary, it is more likely that the enhanced awareness of group forces, conscious or unconscious, can only contribute to the individual's ability to escape the potential tyranny of the group. And Piper's research (1993) corroborates the belief that group-as-a-whole thinking and interventions make a valuable contribution to the therapy process.

Finally, several writers have raised the objection that the GAW approaches tend to lead into traps of over-generalization. They say that the therapist who assumes a common group tension or a group focal conflict falls prey to squeezing his patients into a Procrustean bed since he bases his inference upon the behavior of a small number of patients (often only two or three) and generalizes to the entire group. They also make the important point that silence does not always indicate assent and therefore one is not justified in drawing conclusions about those who fail to express themselves.

This objection certainly has partial validity insofar as the holistic method invites more generalization than does its individualistic counterparts. On the other hand, the silent patient is not exactly a tabula rasa on which anything can be writ. The therapist may not have at his disposal a patient's verbalizations, but he is able to observe a whole variety of non-verbal behaviors including his attentiveness or inattentiveness, reactions of approval or disapproval, his posture, his facial expression, and other significant non-verbal behaviors. Even more important is the fact that the therapist acquires over a period of time a fund of knowledge about each patient's conflicts, attitudes, and reaction patterns so that on those occasions where speculation is indeed being made, he is not manufacturing his inferences out of whole cloth.

Critique of the Tavistock-Ezriel method

As indicated earlier, the group-as-a-whole point of view provides some outstanding advantages to a therapist who is attempting to integrate group forces with individual psychology. But a group centered approach also opens the door to serious shortcomings which require careful examination. Much can be learned from an examination of the Tavistock-Ezriel approach which has now fallen out of favor at the Tavistock Clinic.

Therapist participation excessively restricted

Ezriel asserted that the therapist should refrain from any participation until he has understood the common group tension as well *as* the idiosyncratic individual reactions of each patient. The task is made even more complicated by the requirement that the therapist understand the particular impulse-defense-anxiety configuration in each of his patients, which Ezriel refers to as the "desired-required-calamitous" relationships. Furthermore, the therapist is restricted in his role to making only transference interpretations.

Although there may be some difficulty in distinguishing between Ezriel's stylistic preferences and the dictates of a special model, one is struck by the restrictions imposed on the therapist's role, reminiscent of the rules of abstinence and anonymity in psychoanalysis with the individual patient which has been significantly modified in recent years. The findings of the Menninger Psychotherapy Research Project, for example, indicate that supportive interventions as well as interpretations are an important part of the analytic process (Wallerstein, 1986). In accordance with the Ezriel model, the therapist becomes a prisoner of his method. He is not permitted to engage in the variety of interventions which might help patients to deal with excessive anxiety, perhaps even the threat of serious decompensation. The therapist is not able to act as a catalyst to promote interaction and spontaneous participation and he is not permitted to interrupt resistant-avoidant behavior until he sees the whole picture.

It is inappropriate here to engage in an exhaustive comparison of Ezriel's method with individual analysis, but even the rule of abstinence in individual work is not meant to be applied as rigidly as his method prescribes. This effort to transpose a classical psychoanalytic individual situation, now outmoded, to a group setting seems unduly frustrating for the patient. In psychoanalysis the patient has the therapist's exclusive attention for an hour at each session, a basic underlying gratification inherent in the process. Although there are certain inherent gratifications involved in group, there is the fundamental frustration of being one among several. Even the most intact patient would have difficulty in tolerating the kind of deprivation imposed by his method.

But the most solid evidence for the weakness of the Tavistock-Ezriel approach is the research by Malan, Balfour, Hood, and Shooter (1976) in which a representative sample of patients was studied two to twelve years after completing their group psychotherapy at the Tavistock Clinic. The results were less than encouraging for the majority of the patients interviewed. The common complaint, repetitively voiced by patient after patient, was the low profile maintained by the therapist, leading to a frequent perception of the therapist as unduly detached. Furthermore, many felt that the therapist had little or no concern about them as individuals. The authors' conclusion was that the attempt to transpose an individual psychoanalytic method to the group situation is unwarranted and that modifications are necessary to overcome patients' feelings of excessive frustration and impersonal treatment. The Ezriel method required the therapist to be silent until he formulated a complete, definitive, all-inclusive interpretation and thus unduly frustrated his patients.

Malan, Balfour, Hood, and Shooter (1976) summarize their conclusions as follows:

> It does seem possible that therapists ought to feel less constrained by what they have learned in their classical psychoanalytic training— and should feel free to offer greater warmth and encouragement, greater participation in the group interactions, and provide individual sessions when the need arises, without the fear that such interventions will result in disruption of the group or interference with the group transference relationship. (p. 1315)

Individual needs ignored

An objection related to, but different from, the therapist's overly limited participation, pertains to the quality of the therapist's interventions. He was often seen by his patients as providing input only within the framework of the whole group. According to the Ezriel method, comments about individual patients are given exclusively within the context of a group centered intervention. The paradigm used is that the whole group is dealing with a particular kind of conflict (the common group tension) and only after such a framework is established does the therapist go around the room delineating individual and idiosyncratic reactions to the shared conflict. Even though interpretations were indeed individualized, the obvious impact on large numbers of patients, at least in retrospect, was that the therapist rarely addressed a truly personalized or individual comment to them. In the Malan, Balfour, Hood, and Shooter (1976) study, they tended to experience the therapist and group as ignoring their need for individualized attention and concern. Many of the patients in the Malan study might just as well have been treated in a Bion study group, where interventions were solely addressed to the group as an entity, since the overall impact was that the therapist never spoke to them personally but only to the entire group. In other words, there is some evidence that the technique of intervening solely and exclusively within an explicitly stated common group tension has the psychological effect on the patient that his individual needs are being underplayed or even ignored in favor of some vague group ideology.

Omniscience of therapist

Another objection related to the therapist's infrequent interventions, and to his highly comprehensive (and lengthy) statements which integrate and presumably explain everything that has transpired within the group, is that the method tended to infantilize the members by contributing to the already existing transference disposition that the therapist is all-knowing. One objective of psychotherapy is to help a patient overcome his dependency wishes and to view himself as a capable, self-sufficient adult. Group psychotherapy has the special virtue of providing members with the opportunity to have a real experience of offering help and understanding to peers. This experience in itself provides a growth opportunity and contributes to enhanced self-esteem for each patient.

The therapist's long periods of silent observation followed by oracular pronouncements contributed to the regressive dependency of the patient. The patient as a therapist-surrogate in the constructive healthy sense was not exploited fully in the early Tavistock model (Bacal, 1991). It is not unlike the effect of the gestalt therapist, whose method is active, managerial, and intrusive; the Ezriel model conveys that the therapist, not the patient group, is the "smartest one in the room", the only one who has the requisite understanding, skill, and wisdom to provide help.

Neglect of peer transference

Most group therapists accept the formulation that three kinds of transference develop in a group: toward the therapist, peers, and the whole group. Ezriel's writings suggest that the latter two forms were considered displacements from the really essential therapist transference. He cautioned that the therapist must be ever alert to transference manifestations that are being diluted by references away from him, that is, toward persons outside the group or even within the group. He went on to say that only interpretations coming directly from the therapist, and pertaining to the therapist transference, have a mutative effect.

Various formulations have been proposed regarding the relationship between therapist and peer transference. Stein and Kibel (1975) took the position that peer transference was a defense against the underlying therapist transference. While their basic understanding had some similarities to Ezriel's, their technical suggestions were quite different since they proposed that the therapist must work first with the defensively displaced peer transference before he interprets its significance vis-a-vis the therapist. Ezriel tended to view peer interaction as generally involving the therapist in some way (like struggle to be the favored sibling) and therefore he did not propose a sequential ordering of interpretation.

Some early writers, including Scheidlinger (1982b) and Ganzarain (1989) have observed a special type of pre-genital mother transference elicited by the patient's feelings toward the group as an entity. When the emphasis is on the positive, nurturing perception of the good mother, as exemplified by Scheidlinger, the group-wide transference is regarded as a supportive background factor that is left uninterpreted and used to help further the therapeutic process.

Bacal (1975) proposed that peer transference may be a significant phenomenon in its own right at certain times. In fact, says he, the therapist transference may sometimes be a defense against peer transferences. Bacal goes on to propose the concept of "transference structuring" which may either be basically therapist-oriented or peer-oriented. I would add the third alternative of a combined therapist-peer structuring where, for example, sibling competition to become the therapist's favorite may become the predominant theme.

A valid criticism of the Ezriel method is its neglect of peer relationships in favor of the therapist transference. The latter may sometimes dominate the scene, qualitatively and quantitatively, but it would be an error to permit it to entirely preempt peer transferences.

An inductive group centered approach

The author's experience with the Tavistock-Ezriel method led him to appreciate the usefulness of group centered interventions while recognizing the restriction the method places on the therapist's input and activity. As for the patient in a Tavistock-Ezriel group, he frequently experienced himself as only a spokesman for, and subordinate to, a group-wide theme and not as *a* separate, autonomous individual who spoke for himself. The paradigm of interpretation presented by Ezriel was essentially deductive: the contributions by several members were permitted to develop with little or no comment from the therapist until the group theme emerged. Individualized comments were only made after the common group tension became clear and was interpreted.

The method proposed here is that an inductive paradigm be used: A member's contribution should be dealt with initially in terms of the patient's individual, idiosyncratic, characterological features. As the contributions increase, and preferably within a single session, the therapist may generalize from the individual instances and formulate interventions of a group-wide nature. Usually these observations will stimulate other members to respond with their dominant affective reactions, which in turn will further elaborate the group theme.

Working within a Foulkesian framework, Karl Konig (1991), a German psychoanalyst and group therapist, has proposed a model similar to my inductive framework with rationales that match mine. First, he observes that "the common group phantasy" is not readily observable by either therapist or patient in the early stages of the group process. Only after a number of interactions have occurred between members and therapist as well as members and members will the shared fantasy of the whole group begin to emerge and at that point the members of the group will be more prone to accepting such an interpretation. He further elaborates the common group fantasy as partaking of a deeper unconscious content than the more surface material that appears in the initial interactions. "Part of what is unconscious in each individual member relates to a common group phantasy: the rest relates to each member's biography ..." (p. 113). He thus endorses both the idea of searching for the shared fantasy of the whole group as well as the importance of first exploring and interpreting the psychodynamics of the interacting individuals before delving into the depths of the group-as-a-whole.

The current therapists at the Tavistock Clinic have published a most useful book (Garland, 2010) on their current perspective and techniques of group work. Like my inductive group centered, they believe it is important for the therapist to address individuals at certain times, with the understanding that individual interventions are useful in providing each patient with a sense of personal recognition while also recognizing such comments have a group-wide effect. But they clearly seek out the "common group tension" which they believe deepens the process and stimulates the group to reflect about their own personal reactions. Francesca Hume (2010), a Tavistock senior faculty member, writes that they use a model which is a "flexible integration of Bion's theory of group process and his psychoanalytic understanding of the material with a clinical style that owes more to Foulkes" (p. 126). They concur with Hopper (1985) that talking to one person is not at odds with the concern for the group-as-a-whole.

A further illustration of the value of the inductive approach is given by Schermer (2005) who related that he offered an interpretation to a patient that he was being a spokesman for a group resistance and the comment fell flat. When he changed tactics and worked one-on-one with the patient's self-esteem issues, both the patient and the group became engaged in a group-wide issue regarding ambivalent feelings toward the leader. "Thus the group-as-a-whole interpretation was more effective after the individual and interpersonal concerns were explored" (p. 231).

Writing from a self psychology perspective, Walter Stone (2009) comments approvingly of the recommendation that individualized comments should generally precede interpretations to the GAW, on the basis that empathy should ideally come before explanatory interventions.

A final cautionary note in applying this inductive approach: No single rule of technique covers all therapeutic instances. We are not proposing to substitute one rigid formula for another. A common group theme does not always emerge within a single session, so that a group centered interpretation may not be made. Also, we must sometimes allow for the possibility that a group centered theme is not functioning overtly at a given point and the therapist may therefore necessarily be operating on a more individualistic basis. In other words, the technique must never force itself upon the presented material. The tail of the technical principle should not wag the dog of the presented clinical material. We concur with the observation by Foulkes (1969) that a group therapist must always permit himself to experience surprise, to welcome the novel and unexpected.

Case illustration

To illustrate the method, I shall present the content of one session in which an individualized inductive method was used within a group centered approach. In this six-member group of young adults, the youngest and most pollyannaish patient, Kate, started the session. She had lately been visiting her mother and three younger sisters a good deal and had become upset by the family fighting and bickering. They were constantly trying to hurt each other and she found herself drawn into their arguments as a well-meaning but ineffectual "peacemaker". One patient expressed sympathy for Kate's mother, who had to contend with the stress. Another wanted to know if this was a repetition of Kate's previous role when her parents were getting a divorce. The subject elicited a lively discussion between Kate and the other members in an effort to understand the problem better. Why was she spending so much time at the family home when she had her own apartment; some sympathetic comments about how family members tend to go their own ways instead of pulling together; questions about the good feelings among her family members at certain times. The therapist mostly observed the ongoing interaction, entered a question or two about Kate's difficulty in giving up her peacemaking role, and later he asked, "Why now?" Kate could not explain, and the therapist then suggested that the reason might have something to do with the family-like tensions within the therapy group. The therapist believed, but did not state at that time, that Kate was feeling like an outsider in the therapy group and was unconsciously attempting to direct our attention to that.

This comment led another member to observe that at the end of the last meeting everyone had exchanged pleasantries upon leaving except for Dave, who had seemed sarcastic and depressed. This provided an opening for Dave, a new member, to express his dissatisfaction with the group. He did not know what he was supposed to be doing in order to get help: he felt that nothing got explored in depth and he found it difficult to express what was on his mind. Upon questioning by the group, he acknowledged that he had been feeling more isolated from the group lately, that the other member who had entered the group with him was becoming more integrated than he was.

The therapist used Dave's report of alienation from the group to note that Kate had implied something similar. Kate had mentioned that other group members had been feeling "good with their families" and that perhaps she was experiencing a sense of isolation within the group insofar as several people had reported in the last session that their lives were going well. Kate acknowledged that she had recently begun to feel less assertive than others, at work and in the group. The group returned to exploring Dave's feelings of dissatisfaction. He again criticized the group members for being too superficial in their discussions and for insufficient help forthcoming when people introduced problems. But he quickly shifted from criticism to self-criticism: his own feelings of helplessness with regard to helping other people. He felt at a loss to contribute anything to anyone in the group regarding problems they were raising. He continued to press the therapist for some clear answers about how talking is supposed to help and requested concrete suggestions on how to improve his participation. In his exchanges with other members, he expressed the idea that this process was like a religious experience in which members are asked to place their faith in the hands of an authority.

The therapist interpreted Dave's underlying wish for the therapist to be a supreme authority figure. And the more dissatisfaction he experienced with not getting the magical solutions he was seeking, the more he felt he himself should be able to perform miracles for others in the group. Such an impossible demand on himself made him depreciate the real help he might offer others as worthless. Then the therapist noted the similarity to Kate's feelings of frustration and helplessness in alleviating her family's problems and her unrealistic expectations of herself in helping them.

Dave was dissatisfied with the interpretation and failed to understand why the therapist or the members should not be giving "constructive answers" to each other. A dialogue ensued in which the other, more experienced members attempted to convey that authoritative answers and pat solutions were neither available nor appropriate, and that his passively awaiting help without working at it was self-defeating. Finally the therapist told him that his difficulty in bringing in his really vexing problems to the group, such as his hurt feelings about his recent divorce, was the result of expecting to be frustrated if he voiced any of his demands, so he tended to withhold expression of his real needs. The therapist then generalized this further to a tendency within the entire group to avoid expressing their needs in the group because of expected frustration. He described how another member, Mike, had been relatively silent and withdrawn in this session presumably because the therapist had not given him an answer he had requested in the last session.

The final segment of the session consisted of Judy relating a rather dramatic change in her behavior with her three children. Instead of continuing in the role of a "fourth child" in relation to her husband, she had begun taking her children to task for not discharging their responsibilities. She felt pleased with her newfound maturity, but also experienced considerable uneasiness. After a brief exchange with the other members, the group was adjourned.

The major point regarding technique illustrated in this session is the focus upon individuals, by the group and by the therapist, before a group-wide interpretation is made. Thus, Kate's inability to stay out of the "peacemaker" role was explored at the beginning in terms of some vague dissatisfaction with what she was getting from the family, and, by a slight inferential leap, from the group. After Dave, a new member, made clear his frustrated dependency wishes in the group, the members were able to help him see his growing feelings of isolation from the group, especially in light of another new member's (Judy) growing feeling of integration within the group. This observation helped to clarify further the nature of Kate's frustration within the group: the fact that a few patients in the last session had reported on progress related to their treatment.

When the group returned to further exploration of Dave's dissatisfaction, the theme of wanting "divine guidance" from the therapist was more clearly evident. It was handled partly by the group's explaining that such wishes were unrealistic and later by the therapist explaining how Dave's withdrawal from seeking help in the group (not discussing his recent marital failure, for example) was the result of his expecting frustration of his demands. The similarity between him and Kate in their excessive expectations of themselves in helping others was also mentioned.

Only after these two patients had had an opportunity to explore their current feelings and preoccupations in detail and only after the therapist had interpreted the underlying motivations of their behavior, did the therapist introduce a group-wide interpretation, that is, the common thread running through both patients' reports was generalized to the group: Strong disappointment that the therapist is not removing their distress magically was producing withdrawal, depressive, and compensatory behavior both within the group and in their lives outside.

The generalization that the whole group was to some extent involved in the same conflict was based only in part on the material presented in this summary. It also derived in part from a previous session in which another member had all but pleaded with the therapist for an answer regarding the advisability of termination and his turning away sullenly in this session because the solution had not been given.

The group-as-a-whole interpretation is designed to stimulate further those affects and memories already being stirred through empathy and identification with fellow members. That the general group-wide comment served this purpose is suggested by the content elicited from Judy. Like the other two patients, Judy was dealing with her own strong wishes to be another child in the family by using reaction formation, at least to some degree. However appropriate to her life situation, the parental role she was assuming (like Kate's peace-making role) had the anxiety and excessiveness which suggested that it was partly a reversal into its opposite. Thus, all of the members mentioned were struggling with dependency needs in their own idiosyncratic ways.

Summary

An inductive group centered approach to group psychotherapy consists essentially of using a group centered hypothesis which assumes that a group is often dominated by an underlying conflict common to all members. The method is inductive in the sense that in the first phase individual issues are addressed and get used as data for formulating a group-wide interpretation. This group centered model affords numerous advantages to the therapist in understanding and interpreting the behavior of the group. Commonalities among members are highlighted, resulting in greater cohesion, protection or support by the group theme, and enhancement of understanding the full context of each member's contribution. The shortcoming of a previous group centered approach, formerly used at the Tavistock Clinic and originated by Henry Ezriel, is that it tended to be too restrictive and gave the impression to the patient that his individuality was secondary to the group process. The author's inductive approach, unlike the deductive Tavistock-Ezriel approach, begins with an emphasis on individualized work before a more generalized group-wide interpretation is offered. In this way the individual views his personal needs as being attended to and dealt with, while the important group-wide themes also get attention.

CHAPTER SEVEN

Projective identification in groups

A frequent occurrence between two or more persons is the projection of certain mental contents from one individual onto and into another with a resulting alteration in the behavior of both the projector and the targeted individual. The mechanism of projection alone is not sufficient to explain this event since it only describes the process occurring within the mind of the projector but does not deal with the effect upon the targeted person. This complex of processes has been termed projective identification (PI), a concept introduced by Melanie Klein in 1946 when she described the paranoid-schizoid position. It is a defense mechanism as well as an object relationship which occurs in the earliest stages of development, the first year or two of life, before a firm differentiation between self and other has been achieved. A few years later Wilfred Bion (1961), in a series of penetrating observations on the mental life of groups, made this concept into a cornerstone of group behavior.

Despite the apparent usefulness, indeed the necessity, of this concept, it had failed to gain acceptance in either the individual or group psychotherapy literature until the mid-1980s and since that time it has gained wide currency. In individual psychotherapy, the concept had mainly been confined to Kleinian writers like Rosenfeld (1975) who made extensive use of the process in their interpretive work with psychotic patients. Kernberg's (1984) conceptualization of borderline pathology has relied heavily on this and other object relations concepts. Searles (1963) has used an aspect of this concept in his work with schizophrenics, particularly in his emphasis upon the therapist being willing to become a receptacle for his patient's distorted projections. Malin and Grotstein (1966) have suggested that PI is both a normal and pathological mechanism which may be used to conceptualize the therapeutic action of psychoanalysis in the sense that the projected content is processed by the therapist and is reintrojected by the patient in a more mature and adaptive form. But these were relatively isolated contributions which had not entered the mainstream of analytic literature in dyadic work until the latter part of the last century.

Likewise in group psychotherapy, since Bion's original contribution, and prior to the 1980s, there had been only three articles (Masler, 1969; Grinberg, Gear & Liendo, 1976; Gannzarain, 1977) in the group psychotherapy literature specifically focused on this topic. The group relations conferences, initiated at Tavistock and introduced into the United States by the A. K. Rice Institute, have applied this thinking extensively in their study of the dynamic processes in groups (Rice, 1965; Rioch, 1970). But only the field of marital and family therapy has incorporated such thinking via its key concepts of role assignment and role collusion among family members and particularly marital pairs (Dicks, 1977; Mandelbaum, 1977; Zinner & Shapiro, 1972).

How may we understand the slowness with which projective identification was able to gain wide currency as a basic explanatory concept in the psychotherapy literature? One possible explanation may be that it usually refers to early pre-verbal phases of development when self and object are still relatively undifferentiated. Hence, the contents may be archaic and bizarre and often evoke deep-seated aversive reactions against regression to primary process modes by many clinicians. Projective identification refers to efforts by individuals to rid themselves of certain mental contents by projection, and to the anxiety that these contents will be returned in kind, pushed back into them in the context of weak ego boundaries. The rapid oscillations between projector and target may have seemed difficult to accept.

But even for those prepared to accept the idea of oscillating transfers of mental contents in a setting of blurred ego boundaries, there are genuine conceptual unclarities that emerge in formulating these processes. During several years of studying and teaching this concept, I have found it more elusive and confusing than any psychodynamic concept I have encountered. Despite their extensive writings on this subject, and their own intramural understanding of the complex processes involved, most Kleinians have failed to make a comprehensive and lucid explanation of this concept. These unclarities seem to be based upon the following factors: (1) Unlike projection, the defense of PI stems from a variety of motivations and not just the wish to rid oneself of unwanted impulses like aggression and sadism. The wish to dominate, devalue, and control based on primitive envy, and the wish to cling parasitically to the valued object are among the other motives. (2) The identification part of the concept requires special clarification since its usage differs from most psychoanalytic definitions and one is frequently at a loss to know who is engaged in the identification. (3) Probably the basic unclarity is the fact that projective identification is not simply a defense mechanism involving internal or intrapsychic transformations as is true of most other defenses; rather, it is both an intrapsychic mechanism and an interpersonal transaction which involves transformations in both the projector and target. And further, PI assumes permeable boundaries, at least temporarily, in both parties.

Although the Kleinians used PI extensively beginning with Melanie Klein's introduction of the concept in 1946, the rest of the psychoanalytic community did not embrace it until a few decades later. The first sprouts of the concept were introduced by Kernberg (1975) when he described borderline personality disorder and characterized PI as a primitive defense used by these patients. A few years later Ogden (1979) described the concept in even greater detail and generalized it to the functioning of all individuals who are in close interactions with each other. The present writer followed with a description of how PI manifests itself in a group setting, elaborating the work of Wilfred Bion. Subsequently, there was a proliferation of articles dealing with its manifestations both in dyads and in groups. (Ganzarain, 1992; Goldstein, 1991; Malcus, 1995; Zender, 1991; Meissner, 1980; J. Scharff, 1992).

In her extensive survey of the literature, Scharff (1992) describes her difficulty in grappling with and clarifying the concept of PI and actually concludes that, because of its complexity and lack of clear consensus among contributors, there may be a value in embracing some looseness so as not to foreclose all of the meanings of this rich and complicated human transaction. She notes differences among contributors in terms of a one-person *vs.* two-person phenomenon, whether it is interpersonal or intrapsychic as well as disagreements about where the identification process is located. However, she proceeds to present a very complete account of the transactions involved while applauding the resilience of the concept in refusing to be "nailed down".

As the discourse increased there were two issues that divided writers on this complex concept. First there is a divergence with regard to whether the mechanisms involved are only manifested in pathological individuals as opposed to the view that PI is a universal phenomenon found in all interactions, particularly intimate ones. Meissner (1987) is the main spokesman for the more restrictive usage, contending that the broader definition can be explained by remembering that we are speaking of separate one-person reactions in which one party is engaged in projection and the other party experiences some form of introjection. But there is much evidence from marital therapy (Dicks, 1977) and in formulations regarding the mechanisms of psychotherapy (Malin, A. & Grotstein, J., 1966) that the broader concept is useful to understand human relationships in general.

The second is a related issue that pertains to the blurring of ego boundaries. There is the view that PI occurs only in individuals with weak, permeable ego boundaries which permits the rapid alternation between introjections and projection. I agree with those writers who believe that PI may occur more readily in psychotics and borderlines where ego boundaries are compromised; however, I believe that the same mechanisms occur in all intimate relations regardless of ego strength. In better integrated individuals the blurring of ego boundaries is likely to be transitory and reversible.

Bion's application of Kleinian concepts to group mentality and group behavior alerted group therapists to a number of seminal and provocative ideas. A brief resume of his main line of thinking cannot do justice to the richness of his ideas and can only suggest the direction of his thinking. He believed that groups tend to arouse fears and wishes of a primitive regressed nature and, in particular, the group-as-a-whole stirs archaic fantasies about the contents of mother's body. While such reactions are most easily observable in groups composed of more regressed individuals, says Bion, they may also be uncovered and shown to occur in groups of well-integrated people. These primitive fantasies not only operate on group members but on the therapist as well. When projective identification occurs, the group therapist has the experience that she is being manipulated to play a part in someone else's fantasy. Bion concluded that the ability to shake oneself out of the "numbing feeling of reality" that is a concomitant of this state is a prime requisite of the group therapist. Bion leaves no doubt that projective identification is the cornerstone conception in the functioning of groups and that the group therapist must observe its occurrence within herself, be able to take distance from it, and rely upon her affective experience as a major source of her interpretations.

Bion's description of projective identification puts its major emphasis upon the interpersonal, as opposed to the intrapsychic, aspects of the transaction. Although the process starts with a person projecting a part of his self onto and into one or more other persons, it is the impact of the projected contents affecting the other person which is of special interest. In other words, projective identification may be divided into two general processes. The first deals with the vicissitudes of the projected material as it affects the subject himself, where the external object is not the focus of interest. The second important aspect is the effect of the projected material on the external object itself. The other person, or target, undergoes an identification or fusion with the projected content and its unconscious meanings, and thus has the experience of being manipulated into a particular role. In discussing these two facets of the process I shall first describe the behaviors where they were first discovered, that is, in a dyadic relationship, and then elaborate on their occurrence in a group context.

Effect on the self: the intrapsychic reaction

There are a wide variety of fantasies which accompany the subject's projection. Often they lead to persecutory anxieties concerning retaliation by the external object, and hence the process may be accompanied by a heightened need to control and dominate the object. A frequent fantasy is that parts of the self are intruding into alien territory and, therefore, run the risk of becoming entrapped much like a spy dropped behind enemy lines. When the bad, aggressive self is projected, the individual may experience a depletion of energy and a loss of assertiveness as he rids himself of these impulses.

Following the initial projection onto the object, the subject identifies himself with the projected material; that is, he reintrojects the aggression, or other content, attributed to the external object. This process has been characterized as an "empathic" response (Kernberg, 1975) and becomes the prototype for later, more advanced forms of empathy. In this instance, the subject experiences his own projected aggression which he has taken back into the self. Because the projected content returns to the self, projective identification has been referred to as "unsuccessful projection" and is another distinguishing feature from projection per se.

One might well ask why an individual, adult or infant, would reintroject material which he or she has sought to be rid of. Why engage in behavior which essentially undoes the primary defensive motive? The answer, quite simply, is that the permeability of ego boundaries, the relative lack of differentiation between self and object, associated with regression to the earliest stage of development permits and encourages a rapid oscillation of projection and introjection, so that contents are moving back and forth with relative lack of resistance. Hence, successful projection cannot occur. One might use the analogy of a leaky heart valve which permits some of the blood circulation to move in the wrong direction.

The processes described in this section are best summarized in a quotation from Hanna Segal (1973): "Projective identification is the result of the projection of parts of the self into an object. It may result in the object being perceived as having acquired the characteristics of the projected parts of the self but it can also result in the self becoming identified with the object of its projection" (p. 1267).

We should note here that Segal was referring only to that aspect of projective identification which had an effect upon the self and not upon the external object. She was referring to the intrapsychic side of the process, not the interpersonal. Her failure to make this distinction clear is an example of how conceptual unclarity surrounding the concept has developed.

Effect on the external object: interpersonal transactions in dyads

The second phase of projective identification, its effect on the external object, is of special importance since it underlies a variety of group dynamic phenomena as well as essential aspects of dyadic relationships. The content projected by one individual upon another begins to influence the behavior of the target individual who then becomes

PROJECTIVE IDENTIFICATION IN GROUPS   105

the repository of the unwanted contents. The identification aspect of the process is one in which the projections emanating from the subject become fused with the characteristics of the object and thus, the external object begins to take on the characteristics which have been "put into" him. This is the reason that Bion describes the target individual as having the experience of being manipulated in somebody else's fantasies. Segal (1973) defines this aspect of projective identification as follows: "Parts of the self and internal objects are split off and projected into the external object which then becomes possessed by, controlled, and identified with the projected parts" (p. 14).

The language most often used to describe this interpersonal occurrence is that certain mental contents are "put into" the other person. The quotes are used to recognize that the phrase is a metaphor of an end product and is neither a valid description nor explanation of what occurred. Rather, the person behaves as if the mental contents had been put into him. A dynamic explanation of this behavior will be attempted in the final section of this chapter.

In a penetrating analysis of marital interaction, Henry Dicks (1977) of the Tavistock Clinic made extensive use of projective identification as not only the cement which binds marital partners in their love-hate interactions but also supplies the potential for the conflicting tensions which impinge on marital pairs. Typically, in accordance with the well-known principle of the attraction of opposites, A selects B as a spouse because of his or her potential for acting as the container of part of A's internal being which A cannot tolerate as part of his or her conscious self. A then strives to induce B to become the embodiment of the fantasied other in order to complement an identity which A cannot sustain. A permeability of ego boundaries between the two individuals develops so that each becomes a representative of the other's self (or parts of self) which are ambivalently held. With the blurring of ego boundaries which occurs to some degree in all marriages, each partner feels the other to be a part of themselves. Insofar as these projected qualities are unacceptable to A, he proceeds to scapegoat B, and the intensity of the hostility is proportional to A's ambivalent investment in these rejected qualities.

The wife who is strongly attracted to, and at the same time repelled, by her authoritarian, domineering husband, both encourages him towards a strict parental role and at the same time undercuts his controlling behavior. Thus, she not only projects her ambivalently held object representation onto her spouse but encourages and manipulates him to assume the desired role.

Even though the concept evolved in the context of studying primitive psychological processes, it is also useful in understanding certain kinds of higher level functioning. Indeed, projective identification is a prevalent aspect of the psychopathology of everyday life, particularly in regard to intimate relationships like marital and family transactions, and interactions among close friends. In these situations, a permeability of ego boundaries occurs and the conditions are ripe for well-integrated persons to transfer a whole range of mental contents, be they primitive or mature.

In a good marriage, for example, it is not uncommon for a spouse to experience vicarious gratifications of a motive with which he is not entirely comfortable, or perhaps unskilled, in expressing. Such situations often reflect neurotic trends but of a relatively benign kind. The wife who is uncomfortable with her own competence in intellectual activities may find gratification by encouraging her husband to act for both of them in such matters. If it is an area of great intrapsychic conflict for one or both of them, there is danger ahead. But if the activity is only mildly conflicted, a stable and mutually gratifying arrangement may be formed. Here we have projective identification of a relatively normal kind in which behavioral needs are complementary and roles are mutually adaptive. In fact, says Henry Dicks, a marriage without such reciprocal involvement is a crippled or stunted relationship. It is the basis for the sage observation that the opposite of love is not hate, it is indifference. Projective identification grows only in the soil of intimacy, caring, and intense involvement.

Turning to another dyad, the therapist—patient pair, Racker's (1968) contributions in the area of counter-transference have also made extensive use of projective identification. He describes two kinds of counter-transference responses, one based on concordant identifications and the other on complementary reactions. The concordant identification results from the analyst's effort to understand and empathize with his patient, to be in tune with various aspects of the patient's psyche and personality. To some extent an identification process occurs in each segment of the analyst's personality with the corresponding part in the patient: his id with the patient's id, his superego with the patient's superego, and his ego with the patient's ego. Ideally, these identifications occur mainly on a conscious level. But to the extent that the analyst fails in his concordant identifications and rejects them, complementary identifications become intensified; that is, the therapist begins to assume some of the characteristics of the patient's undesirable internal objects and the patient, in turn, begins to view the analyst as similar to the patient's internal objects. Thus, if the analyst is unable to empathize concordantly with the patient's aggression, the patient will begin to experience him as a rejecting and punitive figure and a process occurs in which the patient projects his unwanted perceptions into the analyst who is manipulated to take on the characteristics of the patient's rejecting superego. In this way the analyst becomes the embodiment of the patient's internal object and a complementary identification has occurred.

It should be clear by now that the identification processes referred to in projective identification apply to both the subject and the object, the projector and the target, to the intrapsychic as well as the interpersonal aspects. The subject identifies himself with his own projection after it returns to him as a reintrojection. On the other hand, the external object is manipulated to behave in accordance with the subject's self-representations or object representations and identifies himself with these projected contents. Thus, identification is alternately used to refer to one aspect or the other, the projector or the target, without always making clear the locus. Furthermore, the accepted definition of identification is that it is a transformation in a subject's ego or superego in which the subject takes on certain characteristics of the object (Kernberg, 1976). But in contrast to introjection, identification occurs in the context of relatively well-differentiated boundaries between self-representation and object representation. Thus, projective identification could have been more accurately named projective introjection.

A group dynamic triad

Only when we are aware that individuals in interaction may transfer mental contents one from the other and back and forth may we appreciate the full complexity of behavior in a group setting. We may then fully understand Bion's observation that each individual contribution adds to the reservoir of the group mentality. One of the fascinating experiences in group work is to find that the key to fully understanding one individual's contributions is to hear later associations and reactions of other members. The dynamics of A's quarrel with his boss, for example, often becomes more comprehensible later in the session when B and C engage in a heated interaction between themselves, and for example, the struggle pertains to the wish to be the favorite of the therapist. Quite often, this dynamic may be part of a group theme which helps to explain A's earlier contribution. The therapist often undergoes an "ah ha" experience as he attempts to piece together the contributions of various members. This kind of unitary functioning in a group has been described by such hypotheses as Bion's basic assumptions (1961) and Ezriel's common group tension (1950). It is not only possible, but likely, that the mechanism underlying these shared fantasies of group members is their capacity to put certain mental contents into each other.

Role-suction was first introduced by Redl (1963) and is related to an earlier conception called billet proposed by Arsenian, Semrad, and Shapiro (1962). These authors observed that there are necessary roles to be filled in a group and that the group in its wisdom selects its most likely candidate to fill a particular function. The term suction graphically suggests the idea that group forces may sometimes act in powerful ways to pressure an individual into a needed role. Projective identification adds a further dimension to this process by introducing the idea that the individual who is thus "suctioned" has also become the repository of the projections of others and is being manipulated to engage in needed roles and behaviors.

With regard to the second related phenomenon, a spokesman is one who assumes a leadership role in expressing the dominant theme of the group at any given time. As suggested in the above description of role suction, there is always a collusion between the individual's character style on the one hand and the group's dominant needs on the other. Groups quickly learn which individuals are best able to express anger, who can deal most comfortably with closeness and libidinal attraction, or who can experience dependency with a minimum of conflict. There are varying degrees of awareness on both sides regarding the relative contributions of the group and the individual to the role taken by the patient. More often than not, the group is content to disown the spokesman and vice versa. In fact, the most common error committed by the neophyte group therapist is his failure to recognize that a given individual's behavior is not only a product of his own individual propensities but carries a greater or lesser degree of group freight as well. I have been impressed by the frequency with which we group therapists experience the feeling that there is one particularly noxious and abrasive member, often a monopolist, who is interfering with the functioning of the group and, so the fantasy goes, "all would be well if we were not burdened down by this member". In most instances, the extrusion of the recalcitrant member does not really improve matters since the group will quickly find a new recruit among its ranks and promptly install him as a replacement.

It is appropriate to ask how one might differentiate between the occasions when the individual serves as spokesman and when he primarily speaks for himself. Resistant behavior which is persistent and which the group expects the therapist to deal with is most often being actively or passively encouraged by the whole group. Whether the behavior is that of a monopolist, a silent member, or a chronic help-rejecting complainer, the group's failure to deal with it usually indicates that the member is expressing an important feeling for all. By contrast, the individual who truly speaks for himself often finds little encouragement from his fellow group members, and the group's associations tend to move into other issues which resonate better with the group's central preoccupations.

The third dynamic, scapegoating, is perhaps the most commonly observed and accepted of all group dynamic processes. Whether a therapist is more group centered or more individually oriented, she will have great difficulty in ignoring the process of scapegoating except, of course, when under the pressure of a strong counter-transference response, in which case the therapist may collude with her group in attacking the scapegoat. The most frequent form of scapegoating is the simple displacement of a patient's aggressive or libidinal impulses toward the therapist onto another member, where such feelings will not necessarily elicit retaliation. Projective identification, however, suggests that there is a more complex form of scapegoating which may not be quite as obvious but occurs with considerable frequency. Those individuals who become the carriers of unwanted affects, the spokesmen for desired but threatening impulses, are particularly prone to end up as victims of the group's active effort to repress such ideas and feelings and safely put such affects into the choice member. These patients are often castigated, ridiculed, and even sometimes extruded from the group. Unless the therapist recognizes that the group is enacting a drama in which they are symbolically flailing themselves for their own unacceptable desires, in this instance projected into the victim, the therapist may very well participate himself in the cruel sacrifice. This kind of scapegoating was poignantly illustrated in the classic short story,

The Lottery by Shirley Jackson (1968) in which a community engages in a ritual stoning of one of its members selected by lottery, in order to rid itself symbolically of its unwanted impulses. The two forms of scapegoating mentioned above are described by Scheidlinger (1982) as projection and projective identification.

My thesis is not that the three aforementioned processes—role suction, spokesman, scapegoating—are entirely dependent for their operation upon projective identification. We have seen, for example, that scapegoating may largely be a process of displacing an impulse from one object to another. However it is likely that all three of these dynamisms tend to be affected by projective identification to some degree. The group therapist who fails to appreciate the profound reverberating effects of these intense affective exchanges is neglecting a highly important determinant of group behavior.

Illustrative examples of group behavior

Two vignettes on group functioning, one from a training group and the other from an ongoing therapy group, illustrate the operation of this dynamic triad. The former is an unstructured small group experience in a group relations conference and consisted of a dozen participants whose primary task was to study the dynamics of their group and met daily over a period of almost two weeks. Don was extremely hostile and critical towards the consultant from the outset. At first he made minor jibes at the consultant's interventions and later he made more biting and sarcastic criticisms of his personal characteristics, like his haughty, aloof manner in the group. Ordinarily, the consultant (like a therapist) would have dealt with these attacks as group-wide negative feelings towards authority figures and would have attempted to uncover such feelings when they surfaced. But instead, the consultant, unwisely in my view, began to show obvious signs of irritation with Don, glared at him unappreciatively on a few occasions, and bristled with annoyance when he was being ridiculed. Since the consultant was obviously reacting on a personal level and counter-transference was interfering with his task, the group became increasingly inhibited about expressing their negative feelings towards him with the result that Don became the main carrier of the group's negative affects. As this process continued, Don became alienated and was criticized by the other participants who expressed annoyance with him, at least on a conscious level. They experienced his attacks as unfair, crude, and tasteless. Finally, near the end of the conference, Don terminated the group prematurely but only after he had made a farewell speech in which he went around the room and had picked apart each member, describing their Achilles' heels with telling accuracy. One of the more dramatic aspects of this episode was that at the conclusion of his speech he proceeded to commit a symbolic suicide by throwing open the tall french windows in the room and dropping a few feet to the ground below. The triad of role suction, spokesman, and scapegoat emerged clearly in this incident, particularly inasmuch as the consultant failed to deal actively with the contributions of the entire group. The group had put its aggression into Don and as a result he not only expressed his own transference reactions but was also carrying the group's repressed hostility as well.

The second example is from a therapy group which had been going for about a year. The therapist announced that he was bringing in a new member in a few weeks and there was no immediate, visible response. However, in the next session, Ken, a potentially troublesome patient, began to resume some of his previously difficult and annoying monopolizing behavior. The therapist and the group had worked hard during the year to help Ken control his endless obsessional ruminations and now it appeared as though none of the previous work had been done. In this session, Ken launched into a long, ruminative, free-associative monologue about himself, showing no intention to interact with the group, and rather obviously imposing himself in an irritating way. He created in the therapist a feeling of helplessness and revived the therapist's fantasies that the group could function more effectively without this troublesome member. At one point the patient launched an attack about the incompetence of his supervisor where he worked, his inability to perform the job properly and the therapist attempted to interpret the barely disguised metaphoric attack upon the therapist's deficiencies. The interpretation was blithely ignored as Ken proceeded in characteristic fashion to continue his monologue as if the therapist had never said anything. At this point the group howled in amusement as they watched their therapist being treated with disdain and helplessly floundering to find a way of stemming the onslaught. It was now clear that the group was enjoying their spokesman and, in contrast to the first example, were at least partly conscious that Ken was expressing the anger that they were experiencing about the therapist's imposing a new member upon them. After the therapist had overcome his "numbing feeling of reality" that it was Ken alone who was acting destructively, his interpretation about the entire group's resentment was effective in helping to bring the monopolist under control.

In effect, an unconscious collusion between Ken and the group had been established in which his characteristic behavior was used to express what the group was experiencing. The therapist was not getting his usual help from the group in controlling this patient because their partly conscious wish was to find and encourage a spokesman for their negative feelings. When the therapist helped to undo the projective identification involved in this process, when he redistributed the mental contents which had been put into this particular member, the group's anger could be uncovered and dealt with and the therapist's counter-transference towards the annoying member had been controlled. It is manifestly clear that the major technical device for dealing with this kind of problem is to interpret the group's exploitation of the scapegoated member in getting its needs expressed.

Towards a dynamic explanation

The phenomenon of projective identification, and its effect on the interactions within groups, seems well established as an observable phenomenon. The target of the process does, indeed, experience a change in his psychic functioning due to the intrusion of mental contents from one or more other persons. Most authors describe this process as certain material being "put into" the other individual. Projection per se is described with the preposition "onto" to indicate that the projected content does not necessarily penetrate the recipient, that it only affects the projector's perceptions of the target. In contrast, projective identification is more appropriately described as a projection "into" to indicate that it sinks below the surface of the target and modifies her behavior. These metaphors may be graphic and descriptive but they fail to explain the actual process whereby an individual experiences Bion's "numbing feeling of reality" associated with introjecting someone else's projected contents. How may we understand and formulate a causal explanation of this important aspect of mental life?

We should first clarify that not all interactions between two or more people in which someone's behavior is markedly influenced by identification necessarily involves projective identification. One can identify oneself with another person without projectively identifying.

Insofar as we share common object relations paradigms with each other, that is, common ego states, we are capable of reacting empathically with other people's affective states, currently referred to as mentalizing (Allen, Fonagy, & Bateman, 2008). When a member of a group begins to communicate dependency longings, or the fear of the consequences of expressing such needs, these expressions will resonate with similar experiences in others. With varying degrees of consciousness, the other members will become aware of their dependency wishes, or their defenses against such wishes, as they get filtered through their own individual, idiosyncratic character structures. Ezriel (1973) describes this process as a fantasy in one group member, usually unconscious, which begins to "click" with a similar fantasy in another. It is possible to conceive of a higher level identification process occurring here, one in which the self-other differentiation has not been significantly altered, where empathy, but not projective identification, has occurred.

It is also conceivable that one could find occurrences of mixed internalizations in which the higher level identifications occur simultaneously with lower level introjections, the latter associated with projective identification. One could assume a continuum of internalization processes from the most to the least differentiated with the possibility that at any given moment there may be a broader or narrower span of response.

Let us consider some possible explanatory models. Masler (1969), in the earliest paper following Bion written on projective identification in groups, proposed that a patient initiates the process by "training" others in the group to react in a manner complementary to his projections. Thus, a patent who exhibits abrasive behavior which has the effect of evoking criticism and censure from his peers, is training the group to react to him like his own superego does. In effect, the patient has projected his superego into the other group members and has "manipulated" them into punitive reactions toward him. Although the effect of this "training" procedure may be similar to what occurs in projective identification, there may be a basic difference in the mechanism. In Masler's (1969) illustration the patient provokes a wished-for superego reaction and thus externalizes an internal conflict, with the result that a complementary identification does indeed occur. What is not clear, however, is whether the subject's internal contents are being put into the other person. In other words, we may be dealing only with a reaction to provocation rather than an introjection of another person's internal objects as must occur in projective identification.

Racker's description (1968) of the process involved in counter-transference reactions may bring us closer to an understanding of the complex event whereby one person puts mental contents into another. With regard to the relationship between patient and analyst, the usual process is that the boundaries between the two begin to merge to some extent and there arises an approximate union or identity between various parts of the subject and the object giving rise to a concordant identification. However, the interferences that occur as a result of the analyst's own blind spots and counter-transferences will interfere with the ideal situation and the patient will react by beginning to treat the analyst as one of his internal objects. In consequence of feeling treated as such, according to Racker, a complementary reaction occurs in which the analyst begins to identify himself with the patient's internal object. This kind of reaction is not only a function of the therapist's counter-transference but also a function of the permeability of the ego boundaries between them, the congruence between the projected material and the therapist's own psychological terrain, and the intensity of the patient's projection.

In a personal communication, my colleague Donald Colson has suggested that we may think of two distorting mirrors facing each other and producing increased distortions as the reflected images bounce back and forth. Thus, the patient feels angry at the therapist and has the conviction that the therapist is cold and indifferent. The therapist in turn feels unfairly accused and begins to get irritated. The patient then not only reintrojects his projected anger but begins to sense the therapist's real irritation, feels more justified in his accusations, and experiences a heightened sense of mistreatment which he directs at the therapist. The therapist, on his part, experiences increased counter-transference and, hence, a greater "identity" with the patient's views of him. Thus, an escalating cycle is set in motion. This series of provocations and reactions leads to ever increasing distortions and pressures which ultimately push the therapist toward identifying himself with the patient's internal object and begins to feel similar to the way the patient was perceiving him.

Such a formulation is certainly consonant with the experiences of all clinicians, particularly those who have worked intensively with border-line or psychotic patients, where the intensity of primitive transferences promotes a blurring of ego boundaries. Therapists are often left by their patients with the disturbing feeling of having become the angry, punitive, withholding parent, and such reactions may vary from fleeting and transitory to more long-lasting experiences. Under ideal circumstances, the therapist is able to use these reactions in the service of better understanding the dominant transference-countertransference situation and will be able to shake himself free of these disturbing introjections.

Applying this dyadic process to a group situation, we must remember that even in a collection of well-functioning and well-integrated patients, there are a number of strong regressive forces which propel members into acting and reacting with developmentally early layers of their psychic functioning. The contagion effect of group emotion, the threats to the loss of one's individuality and autonomy, the revival of early familial conflicts, and the prevalence of envy, rivalry, and competition—all contribute to the regressive reactions in a group. Small wonder, then, that Tavistock group relations conferences where unstructured groups, both large and small, are a prominent part of the format, often induce temporary regressed reactions in some members who are ordinarily well-integrated and high functioning. Usually they result from these individuals becoming the carriers of the group's feelings of chaos and disorganization, victims of projective identification. Such instances, however painful, are instructive lessons in the regressive potential of the unstructured group and, in particular, the impact and potency of projective identification. Of course, the group leader's style, particularly his tendency to frustrate the group, may have an iatrogenic effect and contribute to regressive reactions.

Thus, the intensity and primitiveness of the projection is capable of eliciting in the target person varying degrees of transformation. Such changes may involve the target person beginning to feel and act as though he were like the projected object. Malcus (1995) has been able to build on Bion's view of the role projective identification in groups and integrating it with the views of several others who conceptualize the group's mother transference. As patients begin to elaborate their reactions to a growing theme in the group, the transference paradigm of the entire group becomes filled with good mother or bad mother introjects that begin to affect each patient. The group responds to these increasingly intense affects with an effort to project their unwanted wishes and fears into a scapegoated member whom they then attempt to reject and even extrude. It becomes the task of the therapist to observe and interpret this defense and help his patients to reintroject their projections from the more metabolized and integrated identification of the therapist, thus helping patients to acquire a more mature and higher functioning self-concept. In this formulation Malcus was able to integrate the concept of projective identification with the view of the group acting as an integrated entity, and more specifically, the view of the whole group as representing either the holding, containing good mother or the punitive, rejecting bad mother.

The above model appears to be currently the most specific and comprehensive view of projective identification and how it functions within a group-as-a-whole model. Malcus' clinical example of this formulation describes a group in which a number of members express the fear of trying to express themselves openly and members are "wanting to protect themselves by hiding in silence" (p. 65). Finally Dawn is induced by members to start talking (to become "bad" in the eyes of the group) and she is then scapegoated by the others who critically remind her of her previous efforts to be silent as a way of testing the interest of others. One member expresses the belief that his life has been full of monsters and that if he were to attempt to slay the monsters he would destroy himself. Another spoke of her hypercritical father for whom she had to be perfect; still another patient chimed in with his being expected by his parents to be perfect and avoid sinful behavior.

A few sessions later Dawn, the scapegoated member, announces her intention to leave the group and despite the efforts of the group and the therapists, she interrupted her treatment because she experienced the group as the increasingly invasive and demanding bad mother. On the other hand, the other members viewed the group as the boundlessly nurturing mother. In retrospect, Malcus observes that he could have "fostered an exploration of other members' frustration, disappointment, and anger with the group. Such work would have attenuated the split-off, bad mother projections that suctioned Dawn into the role of the indirect scapegoat by pressuring her to introject and articulate these projections" (p. 69). That work, he suggests, hopefully would have permitted her to remain in the group and would have permitted the entire group to experience the good mother who could tolerate both their hostility and their love.

The field seems to be moving ever closer to a dynamic explanation of how the all-important concept of projective identification operates.

At this point, the analogy of the reflections of distorting mirrors appears helpful. More recently, a formulation in terms of the group-as-a-whole perception of the good or bad mother group which then gets attributed to a scapegoat also provides a further contribution to understanding how this powerful phenomenon develops.

Summary

I have attempted to explain why the concept of projective identification has often been a source of confusion among dynamically oriented psychotherapists. Unlike other mental mechanisms, it is a concept which is both intrapsychic and interpersonal. Like the quality of mercy, it is twice "blessed"; it blesseth him that gives and him that takes.

Projective identification has been defined alternatively with a focus upon the effect on the self, and at other times, in terms of its impact on the external object. Confusion has often resulted from not making clear which aspect of the process was being described. The identification part of the term refers to the introjection and fusion which affects both the self which projects (and reintrojects) and the external object which introjects the projected content. It is a concept which elucidates the behavior of regressed individuals but is equally important in the understanding of intimate relationships within the normal range, such as transference and counter-transference phenomena as well as family and marital interactions. It plays a major role in the dynamics of a group insofar as mental contents of one part of the group are put into another part and underlies such occurrences as role-suction, the spokesman phenomenon, and scapegoating. An understanding of this all-important dynamic is essential to a full appreciation of the complexities of behavior within a group. Various mechanisms of its operation are described and it appears that the most comprehensive explanation at this time is one which integrates PI with the concept of transference to the whole group as the good or bad mother.

CHAPTER EIGHT

Depth of transference in psychotherapy groups

In deciding about the treatment of choice for a patient, one must give consideration to how individual and group psychotherapy compare with regard to the transference regression that occurs in each modality. Patients who are candidates for intensive-expressive treatment require a regressive experience in order to uncover the repressed unconscious conflicts that produce pathological symptoms or behavior. If the group situation does not permit a therapeutic regression to the early levels of development, the group modality would be relatively ineffective for exploratory, uncovering work. Writers who have compared group and individual treatments with regard to their potential for eliciting therapeutically useful regressions have derived quite different conclusions. The contrasts cover several related dimensions, such as the depth of transference regression, levels of cognitive functioning, and the mode of therapeutic action. All of these factors converge on the issue of the potential for transference regression of a group compared to individual treatment.

Historical background

There is one school of thought that contends that transference regression to earlier and more primitive levels of functioning in a group tends to be more limited than the kind of regression seen in a dyadic relationship. The classic paper cited is that of Spanjaard (1959) who compared a closed group of five men that met four or five times a week with reactions of comparable patients to a standard psychoanalytic process. His observation was that the age regression in the group was limited to early adolescent reactions and that the reality pressures in the group prevented the members from regressing to earlier levels of development. This position stands in contrast to the view of Bion (1961) who contended that the ever-present group mentality associated with projective identification exerts a strong regressive pull on the individual patient and hence the reactions that are elicited or defended against are at least as primitive as those elicited in individual treatment.

Likewise, group psychotherapists tend to be split into two polarized camps with regard to the depth of the transference that develops in groups, especially compared to individual psychotherapy. On the one hand, there is the belief that the multiple transferences in groups (therapist, peers, group-as-a-whole) are necessarily diluted by the realistic demands of the situation. These pressures make it necessary for each individual to restrain his more primitive and narcissistic wishes in order to preserve working relationships in the group (Foulkes, 1975; Slavson, 1964). In contrast, a number of writers contend that groups are capable of intensifying the transference and of producing affectively intense and highly regressed transference experiences that sometimes may be stronger than reactions that occur in individual treatment. These writers attribute such reactions to factors like a contagion effect, resonances among members, as well as the role of projective identification (Ganzarain, 1989; Horwitz, 1982) These writers believe that behavior in a small group may sometimes be comparable to large group behavior in which the crowd or mob causes individuals to lose their superego restraints and to engage in behavior that would ordinarily be unacceptable to themselves in a smaller context.

Similarly, there is a long-standing split among group theorists regarding cognitive efficiency in groups. The Tavistock and A. K. Rice Human Relations Conferences, tied largely to the theories of Bion, find cognitive de-skilling, reduction in intellectual efficiency, and an aversion to clear thinking among the participants of their unstructured groups. In contrast, advocates of brainstorming and other kinds of group problem solving contend that the diverse inputs of a heterogeneous group make for a creativity and productivity that is unmatched in individual or dyadic problem-solving activity. Of course, problem solving groups with set agendas are quite different from unstructured therapy groups.

Several writers have attempted to compare the curative process in group and individual modalities, and once again those who emphasize the strength of the regressive potential in groups believe that group patients reach levels of insight that are quite primitive. Thus, they are able to heal their personality splits and develop more effective ego structures to a degree that is comparable to an expressive, individual psychotherapy (Durkin, 1964; Glatzer, 1969). On the other hand, writers like Foulkes and Anthony (1973), and Scheidlinger (1968) take the view that limitations in the time available to explore the genetic roots of a neurosis prevents the group patient from engaging in the working-through process necessary for change associated with insight. These writers emphasize the opportunity for changes of an experiential and behavioral type, particularly associated with the pressure of the group to appreciate the needs of others.

The common thread running through all these polarized positions has to do with regressive pressures versus reality pressures in group functioning. Assuming that both positions have some degree of validity and each may be describing "a different part of the elephant", is it possible to synthesize these discrepant observations into a more understandable, explanatory framework? In this chapter I shall focus first on the theories concerning the levels of functioning, primitive and mature, that characterize group functioning. Then I shall focus on the issue of transference dilution versus transference intensification in groups and attempt to demonstrate that both forces are capable of operating, partly depending on the patient's ego capacities and in part a function of the therapist's technique.

Levels of functioning in groups

Before dealing with the issue of transference dilution *vs.* intensificaion, let us first examine the major theories regarding levels of group functioning. A central proposition in psychoanalytic thinking, reflected in the topographical point of view, is that all mental events can be described with regard to the relative contributions of conscious and unconscious processes governed according to secondary-process or primary-process principles. When a clinician listens with the third ear, he or she is attempting to discern the latent, unconscious content that is operative but repressed behind the more conscious, manifest content. This view has been transposed to the group setting by several theorists who have observed the simultaneous occurrence of advanced and regressed levels in groups.

The earliest contribution is the observation by Bion (1961) of the higher-functioning "work group", which is the rational aspect of the group's activity, directed toward completion of the task, where members are cooperative and mature, and time considerations are ever present. On the other hand, the "basic assumptions group" is an ongoing form of group emotionality that is under the grip of primitive impulses such as dependency, sexuality, and aggression, and presses for immediate gratification. It is a defensive reaction which grows out of the anxiety of losing one's individuality through becoming submerged by group forces. The work group is under a constant threat of being intruded on and weakened by the powerful regressive forces of the basic assumption group.

Scheidlinger (1982) presents a somewhat similar duality in group functioning. He describes a "contemporaneous-dynamic" level where expressions of conscious needs, ego-adaptive patterns, and realistic group-situational factors predominate. On the other hand, the "genetic-regressive" level is characterized by unconscious and preconscious motivations, defensive patterns, and conflicts and is more apt to emerge in situations in which defenses have been loosened up. Scheidlinger emphasizes the dichotomy between the conscious, rational, and adaptive level as opposed to the unconscious, primitive, and defensive mode of functioning.

Although most writers describe a division that is dichotomous, there are degrees of regression within the unconscious level that get elaborated by other theorists. Another early contributor Foulkes (1975) presents four levels of group functioning going from surface to depth. First is the "current level" in which the group represents community standards and the members view the conductor as the authority figure. Second is the "transference level" in which the therapist and members represent mother, father, and siblings. Third is the "level of bodily and mental images" in which primitive object relations occur and peers in the group may reflect unconscious elements of the individual self, whereas the group-as-a-whole often represents the mother image. Finally, he describes a primordial level based on the Jungian idea of a collective unconscious.

In his comprehensive review of the application of object relations concepts to groups, Kibel (1992) emphasizes how the individual's attachment to a group results in a variety of transferences, ranging from primitive to mature. The more advanced levels are represented by the need for acceptance and belonging, whereas the more primitive transferences involve the group-as-a-whole being unconsciously perceived as an early mother imago, an idea that is accepted by most theorists. Bion thinks of the basic assumptions as defenses against regression to a psychotic level of perceiving the group as embodying the contents of mother's body and of the struggle against merging with, devouring, and destroying it. Somewhat similar is the view espoused by both Durkin (1964) and Glatzer (1969) who attribute to the group-as-a-whole the conception of the hostile, attacking, bad-mother image. They view much of the defensive behavior within the group as an effort to appease and pacify the "witch-mother" that unconsciously is represented by the whole group. Scheidlinger (1982) also espouses a mother-group theory, but in contrast to the others, believes that the whole group represents a primitive identification with a need-gratifying object, that is, the good mother. In his view the group-as-a-whole becomes the protective envelope within which the hostile and threatening therapist and peers are experienced and dealt with.

Although these various writers differ from each other in detail, there are at least three clear levels of functioning that have been delineated: a conscious, reality-oriented, mature, adaptive level; an oedipal transference level that emphasizes earlier relationships with paternal and maternal figures; and a preoedipal transference level in which the split good and bad mother images predominate.

An important consideration regarding these levels of functioning, and one consistent with the principle of multiple determination, is that all of the levels are likely to exist simultaneously although usually there is a predominance of one particular aspect of the spectrum, a "point of urgency" that requires the therapist's attention and possibly intervention. This conception is not unlike the view regarding the multi-determined contribution of primary and secondary process factors involved in a Rorschach response. All levels usually contribute but each response is characterized by the dominance of one particular aspect.

Of the three levels cited above, paradoxically the most difficult to define precisely is the "surface level" characterized by the above writers as the "work group", the "contemporary-dynamic", and the "public level". All of these formulations involve an emphasis on a reality-centered dimension, a focus on the primary task of the group, and an appreciation of the true role of therapist and patient. The problem is that this reality level is constantly being intruded on by the other more primitive levels. For example, group patients who are collaborating with the therapist and their peers in reporting significant events in their lives and their emotional reactions in the group may also be influenced simultaneously by competitive strivings and envy toward their peers as well as a wish to achieve the favored position among their siblings.

Factors promoting transference dilution

Certain features of the group situation, compared to the dyad, reduce, control, or inhibit the intensity of the patient's primitive, regressive reactions. In some contexts and with some patients, groups are capable of contributing to a reduction of paranoid, aggressive, fearful, or erotic feelings. The major factors contributing to this development are the greater reality inputs present in groups as opposed to dyads as well the opportunities the patient has to regulate the distance and closeness he wishes to permit in his participation.

Greater reality inputs

The major factor contributing to dilution is the presence of increased reality inputs compared to individual therapy, and these reality pressures will often inhibit the development, growth, and intensity of the transference, as illustrated in the above example A frequent observation in groups is that often the therapist "looms less large" compared to a dyadic situation. Borderline patients in groups, for example, often feel more comfortable dealing with the therapist in a group rather than individually. Idealizing as well as fearful transference reactions seem to be less intense in a group setting, and helps the patients to be more relaxed and productive. A similar observation was described by pediatrician

Benjamin Spock who noticed that his counseling sessions with parents, when seen individually or as a couple, were generally restrained and unquestioning of his authority. When these same parents met with him in a group setting, the inhibitions were decidedly less prominent and the participants felt much freer in expressing their skepticism and disagreement with the famous doctor's pronouncements.

A number of factors contribute to this decrease in the idealizing transference. One is that the group situation places the therapist in a considerably greater position of exposure. The patient is able to sit back and take the position of an observer who may scrutinize the therapist as he or she interacts with the group or with a particular patient. The patient thus has the opportunity to observe the therapist's personal style and characteristics in a more detached way than would be available in a dyad and thus is more able to view the therapist as a real person. Also, there is the modulating effect on the transference of hearing the reactions and viewpoints of other patients and their unique perception of the therapist. Each patient's special view, distorted or accurate, of the therapist often tempers and modulates the reactions and perceptions of the other members.

Another way of conceptualizing the group as imposing greater reality testing and thus mitigating transference developments was suggested by Kosseff (1975) who described the group as similar to a transitional object insofar as the patient's fantasies may get tempered by reality pressures. Severely schizoid or borderline patients in individual treatment sometimes develop an insoluble transference neurosis because of the fear of getting too close or too dependent. The introduction of the group modality (usually concomitant with individual) helps to reduce the intensity of these transference fears. Fantasies of destroying and being destroyed by the therapist are mitigated by the presence of other members who contribute to the reality of the situation and make the therapist a less fearsome figure. Also, an individual's distorted split images of self and others tend to become more integrated by identification with the healthier, more reality oriented perceptions of other members.

Another facet of the increased reality orientation that prevails in group, compared with a dyad, is that narcissistic fantasies, often stimulated within a group situation, may get attenuated because of the presence of other patients. The frequent wish to be the exclusive object of the therapist's interest, or the wish to be the therapist's favorite, often expressed in the tendency to monopolize the group's time and attention, are counteracted by the presence of others who share similar wishes and frequently express their displeasure with the monopolist.

In addition, peer pressures tend to decrease transference resistances and other regressive behaviors. The norms of punctuality and regular attendance are frequently enforced by the peer group and become an obstacle to acting out. In a similar way, pressures for member self-disclosure are often difficult to resist in the group because the patient's acceptance in the group is threatened unless he or she engages with the group at their general level of self-disclosure. For example, a patient who was fairly new in the group reacted quite negatively to the group's discussion of intimate sexual fantasies, terming them "inappropriate and disgusting", but she soon found herself, against her better judgment and certainly her predilection, bowing to the group pressure to describe her sexual experiences and fears. Also, the erotized transferences that frequently develop in therapeutic situations, as mentioned earlier, similar to the narcissistic transferences, are necessarily modulated and attenuated by the presence of other members.

Caroline Garland (2010) of the Tavistock Clinic made the cogent observation that projection and introjection are inevitable developments in a group therapy setting and they are the "glue" of any group. But the presence of a peer group places pressures on group members that mitigate the effect of the transference distortions that develop.

Opportunities for withdrawal

Individual patients in a group are provided a broad repertoire of vehicles for detaching themselves from deep involvement with the group. If attachment and affective involvement are excessively difficult, the patient is able to limit the intensity of his or her involvement without necessarily dropping out of the group. Absenting oneself from the group by missing sessions is usually easier in a group than in individual treatment.

If the patient attends, he or she may remain relatively silent, stay in the role of observer, or more subtly, become the therapist's assistant. Patients in combined or concomitant individual and group psychotherapy often limit their participation in the group with the rationalization that they will have ample opportunity to do the necessary work with their individual therapist. The opportunities for withdrawal and limiting one's participation are often considered the primary reasons for using group psychotherapy as the ideal modality for certain borderline patients who have a need to maintain more emotional distance than is available in the individual therapy situation.

A narcissistic patient who was fairly new in the group and took the attitude, barely concealed, that he was superior to the other members insofar as he was less needy of help than they were. On one occasion the therapist made a group-wide interpretation regarding how people were reacting to the therapist's announcement of a planned absence, noting a muted anger in response to his announcement of the interruption. This particular member made it clear that he had no such reaction and separated himself from the rest of the group, a nice example of the how the context permits members to dismiss or deny interventions offered by the therapist that are not acceptable.

To summarize, the factors contributing to transference dilution in a group consist of a variety of reality pressures, such as a greater exposure to the real personality of the therapist, feelings of greater safety among peers, the modulating effect of multiple viewpoints, the use of the group as a transitional object, and the presence of other patients as a mitigating factor of narcissistic and erotic transferences. In addition, the greater opportunities for withdrawal and detachment in the group situation as opposed to individual treatment, may attenuate transference intensity.

Factors promoting transference intensification

There are several forces that operate in the reverse direction and contribute to an intensification of regressive transference reactions. These elements consist mainly of various affective stimuli not present in dyadic therapy. In psychoanalysis, for example, the regressive pressures are derived mainly from stimulus deprivation. In contrast there are a variety of group-specific phenomena that promote regression and transference intensification due to a multiple stimulus inputs.

Mutual stimulation and contagion

All writers on group psychotherapy, whether or not oriented to exploiting group processes for therapeutic purposes, emphasize the presence of a contagion effect that operates in a significant way. This effect occurs in groups large or small, therapeutic or problem solving, but mainly it is a property of unstructured groups. There are many diverse views regarding the phenomenon itself, as well as its underlying mechanisms, and most probably it is a multifaceted effect. Freud's foray into the psychology of groups (1921c) described the libidinal ties among members of large groups, using the army and the church as his prototypes, based on superego identifications with an idealized leader. Under these conditions members experience heightened emotionality, decreased intellectual efficiency, as well as a regression toward dependency resulting from their feelings of closeness toward their leader, which in turn resulted in increased libidinal ties among the peers.

There are probably two underlying processes involved in the contagion effect. The first is the all-important phenomenon of projective identification as described in the preceding chapter and originally derived from the Kleinian theory of individual development. The early view is that the pooled projective identifications of the group constitute the regressive group mentality. This concept has been further explicated as a dynamic in groups by several other writers (Ganzarain, 1989; Horwitz, 1983) and is viewed as both an intrapsychic defense as well as an interpersonal pressure on others in the group to respond in a desired way. Scheidlinger (1982b) has described the process of scapegoating as based on the operation of both projection and projective identification and believed that the latter is associated with a chronic collusion between a susceptible individual and the group's need for a repository of its unwanted emotionality. Most group therapists have long recognized the hazard for therapists to act out their counter-transference by unconsciously encouraging the group to scapegoat a patient who has become a troublesome member while at the same time offering himself as a sacrificial lamb. This dynamic has been described as "role suction" and as a "group billet"; concepts that capture the group's need to find an outlet for the expression of certain dominant group emotions be they dependency, hostility, or sexuality. Thus, the group, and regrettably sometimes the therapist, encourage their most susceptible members to express or act out such roles.

The second mechanism underlying mutual stimulation and contagion is based on identification processes, either concordant or complementary. The mechanism of resonance, as described by proponents of Group Analysis, is based largely on identification among members in which one patient's conflicts, anxieties, and defenses reverberate consciously and unconsciously with similar affects within other group members. When one member begins to express his dominant wishes and fears in relationship to his mother, for example, it is inevitable that others will find themselves resonating with similar issues, however differently experienced or handled, Identifications may be complementary or concordant in the sense that individuals may either empathize with the speaker's point of view or identify with the role of the offending object. In the latter case, exhibitionistic impulses in one patient will frequently stimulate voyeurism in others or masochistic expressions could elicit complementary sadistic impulses.

Frustrating inputs

Group patients endure certain frustrations that do not occur in a dyadic relationship. Most obvious, of course, is the need to share the time and attention of the group and the therapist. These group pressures induce a variety of anxieties and resonate with patients' conflicts at various levels of functioning. Oedipal rivalry produces competition among members as well as between member and therapist as individuals struggle to triumph over fantasied rivals or defend against such triumphs by passivity or helplessness. Or they might view the therapist as attempting to keep them in a subordinate and helpless position. Preoedipally, one sees a variety of issues relating to narcissism, dependency, abandonment, greed, and envy. The fear that the limited supplies in the group will be depleted by others and nothing will be available for oneself; the wish to be the favorite child, or at least the first among equals; the envious antagonisms that are set in motion when others are receiving desired supplies—are typical reactions stimulated by group membership. Thus, one group member struggled to deal with his intense ambivalence toward his mother, feeling both the wish to be soothed and nurtured as well as his resentment over his mother's tendency to be overprotective in the service of her own narcissistic needs. The therapist responded to this material with an interpretation linking this genetic material to the patient's current struggles with his girlfriend concerning the wish for and fear of intimacy. Subsequently, the entire group, sensing the potential value of the interpretation, felt both jealous and needy to gain similar "gifts".

Identification in this context is being described with regard to its potential for generating envy, but there are adaptive aspects of identifications as well, particularly in patients with ego defects (Pines, 1990). The individual who lacks the capacity to deal effectively with certain conflicts begins to identify with group or individual solutions, a process similar to supportive individual therapy, where identification with qualities of the therapist is a growth-enhancing experience.

In addition, there are experiences not only of inevitable interruptions of sessions as in individual treatment, but the occasional arrival of a new member and departure of an old one. New members characteristically deepen transference reactions that typically stimulate feelings around the birth of a new sibling. Threats to one's position vis-a-vis the therapist, fears that the new member will preoccupy the group and the therapist, or that the already limited supplies within the group will become even more scarce—are the dominant reactions. The departure of an old member, whether therapeutically indicated or not, commonly stimulates envy of that individual's fantasied or actual achievement, as well as experiences of abandonment and loss. His or her contributions will no longer be available and the loss of accustomed support and affirmation will now be experienced as a deprivation.

A male patient with a chronic sense of having been deprived of good caretaking had a strong reaction to one member's announcement of her intention to terminate. This woman was an older person with a nurturant personality who was viewed by others as the mother figure in the group. The man freely expressed his heightened sense of loss of the woman's contributions to his comfort and well-being.

Protection and support of shared group affects

Universalization is characterized by a sense of belongingness because others in the group experience the same conflicts, symptoms, or behavior as each other. The shame, inadequacy, and fear of catastrophe if exposed, are diminished and this phenomenon becomes an important stimulus toward self-disclosure. It is a mechanism that leads to group attachment or cohesion and has an analogy to the therapeutic alliance in a dyadic situation (Frieswyk et al., 1986). In individual therapy, as the alliance grows the patient experiences greater feelings of acceptance by the individual therapist and becomes increasingly confident that he or she will not be abandoned or rejected because of increased self-disclosure. Similarly in groups, trust is enhanced, and the conviction grows that hidden and unacceptable parts of the self may be admitted both to self-awareness and to scrutiny by the group. Both the group therapist and the group members begin to be perceived mainly as supportive and soothing figures who facilitate increasing closeness and intensity of affective reaction.

The exploitation of this particular facet of group functioning by group centered therapists provides us with an explanation for why many of these theorists tend to emphasize the potential in groups for increased openness and self-disclosure. For the most part, group centered therapists like Horwitz (1992) and Ganzarain (1989) tend to emphasize an intensification potential in therapeutic groups. Their concern with group-wide phenomena and their technique of seeking out shared, universal fantasies and conflicts (group mentality, common-group tension, focal-group conflict) not only encourages contagion and resonance, but also provides a significant supportive envelope that enhances a sense of safety and lowered defensiveness, a feeling of protection by the group theme. In contrast, it is interesting that those theorists who were most adamantly opposed to the use of group dynamics and who emphasized doing individual therapy in the group were also the therapists who most strongly emphasized the transference dilution effect in groups.

A synthesis

1. Both transference dilution and transference intensification exist as potentials in a group setting, coexisting and sometimes acting simultaneously, although one or the other may be dominant at any particular time. This situation should not be surprising, insofar as all human interactions and mental events partake simultaneously of varying levels of consciousness, repression, and depth. In individual psychotherapy either a predominantly supportive relationship or a mainly uncovering-expressive process will occur as a function of the kind of patient one is dealing with, his or her special needs and limitations, as well as the specific techniques the therapist utilizes. The individual therapist usually titrates frustration and gratification so that neither experience becomes excessive for a particular patient. Dilution and intensification factors in groups, based on reality and regressive pressures, generally show more oscillation than does the individual transference situation.

With regard to the latter point, it is not uncommon in therapy groups for members to manifest bursts of affectively intense reactions, often stronger in my view, than one is likely to see in an individual therapy situation. A frequent reason is that group patients tend to be subjected to intense stimuli. In one group, a female patient was being left by her only female co-patient, who was terminating. As the only remaining woman, she developed intense transference anxieties of being abused, demeaned, even assaulted by the males in the group, and struggled with the wish to drop out.

2. Transference dilution is fostered by the reality impingements of the group structure and by the supportive techniques used by the therapist. Group centered techniques generally tend to engender more intensification, whereas more individually centered approaches produce dilution effects.

Whether intensification or dilution occurs may be determined by what the patient is capable of using from among the smorgasbord of elements that are available in the group experience. Many patients are capable of extracting what they particularly need and ignoring those parts of the experience that may be noxious or not helpful. This is not an unvarying reaction, of course, but there are some indications, particularly in mixed groups of neurotics and borderline patients, that such a situation often prevails. In general, one would expect neurotic patients to profit from expressive, insight giving elements, whereas more fragile borderline patients, as well as some narcissistic patients, respond primarily to the supportive aspects.

In one group of mainly neurotic patients, a borderline young man, who was highly schizoid and obsessional, listened to the therapist's group-wide interpretations without ever permitting them to apply to himself. Rather, he often became the therapist's assistant in elaborating the leader's observations, particularly as they touched on his own primitive, but intellectualized, aggressive impulses. He was able to profit from the supportive elements in the group, especially the nurturant acceptance he experienced from the group members who recognized that he had special needs.

On the other hand, a more affectively uncontrolled borderline patient in a group of neurotics, and also the newest member of the group, had considerable difficulty in restraining her explosive reactions when she sensed, in paranoid fashion, that she was being criticized, or worse, ignored. In the brief period that she was in the group before she impulsively dropped out, the dilution effects in the group did not take hold for her, and her ability to use the group was severely compromised by her tenuous alliance with the group and the therapist. The patients viewed her as a monopolist who showed no interest in others and they showed no disposition to encourage her to remain in the group. I had some initial misgivings about accepting her as a member but I mistakenly thought that her relationship with her individual therapist could support her in tolerating the stress of entering an ongoing group. Borderline patients who are at the lower end of the diagnostic spectrum and who engage in intensive splitting often develop a strong negative transference reaction that is difficult to contain.

3. The transference intensification aspect of the group is fostered not only by the dynamics of mutual stimulation, contagion, and protection of the group theme mentioned above, but is also fostered by the therapist's effort at uncovering of regressive transference fantasies. Even though the group therapist is definitely more "exposed" in the group situation than in a dyad, and the increased exposure lends somewhat more reality to the patient's experience of the therapist, the experience will not hamper the development of transference reactions. It is possible that transference reactions in a group, based on the intensification phenomena cited above, may give rise to intense reactions to peers or therapist.

That is not to say that one can expect to elicit or analyze a transference neurosis comparable to the work in an analytic process. First, most expressive groups meet only once a week, rarely more than two times per week and, as in individual treatment, intensity and regression are partly dependent on the frequency of meetings. Second, most expressive groups are slow—open; that is, they fill vacancies from time to time. These events alter the therapeutic alliance in the group, at least temporarily, and thus impede the systematic analysis of the transference. And finally, groups do not easily lend themselves to the kind of continuity seen in intensive dyadic analysis. The vicissitudes in the lives of its several members will necessarily introduce diversions from a particular theme and thus group transferences tend to arise in sporadic and often intense bursts with the result that the working-through process is more irregular than in individual treatment.

4. The observations of many writers who describe the special virtues or limitations of group psychotherapy often lead them to adopt certain

techniques that are consonant with their beliefs and expectations. The therapist's format, whether group centered or individualistic, will contribute to a self-fulfilling validation of one's views about how groups function.

In conclusion, therapy groups are not intrinsically vehicles for either dilution or intensification of transference. They promote both factors, often simultaneously, but usually one is dominant at any given moment for a particular individual. One major determinant of a patient's reaction is the extent of the patient's pathology, with strong ego patients tending to use the intensification processes while dilution tends to occur among most patients with fragile egos. A second factor is the therapist's technical approach, in which exploratory techniques, low structuring, and the use of a group centered approach will produce intensification of the transference while a more individualistic stance lends itself toward greater transference dilution.

PART III

CLINICAL

The 1970s heralded significant advances in theory and practice in psychotherapy practice based on two very important contributions. First, Otto Kernberg, working at the Menninger Clinic, produced a number of significant papers and books on object relations theory which provided a breakthrough in our understanding of borderline personality functioning. Mainly, he used Melanie Klein's discoveries of early personality development, particularly splitting, and applied it to the symptoms of borderline pathology. He contributed to a major advance in how clinicians began to view the "stable instability" of these patients.

And during the same period Heinz Kohut moved the theory of narcissistic pathology ahead in a most significant way. His major contribution was to call for the recognition of narcissism as more than a nuisance in treatment to be brushed aside and to view it as a pathological development, a developmental arrest, that required slow working through. A major debate ensued between Kohut and Kernberg about understanding narcissistic defenses, like idealization and grandiosity, with Kohut emphasizing arrested development and Kernberg asserting they were conflict determined. In retrospect both points of view appear to have some validity and narcissism is probably best understood as a product of both processes.

I begin the section with a case illustration of my inductive, group centered approach (Chapter Nine). This clinical section also reflects my effort to deal with the borderline and narcissistic syndromes. I became convinced that group treatment had something special to offer both types of patients, provided one was careful in selecting them as discussed in Chapter Ten. Obviously not all borderlines nor all narcissists can be successfully integrated into a group.

My first venture into formulating my views about the group treatment of borderline patients occurred when the Menninger Clinic sponsored a major conference on borderline disorders and I was invited to make a presentation. We were honored to have Wilfred Bion accept the invitation to give the keynote address, a memorable occasion for all those in attendance since this dignified and formal Britisher shocked the audience with some unexpectedly racy language to characterize the issues that borderline patients need to deal with. These issues are presented in Chapter Eleven.

Over the years I developed an increasing conviction that many narcissistic patients, and indeed much narcissistic pathology, can best be treated in a group setting (Chapter Twelve), This point of view is illustrated in a case presentation in Chapter Thirteen. Such patients are often troublesome and irritating, but if they are capable of tolerating the group and the group is capable of tolerating them, they frequently are able to show significant adaptive behavioral change.

Chapter Fourteen, The Self in Groups, is based on my presidential address to the American Group Psychotherapy Association. Self psychology was just gaining prominence in psychodynamic circles and the concept of the self was very much in the air. It appears as though the idea of a superordiate self which includes the self as agent as well as the various layers of an individual's self-concept, has gained a prominent place in analytic theory.

As a result of my work in the Menninger Psychotherapy Research Project, I became interested in how narcissistic therapists hinder the treatment process. Owing to the influence of relational psychology and intersubjectivity, the mental health field has been more open to exploring how the personality organization of the treater impacts the therapeutic process, whether in groups or in dyads. My thoughts about this issue in the group setting are presented in Chapter Fifteen.

CHAPTER NINE

An integrated group centered approach: a clinical illustration

The debate among analytic group therapists has shifted from the issue of which orientation to emphasize—individualistic, interactional, or group-as-a-whole—to the question of how best to integrate all three into an effective rationale for understanding group behavior and intervening most effectively. In the early days of group psychotherapy, polarities tended to be set up, particularly between those with a group-as-a-whole orientation and those who focused on individuals. As in the polarities that often emerge in patient groups, not to speak of political partisans, each of the two camps tended to see all the virtues in its own position without recognizing its shortcomings. The now outmoded Tavistock method of group psychotherapy made a genuine contribution to the theory of the system properties of groups but failed to appreciate the absolute necessity of working with individuals in a way that made them feel that their needs were distinctive and not subservient to the needs of the group entity. Similarly, the early proponents of individualistic group work took a vigorous position against recognizing or using the dynamics of groups in group treatment and, in my view, failed to exploit the powerful therapeutic effect of a group's system properties.

139

In recent years, there has been a shift toward greater recognition in many quarters that one should understand and utilize group dynamic forces in order to do optimal therapeutic work. The concept of role suction, whereby an individual's behavior is viewed not simply in terms of his or her personal dynamics but also in terms of pressures within a group for certain roles to be filled, has become an important working tool for the group therapist. A corollary concept is that of the spokesperson who is speaking not just for himself or herself but on behalf of a segment of the group that is striving to find expression. Further, there is greater acceptance of the importance of the scapegoating phenomenon, in which ambivalent attitudes toward unconscious impulses get played out by first eliciting the expression of such drives through role suction and then attacking any individual who personifies that position (Scheidlinger, 1985).

As described earlier, the Ezriel model had been found wanting by a number of writers (Malan, Balfour, Hood & Shooter, 1976; Horwitz, 1977; Day, 1981; Garland, 2010). Using research data gathered at the Tavistock Clinic, the Malan group (1976) found widespread dissatisfaction among former group therapy patients with the method of the group therapy that prevailed in the first few decades. Patients experienced their group treatment as focused mainly on how the group was functioning and only incidentally on the psychological needs that they brought to the group. Working with a group centered orientation in Boston, Day (1981) reported that he gradually became disillusioned with the efficacy of a method that focused on the dynamics of the group, because his patients tended to feel that their individual needs were slighted. A similar experience was reported by the present writer (Chapter Six), who found that group-wide interventions must first be preceded by individualized work and liberally interspersed with comments to single patients so that members will feel that their idiosyncratic needs are not being ignored and that the therapist is empathic and responsive to them as unique persons.

The early Tavistock model was a deductive method of interpretation in the sense that a generalized principle, the common group tension, is the bedrock, or foundation, on which the individual comments rest. I have proposed that the interpretive sequence be reversed and that an inductive method be used in that only after working with two or more individuals would the therapist introduce a common theme that binds them together.

Superficially, the inductive method may not appear too different from a purely individualized approach that does not attend to group-wide properties. Certainly when an individualized interpretation is offered to a patient, one might be hard put to distinguish between a group centered and an individualized approach. The group centered therapist will not stop, however, with individualized interpretations but, rather, will silently begin integrating the common threads among individual productions as the session proceeds, a process that eventually culminates in interpreting the common group tension. In this sense, the group-centered therapist is constantly attending to the common underlying themes expressed by the patients as a whole while addressing his or her interventions to various individuals. In other words, the group-centered therapist's manner of conceptualizing the process, thinking about it and mentally organizing it, is quite different from a purely individualistic model.

An important facet of the inductive method is that once the therapist has identified a common theme and interpreted it to the group, any number of patterns of moving back and forth between individual and group comments may follow. More often than not a particular common group tension will prevail in a group for more than one session, even though one might expect that each of these sessions is likely to show some facet of the group-wide conflict emphasized more than others. But once a given theme has been uncovered, the therapist will usually be offering some combination or integration of individual and group interventions.

An illustrative group session

The session to be described is from a group of six patients, three male and three female, in an age range of approximately twenty-five to forty, and length of membership ranging from less than one year to about five years. Diagnoses are mainly character disorders within the neurotic range, with the exception of one patient who suffers from a borderline personality disorder. The group meets twice a week. The quoted remarks are derived from a videotaped recording, a procedure which had been occurring for over a year.

The important events preceding the session to be reported are, first, a month-long vacation break that had ended two weeks before and, second, that a couple of months prior to vacation, one of the patients who had had the longest tenure in the group had begun making plans for discharge, the termination date being set for about one month after the vacation break was over. When we resumed after vacation, his attendance became somewhat sporadic, and he was absent without explanation from the current session.

During the three sessions preceding the present one, the group was mainly dealing with its hurt feelings about having been abandoned for a month by the therapist. The theme that was developing was the wish to put one's worst foot forward in order to test the devotion of loved ones. Each patient wanted proof from a significant person in his or her life or from the therapist that he would stick by the patient despite the patient's anger, his or her childishness, or any other troublesome behavior. This theme had been played out and interpreted by the therapist in two preceding sessions and continues into the session being reported.

The session is opened by Carol, a stout thirty-two-year-old divorcee with a ten-year-old son. She says she doesn't understand the theme that occurred in the group last week. In particular, she did not understand how she would get any gratification out of becoming even heavier than she is now, because any increase in weight would only depress her. So what would be the advantage of gaining acceptance from others if she can't accept herself? Jim responds obliquely to that question by saying that my interpretation to him had made a great deal of sense. He felt at the time that it captured his situation beautifully even though at the moment he is having some difficulty in holding onto it. Karen comments that she thought a great deal about things after the last session. Jim gropes to remember what the therapist had said, which he felt was quite meaningful to him, and rather than respond to his question directly, the therapist encourages him and the rest of the group to search their memories. The therapist believed that Jim was seeking some comforting words from the therapist, since he and the rest of the group were feeling deprived.

At this point Karen begins a rather long recitation of some recent feelings and events. She first refers to the therapist's comment in the previous session that group members were feeling guilty about their neediness. The other day she bought a moderately expensive blouse and felt terribly upset about all the money she had spent. When she talked to her live-in boyfriend about this, he gave her a hard time about her irrational reactions. Continuing in this vein, she found herself talking to another man. She doesn't think she was flirting, but once again she felt overwhelmed by guilt afterward and was on the verge of tears when she thought about it. In these two comments the patient confirms the therapist's previous observation about guilt feelings over the need for love and attention. She goes on as follows:

> I was reading this book last week, and I was so obsessed with the damn book I couldn't even think of work or concentrate on anything but the book. It's called Touch the Wind, and one part in the book, the reason I didn't bring it up last time—it's so upsetting, it feels like it's really stupid. But in the book this girl fell in love with this guy, and he loved her so much that she was two and a half months pregnant—and I thought maybe this was far-fetched—he knew it and she didn't know it. He knew her so well that he could tell when there was any slight movement or change in her body. For some reason I got overwhelmed with that, feeling that he loved her so much that he could tell that.

Then, with some hesitation and no reference to how her feelings about the story and the next incident are related, she tells of a terrible fight she had with her fiancé. It is necessary for the group to pull the details out of her, and the story is essentially incomplete. She was drinking too much wine and began to berate him. "I'm sure I must have called him every name in the book—a million times". When pressed about what led up to it, she says she is not sure why she got as drunk as she did. She goes on to say that the next night he informed her that if she was ever that bad again, he was going to leave her.

Once again, the theme from the previous two sessions is repeated. Karen is preoccupied, using the metaphor of the story, with finding a man who would be totally devoted to her, merge symbiotically with her, to the extent of knowing her body better than she knows it herself. And this intense wish has two related effects: she uses a form of brinkmanship to test her boyfriend's devotion to her, and she behaves in a thoroughly obnoxious way, which makes her feel extremely guilty.

Jim observes that Karen's anger at her boyfriend must be based on the fact that he is intimidating her or smothering her or doing things that she resents. (Note the readiness with which he makes these observations even though Karen has made no reference at all to provocation by her boyfriend.) Carol disagrees, saying that Karen is "just throwing fits for attention—she wants to be noticed and loved, and she feels so unloved right now". Carol and Jim continue the argument about their respective interpretations, and Jim has the last word: "She needs love—she needs a lot of it. Just like we all do. And he's not giving it to her, and she's very angry about it".

The group decides to check this out with Karen and wonders whether she is feeling sexually gratified in the relationship. She responds that she does not feel as if she is getting what she wants sexually and has felt reluctant since the beginning of their relationship to ask for more sex because of the criticism he had leveled against her earlier for being too sexually demanding. The group begins questioning her about whether her sexual frustration is based on a need for closeness or is something more purely physical. Karen is uncertain but proceeds with some reflection about her feelings toward the group.

> I think he (her fiancé) just gets what is built up in the group. I think the reason I was so angry at the group last time was that I was angry at Cal's leaving. He is the last of the original group, and now there is a part of me that feels like I don't belong here anymore. I guess it's because of the high-level jobs you all have and I feel like I am in a rut with mine (factory work) and I have no desire to go back to school. Part of me feels like you guys all have more in common than I do. I feel a lot of distance from the group. Probably because I feel like I don't belong here anymore. And partly I feel that you're all in a different league than I am.

Gary, an attorney, joins in her feeling of alienation: "Well, I feel the same way, so maybe there's a lot of distance in this group. We haven't gotten back together again since Dr. Horwitz left". At this point, about a half hour into the session, the therapist enters his first interpretive comment, addressed mainly to Karen:

> It is striking to me that you feel you don't belong in this group and that other people in the group are superior to you. Maybe because of your job, but you also imply the feeling that the group is not interested in what you have to say. This feeling has surfaced particularly since we resumed after vacation. You seem to feel that you shouldn't be talking in the group and that you are getting that message from others in the group. It seems like a general feeling that people in the group think they shouldn't be so assertive in here. I think it's related to the wish to get more from the group, to get

more attention, more love, more concern, and again feeling guilty about all that greed to get it all for yourself. We were talking about that particularly with respect to Carol last time, and I think it is coming out again in your relationship with your fiancé where you feel that he's not attentive enough or loving enough or sexual enough and you put him to the test. You get drunk, you berate him, and then if he sticks around, you practically push him over the edge and defy him to leave. The fact that he doesn't, proves to you that you're not as bad as you feel you are.

The most significant aspect of this intervention is the primary focus on an individual with a secondary emphasis on a group-wide observation. The comment is addressed primarily to the main speaker, Karen, and is an effort to explain her feelings of being shunned by the group because of her inordinate wishes for love and nurturance, which induce guilt and feelings of worthlessness. In talking about the fracas with her fiancé, she herself had come close to understanding her frustration with the group and how she had acted out her transference with him. There is an implication in my comments that the patient's feeling of frustration and anger with me around the long vacation separation was a shared feeling in the group, but this is not made explicit and perhaps could have been. Her preoccupation with the story about the lover who knew the woman's body better than she did implies an eroticized transference to the therapist, which also could have been addressed. Probably I was responding to Karen's attributing her frustration to peer relationships, her feelings about Cal's termination, and her sense of inferiority to the other members, so that I focused on her feelings toward the group. In addition, since the group theme had already been explicated in the previous session, the relatively weak emphasis on group-wide feelings may be justified by the fact that each individual is now likely to translate the therapist's comments into personally relevant observations.

Carol responds to the intervention with the observation that she experienced a considerable resentment toward her ten-year-old son last night because he was demanding attention from her and since it was something she was wanting for herself, she had difficulty in responding to him. She was able to understand his special needs and even his right to make these demands. In fact, he has been able to make his transition back home after his annual summer visit with his father more smoothly than in the past. The therapist then encourages her to think about how my comments to Karen might apply to her, and she observes, without much conviction, that she attempts to test others' love by overeating. Gary tries to help her think about this: "How about this? You're making people prove they really like you because they like you even when you're fat". And Carol basically agrees by responding, "She gets drunk and I eat".

At this point the therapist reminds her of the breakup of a romantic relationship that occurred a few months earlier and suggests there is still more work to be done on that. Carol acknowledges the need to do so but rather quickly shifts to Brenda, who has been relatively silent during much of this discussion. Despite being coaxed by the group, all Brenda is ready to say at this point is, "I'm very confused". Jim takes advantage of the lull to announce that he will be absent next session.

Carol asks him for details and Jim explains that he is attending a family reunion. "I don't have much family left. They really care for me". Karen suggests that perhaps he has the desire to go home because of how he is feeling about the group. Jim denies this, stating that he feels as though he has made progress in the group and he hopes his family will notice the difference. The group is not ready to let him off the hook that easily and points out that the fact that his individual therapist (he is the only patient in combined treatment) is gone at the present time also makes him want to go "back to the womb". Jim is aware of such feelings in himself and elaborates that he is not getting what he needs from his girlfriend. "I really don't want to talk anymore. I want so much in here that what I do is become overly aggressive as a way of reaching out and saying, 'Love me, too,' but I get too angry and then feel guilty". Carol reassures him that everyone in here does that. "I eat, Karen drinks".

Gary then joins in to observe that this weekend he drank too much and "maybe it was guilt about wanting so much attention". It was unusual because he has pretty much given up liquor and marijuana. The therapist notes that this is the first time that Gary has mentioned this important change. Gary agrees that he had finally come to the conclusion that being in a half-drugged state was only perpetuating his difficulty in getting himself mobilized in his career. "It's hard to work and be stoned all the time". He speaks of his awareness that his new professional responsibilities require that he be as alert as possible when he is at work. He goes on for a bit about the strains he is experiencing in his efforts to establish himself as a professional.

At his point Karen turns to Brenda and wants to know what is so confusing for her. Benda responds in a distraught and chaotic way that she is feeling terrified, her heart is pounding, and that she is frightened of Dr. Horwitz and doesn't know why. She is feeling discouraged and "really pissed off". Why does she have to be so dependent, she asks. She has the feeling of having to start all over in the group. With some encouragement she begins to relate that as soon as she begins to feel that she is doing well in something, such as her work, she feels the need to start drinking or messing up in some way. She feels unable to stop.

With regard to men she has had some "male acknowledgment lately", but she has just pushed them away and doesn't know why or what she is looking for. Then she reveals that she has been getting a lot of attention from a man she has been seeing lately, the first time she has mentioned him in the group. Karen becomes quite provoked with her for not having discussed it before, and Brenda defends herself by saying that the relationship does not really mean anything to her. She is not interested in him, but he persists, and so she occasionally relents and goes out with him. Under some pressure from the group she acknowledges that she has slept with him on a couple of occasions, and the group, particularly the women, confront her with the fact that she is engaging in some very self-destructive behavior in having a sexual relationship with a man she does not care for. The therapist reinforces this idea by stating "I think what might be going on is that you're feeling badly about yourself for having sexual relations with someone you do not like". The patient acknowledges that she is feeling embarrassed about it, and the group begins to focus on whether this relationship started just before the therapist's vacation. Carole puts it bluntly: "Dr. Horwitz, the love of your life, is gone, so screw him, I'll screw you". Brenda acknowledges her anger at the therapist for leaving and her difficulty in trusting him because "I just didn't want him to leave".

In a somewhat competitive way Jim wants to know whether Brenda has any difficulty in trusting him, considering he will not be present at the next meeting. Brenda is not sure how she feels about that. Carol interprets this question to Jim with the comment that perhaps he is asking if Brenda will still be here when he returns and then generalizes it to the group: Will the group bar the door when he returns? At this point the therapist makes the following intervention, mainly to Jim: "The fact that you hadn't talked about it earlier is also an indication that you think it's not an interesting subject for anybody to care about your absence. After all, it's just for one time and isn't going to make any difference to anybody. Maybe they won't even notice it. It seems as though you almost forgot to tell us about it, and the lack of importance you are attaching to it expresses the fact that you seem to think you have very little importance in this group. Now what I wanted to say to Brenda was that I think your starting this sexual relationship with this man around the time of vacation is expressing the wish to get more love from somebody since you are lacking love from me. But at the same time I think it involves a kind of self-punishment in the same way we were observing from the others, punishing yourself for having such wishes".

Brenda responds by claiming that she has been relatively passive in the relationship with this man, although she is aware that she is doing nothing to stop it. The therapist continues: "Also with this man you're in some ways giving him a signal that you're receptive while at the same time saying to yourself that he doesn't mean a damn thing to me. That may be what you're also experiencing in here, and you're turning the tables on him and treating him in the way that you feel you're being treated in here. Brenda asks for some elaboration. The therapist explains, "Being encouraged to express feelings in here and at the same time experiencing yourself as being rebuffed". Carol attempts to reinforce that point by saying that Brenda is both encouraging this man and at the same time pushing him away. Brenda acknowledges that what she is doing with this man is not something she is proud of, and at this point the time is up.

The last half of the session, which mainly involved Brenda and Jim, was a further elaboration of the theme of hurt feelings experienced by the group in relation to the therapist's vacation. Jim's belated announcement of his plans to be away to attend a family reunion reflected mainly the wish to find a replacement for the nurturance and comfort that he was not getting in the group. My interpretation to him also stressed the low self-esteem that he was experiencing in the group, shown in his minimizing the importance of his absence from the group. This dimension had already emerged earlier in the session with Karen's feelings of inferiority vis-a-vis the other members, seconded by Gary, who also felt that no one really cared to listen to him. Another facet of Jim's absence that could have been further explored was Jim's competitive and retaliative wishes toward the therapist. He seemed to be saying that the therapist was not the only one who could take the initiative in leaving the group, and the theme of guilt and self-punishment was apparent in the group's fantasy of his being locked out when he returned.

Brenda's special contribution to the group theme was not unlike the self-destructive acting out described earlier by Karen. Karen's guilt about her greed for love and nurturance led her to behavior that threatened the stability of a valued relationship with her fiancé. She gained reassurance from his willingness to tolerate her behavior, and she gained self-punishment from his disapproval of her obnoxious display. Similarly, Brenda found a suitor to express his love, but her contempt for the man vented her anger displaced from the therapist. She was both identifying with the therapist as aggressor in leading this man on and at the same time treating herself rather contemptuously in maintaining intimacy with a man who meant nothing to her. Thus, the common threads that ran through the session were the intertwined themes of seeking love and reassurance to compensate for the therapist's abandonment, the guilt for having such intense needs, and the lowered self-esteem in relation to the abandonment and greed.

Conclusion

Earlier in this chapter I emphasized that the ideal model of interpretation is an inductive one in which the group therapist gradually builds up a series of individual interventions before offering an overarching group-wide intervention. The session just described illustrates this model but only in its general spirit and, I hope, not in a rigidified way. First, all models and rationales for clinical intervention are guides and ways of thinking rather than strict rules that must be adhered to at all costs. In effect, group therapists should ideally adopt their own preferred system of integrating the dynamics of the group with interpersonal and intrapsychic material. Once having developed a method, the group therapist should respond flexibly and creatively to the changing context and varying needs as they are expressed at any given moment.

Second, therapy is an ongoing process that should not be segmented into individual sessions. Any particular session must be understood in light of significant events that preceded it. An inductive method is most relevant when a group theme is in the process of unfolding. Thus, the theme in this group had already emerged and had been interpreted.

Hence, my comments involved some degree of moving back and forth between an already explicated common group tension and individual conflicts that were being elaborated by the patients and explicated within a group framework. The therapist's interventions in this session emphasized individual content, but in each case the common group theme was either alluded to or implied.

Summary

There has been an increasing recognition in the group psychotherapy literature of the importance of group-centered thinking and group-centered interventions in trying to integrate the important dynamics of the entire group with the significant intrapsychic dynamics of individual patients. A rather wide spectrum of models has been proposed to effect such an integration. The view expressed in this chapter that a common group tension is usually present at all times, sometimes more visible than at other times. I have attempted to develop the thesis that my preferred conception of integrating group and individual issues is a theory of an omnipresent common group tension, fueled mainly by a process of projective identification, moving back and forth among the various members. Care for the individual needs of each member can best be assured by an inductive method in which a patient's content is interpreted individually until a shared group theme clearly emerges, at which time a group centered intervention is offered.

CHAPTER TEN

Selection criteria for groups with self-disordered patients

This chapter will deal primarily with the issue of selecting patients for group therapy who suffer from a variety of symptoms associated with defects of the self, inasmuch as these patients, usually borderline or narcissistic, are often the problem patients in any group. This category includes a wide variety of psychological and behavioral deficits such as impaired self-esteem, extreme neediness, difficulties with impulse control, tendencies to withdraw from others, to name a few of the problems that such patients present. I will not be attempting to discuss selection criteria in general even though those indicators may often be relevant as well to a broader population. There are a number of excellent writings on selection, including the chapters in the texts by Yalom and Leszcz (2005) and by Rutan, Stone, and Shay (2007). Those authors emphasize that their selection criteria focus mainly on contraindications and this chapter will attempt to include both the cautions as well as those features of self-disordered patients that may especially lend themselves to group treatment.

Self-disordered patients present a "double-edged paradox" for group psychotherapists: The same characteristics that indicate group treatment may also constitute the specific contraindication, depending on the total personality constellation in which those traits are embedded. I will first review the literature on indications and contraindications for group treatment for this type of patient. I will then focus on four characteristics of the self-disordered patient that may be specific indications for group treatment. While these characteristics may put a strain on group members and the therapist, many patients who exhibit them are often quite amenable to group treatment.

Observations by writers on group psychotherapy indicate that many borderline and narcissistic patients respond particularly well to treatment in groups (Grotjahn, 1984; Shields, 2000; Gans & Alonso, 1998). While there is universal agreement that these patients present difficulties in any treatment situation-individual or group psychotherapy, inpatient or outpatient treatment—the group literature tends to emphasize that group psychotherapy is often the treatment of choice for these patients based on: the dilution of the transference, optimal opportunities for regulation of closeness and distance, special ego-strengthening features, and gratification of object hunger needs.

Self-disordered patients, particularly borderlines, cover a wide spectrum of ego strength and weakness and this fact has a strong bearing on the type of treatment they require (Horwitz, 1996). In addition to a range of ego capacity in these patients, there are a wide variety of character traits that they display, such as the overt versus the covert dimension and thin-skin and thick skin, which divide patients with narcissistic pathology.

At the risk of compounding the problem by including both borderline and narcissistic patients in this chapter, we should remember that some, but not all narcissistic patients fall into the borderline spectrum. But grouping these patients together is justifiable, not only because they share significant identity disturbances and suffer from deformation in the development of a healthy, cohesive self, but also because the two diagnostic groups overlap considerably with regard to their pathological conflicts, needs, and defenses.

In this chapter, I will first describe the contexts of group treatment that help to engender positive outcomes followed by those characteristic of the group setting that lend themselves to the special needs of self-disordered patients. Then I will describe the special features of these patients that constitute contraindications as well as indications for group treatment.

Context for treatment

The literature on the special characteristics of this patient population that respond favorably to group psychotherapy describes group treatment in two contexts. First, these self-disordered patients, particularly borderlines, do better when they are a minority in a group of higher functioning individuals. Although some courageous therapists have treated borderline patients in a homogeneous group (Roth, 1980; Slavinska-Holy, 1982; Pines, 1990), most writers believe that more than one or two such patients in a group produces undue stress on the group, as well as the therapist, making it difficult to establish a strong, cohesive unit. Second, there is a consensus in the literature that the borderline-narcissistic patient usually requires individual therapy to accompany their group treatment. Bateman and Fonagy (2001) report considerable improvement in borderline patients who are offered psychoanalytic group therapy as their primary treatment but provided in the context of partial hospitalization. These adjunctive treatments help the individual tolerate feelings of deprivation, narcissistic injuries, and other stresses that inevitably accompany group membership.

Facilitating characterics of groups

Opportunities for regulating distance and closeness

Numerous writers have observed that certain patients become unduly intimidated by the closeness and intensity of a one-to-one relationship in which the individual therapist is viewed as an unduly powerful figure, for good or for evil-more often the latter. These patients crave the development of a close symbiotic relationship but fear the consequences of permitting themselves to submit to, and depend on, a figure whom they also view as capable of doing them harm. Groups permit the patient to either participate actively and intensively or withdraw into a more passive observer role, and this distance-taking feature is often of help to borderline and narcissistic patients.

Dilution of transference

Affectively labile borderline patients are prone to developing highly distorted views of themselves and others, and are therefore in constant danger, particularly in individual therapy, of undergoing either a transference psychosis or a stalemate. This characteristic is similar to Kernberg's (1984) description of the modal borderline patient who typically struggles with intense aggressive impulses and attempts to manage them through primitive and pathological splitting defenses. As noted in Chapter Eight, dilution of the transference is a feature of group treatment that makes it especially suitable for patients with a proneness to distorted reactions and usually the self-disordered patient draws upon the dilution feature of the group.

Gratification of self-object needs

Most writers point out that the ego-strengthening features of group psychotherapy are especially compatible with the needs of self-disordered patients, whose ego structures tend to be quite fragile. These patients often find it difficult to gratify their intense object hunger, their sense of loneliness, and difficulty in feeling a sense of belonging (Segalla, 1998; Livingston & Livingston, 2006). Pines (1978) described the patient who feels incapable of finding within himself or his relationships experiences of maternal sustenance. A low sense of self-esteem is another of their important characteristics partly due to the roller coaster effect of rapid and intense oscillations in their self-experiences (Kernberg, 1984). A similar result occurs when empathic self-objects are not internalized (Kohut, 1984). A common observation is that the group encourages the patient to fulfill an important helping role with his peers, which in itself is ego-strengthening and self-enhancing. When patients become integrated into the group, they feel that their presence is needed by the group and that their contributions are valued. Thus some authors (Segalla, 1995) suggest that narcissistically vulnerable patients are more likely to accept active interpretive work from peers as opposed to the therapist and also experience ego strengthening via the gratification of their affiliative needs when they become integrated into the group.

Opportunities for overcoming withdrawal

This characteristic has often been described as withdrawal from affective contact and entering a "narcissistic cocoon". Such a patient typically seeks a magical cure through association with a powerful helper, the idealizing transference described by Kohut (1984). These patients expect that their passive presence alone will be sufficient to absorb the needed help and change, and they typically believe that their unreasonable narcissistic needs will be gratified rather than confronted or interpreted. Under optimal circumstances, narcissistic patients emerge from their "cocoons" and gradually curb their demands, silent or overt, for gratification of special needs. Macaskill (1982) described affective withdrawal in his research study on nine hospitalized borderline patients assessed after one year of group treatment. One of his main findings was that initially the patients had difficulty developing an interest in and commitment to helping their fellow patients. However, altruistic concern for fellow patients develops most predictably after a patient experiences an empathic response from the group.

Contraindicating patient characteristics

Lack of personal accomplishment

A general contraindication to group psychotherapy is the borderline patient's lack of accomplishment and progress in life as compared to his fellow patients, with the result that his defective functioning becomes painfully apparent to all; such an experience is likely to be countertherapeutic. A related complicating feature is the "fit" of the particular patient with the particular group. Sometimes this contraindication is attenuated by combining the group and individual approaches, so that the supportive aspects of individual treatment enable participation by fragile patients who are unable to tolerate group alone.

Overwhelming affect and anxiety

A more specific contraindication to group treatment is a patient's lack of a sufficient stimulus barrier to avoid being flooded by affect and anxiety. As Pines (1978) notes: "Some borderline patients do seem to be overwhelmed by the group situation for in it they form pathological and overwhelming identifications with all the members of the group and therefore leave a session in a state of confusion and excitement. These patients need to be transferred to individual therapy" (p. 125).

Paranoid tendencies

Similar to this consideration are prominent paranoid trends in those patients whose paranoia tends to be exacerbated in a group situation.

Such people, usually in the minority and often difficult to identify in advance, tend to experience intensification rather than dilution of the transference in a group. In one research study, those patients with the greatest tendency to engage in splitting, primarily of the co-therapists, were also the ones who experienced the greatest sense of badness and distortion in themselves and others (Greene, Rosenkrantz, & Muth, 1985). Borderline patients who rely heavily on pathological splitting might reasonably experience an exacerbation of their difficulties in a group setting. In particular, they would be prone to form troublesome splits, not only between the co-therapists but also between the individual therapist and the group therapist, if they are in a combined treatment situation.

Extreme narcissism

Interestingly enough, Yalom and Leszcz (2005) issue a caution about including "extremely narcissistic" patients in group therapy. These patients' self-centeredness, difficulty in developing concern for fellow patients, feelings of entitlement, and expectations of admiration all conspire to make them experience a stormier time in a group than they would in individual therapy. Burstein and Beale (1975) noted the heavy burden narcissistic patients place on group members and therapists because of their demandingness and their attacks on the therapist and the therapeutic goals. This reaction, however, may occur mainly in patients who do not have adjunctive treatment and hence lack the support and cushioning effect of concomitant dyadic psychotherapy. On the other hand, vulnerable patients, can often be worked with more expressively in a group because of the "contained regression" that develops there.

The above characteristics constitute cautions concerning the recommendation of some patients for group treatment. Patients who drop out prematurely or are extruded by the group suffer a sense of failure and the group in turn will often feel guilty by their inability to integrate the difficult patient. However, there have been some observations that the so-called "troublesome" patient may actually be a boon to the other members of the group. Shields (2000) has made the perceptive observation that these assertively demanding people in a group may set an example for the compliant, well behaved members, that is, that the expression of the less civilized parts of the self can be helpful both to the individual patient who is expressing his primitive "true self" and to those group members who hesitate to expose those unacceptable parts of themselves. Shields emphasizes that these patients are conveying a sense of hopefulness that they might be able to repair and deal better with their personal trauma that troublesome behavior may be conveying. Gans and Alonso (1998) make the same point in their paper on the difficult patient.

Patient characteristics as possible indications

In considering self-disordered patients for referral to group treatment, therapists may frequently be confronted with a "double-edged paradox", mentioned earlier. The same character problems that make borderline and narcissistic patients difficult and problematic in a group are also the problems that may make group psychotherapy the treatment of choice. Conversely, those patient traits that constitute special indications for group treatment may also be the contraindications. The schizoid patient, for example, who has great difficulty tolerating intimacy and who is likely to be an early dropout from group therapy, is often the kind of person for whom a successful group experience could be particularly rewarding. In assessing patients' readiness to enter a group and their capacity to benefit, therapists must consider both the extent of the patient's pathological characteristics and the context of the total personality in which the traits are embedded. Thus, therapists should ask whether such patients show counterbalancing redeeming features that could help them become successfully integrated into a group (e.g., sense of humor, dogged perseverance, capacity to convey appreciation, etc.).

The difficulty in generalizing about self disordered patients is that they fall along a broad spectrum of degrees of pathology and they present varied characterological types. I will present four dominant characteristics found in the self disorders that I believe constitute specific indications for group treatment, provided, of course, that the two caveats, previously discussed, are observed: first, therapists should usually use adjunctive treatment, and second, they must consider the degree of difficulty the patient will present for the group as well as the stress that the patient is likely to experience. The four characteristics are: (1) demandingness, (2) egocentrism, (3) social isolation and withdrawal, and (4) socially deviant behavior. These behaviors are by no means mutually exclusive and more often than not tend to overlap.

Demandingness

People who have been deprived of the early developmental needs of mirroring and of merger with an idealized self object (Kohut, 1984), or who need to defend themselves against aggressive reactions in response to early frustration (Kernberg, 1984), tend to develop insatiable needs for affirmation and validation. They make undue demands for praise and flattery, and they are constantly oriented toward bolstering their self-esteem. Because they experienced severe deprivation in early life, they feel a sense of entitlement and expect to be rewarded beyond their due. In a group situation, they are prime candidates to become monopolists who vie for whatever supplies the group offers: time, attention, and concern. And the covert narcissists with silence and hyper-alertness observe unintended affronts to their self-esteem either by the therapist or by fellow patients.

These experiences are exacerbated in specific group events, such as interruptions of the group, the addition of new members, and even the loss of old members. On these occasions, the common group tensions become most obvious and lend themselves to group centered interventions (Chapter Six). The manifestations of group-wide feelings of deprivation may take many forms. In addition to the usual monopolizing behavior, patients in a group may "take turns" in an unspoken pact among members that entitles each one to a specifically allotted quantity of time (usually a whole session), so that each member is guaranteed an equal share. Another sign of group-wide feelings of deprivation could be the group's unresponsiveness to its members, thus communicating envy and resentment toward the member who is getting the group's valued attention. At the same time the presence of others provides the reality pressures on these patients to adopt a more considerate, less demanding stance.

In contrast to individual treatment, the group is a medium par excellence for highlighting a patient's pathological demandingness, in particular, greed and envy. In a dyadic situation, patients are given the task of communicating their experiences and life problems and, since only one person is present, feelings of being deprived may be less apparent. Groups, on the other hand, tend to stir up fears of being overlooked, of being deprived of what one deserves or needs, of having others preferred to oneself, and of having one's needs go unheeded.

Egocentrism

A corollary of demandingness is a patient's focus on personal needs to the exclusion of the needs of others. Such patients tend to see other people as "part objects", their potential for gratifying the patient's needs and not as "whole objects" with their own needs, aspirations, and constraints. These patients tend to value others mainly in terms of the self-enhancement they afford, the applause they can give, the advice they offer, and the attentive audience they can become. The counterpart of this one-sided orientation of only being able to take or receive is these patients' considerable difficulty in giving. It is not easy for such individuals to listen to the inner experiences of others and to develop a concern and empathy for their affective lives and struggles. These patients are narcissistically sensitive but interpersonally insensitive.

The basis for this egocentrism has been formulated differently by various early writers. Winnicott (1965) describes the capacity for concern as based on the individual's ability to achieve a depressive position associated with the integration of good and bad self and object representations. This developmental phase involves the acceptance of one's destructiveness toward a loved object, where libidinal wishes must outweigh aggressive ones, and being sufficiently capable of successfully repairing the fantasized damage. Also, these egocentric individuals have been described as afflicted with a sadomasochistically colored "zero sum thinking" in which the world is perceived concretely as having limited supplies and any reward or gain by another person is an automatic deprivation for the self. And they have been characterized as constantly threatened by a sense of emptiness and therefore must jealously guard treasured affects and inner experiences lest they feel bereft of valued mental contents.

In contrast to individual therapy, group therapy challenges the patient with the task of achieving some balance between working on personal problems and investing in the problems of others. Narcissistic self-absorption is not always easily apparent in the one-to-one treatment relationship, but it emerges with great clarity from the outset in the group situation. In its most naked form, narcissism was manifested by one group patient who regaled the group with embellished stories of his daily exploits but promptly fell asleep when others began to talk. More characteristic is the self-centered individual who rarely speaks in the group except when prompted by others. Many patients believe that therapy occurs only when they are holding forth about their own problems. On the contrary, a patient's responses to others, or the lack thereof, are significant parts of the treatment process and offer many opportunities for insight and change.

Two major group forces lead to modification of such maladaptive behavior. First, patients who characteristically fail to become involved with the problems of others inevitably find themselves confronted by their fellow patients about this deficiency. While scapegoating as a displacement of the repressed anger at the therapist or other group members is a hazard therapists must guard against, they must also avoid overprotecting patients by not permitting timely and appropriate confrontations. Second, the group situation affords opportunities for patients to experience the gratification and reward of helping another person. Helping others is one of the important self-enhancing agents in a group experience that strengthens self-esteem and permits a patient to tolerate confrontations and interpretations of negative aspects of the self. Indeed, an important sign of progress in treatment is a patient's growing capacity to show concern and empathy for other group members. A significant indication of therapeutic movement is a patient's shift from narcissistic self-absorption to genuine empathic attunement.

Social isolation and withdrawal

Candidates for group psychotherapy include people who are withdrawn and isolated from others, who suffer from social shyness, who fear making close relationships, and who need to avoid intimacy in any form. Social isolation, of course, is a behavioral symptom with multiple underlying causes. It may be associated with phobic anxiety, narcissistic self-protection, paranoid ideation, or marked problems of self-esteem.

One difficulty isolated patients have in group therapy is that they are typically silent and often perplexing to therapists and peers alike with regard to their life experiences and their reactions to group events. They often become a drain on the group's resources because their lack of spontaneity and their inability to openly express themselves makes it necessary to offer them extra encouragement and prodding to engage them even minimally. These isolated individuals are the most frequent candidates for prematurely dropping out of group therapy or for becoming scapegoats in the group. Since their pathology makes it difficult for them to disclose important information about themselves, their integration into the group, in the initial stages at least, is quite tenuous. These patients usually indicate that they need to go slowly in opening up, and this constraint must be respected. But the group also tends to get caught in a bind between respecting the privacy of such members while also trying to convey a continued interest in them. The silence of these patients engenders the free use of projection by others, and these patients become easy targets for scapegoating, often as a displacement from the therapist, who is frequently seen as not disclosing enough and as setting himself above the patient group.

A useful formulation associated with narcissistic pathology is one based on their being encased in a cocoon, a plastic bubble, or a glass jar. They attempt to remain affectively unrelated, sometimes burying their feelings under a plethora of words that reveal little or nothing about their true selves. Despite the wish these patients have to break out of their lonely, self-imposed isolation, powerful inhibitions prevent their doing so because they fear that a free expression of genuine need, their "true self", will elicit increased frustration, anger, and narcissistic injury.

How does the group situation contribute to the modification of this rigid defensive position? First, as in individual psychotherapy, the group atmosphere that usually develops contributes to a therapeutic alliance among group members. Despite the tensions and resistances that arise in an actively interpretive group, nicely portrayed by Nitsun (1996) as the "anti-group", most groups achieve an underlying benign holding environment (often referred to as a transitional object) that engenders a sense of safety and protectiveness. Second, these group members begin to observe that others in the group take risks by openly expressing shameful and threatening feelings, and the "emotional illiteracy" often associated with socially isolated people begins to erode as they identify themselves with fellow patients who have greater freedom of affective expression. Furthermore, such opening up tends to be reinforced by the positive rewards group members typically bestow on each other when a fellow patient makes a significant step forward. These events not only contribute to individual progress, but also add significantly to the cohesion of the group.

A vignette by Segalla (1998) nicely illustrates the usefulness of group for a socially isolated individual. A male patient had been in individual psychotherapy for three years and had made some progress but was still quite withdrawn. He was placed in a group and very slowly began to open up although each step of the way he was quite anxious about how his contribution would be received. The positive response from the group for his new behavior gave him the courage to reach out to other people outside the group and he became a more social, less isolated person.

Socially deviant behavior

Socially deviant behavior refers to strange or abrasive actions which are not bizarre or overtly psychotic. Such behavior elicits irritation and ridicule, often reflects a gross insensitivity to one's impact on others, and usually leads other patients to shun the offending individual.

As with social isolation, this characteristic refers to overt behavior that may be associated with a variety of underlying motives and structures: rebelliousness, negativism, avoidance of a mature role, overpowering narcissistic needs, or gross blind spots in reading social cues. Deviancy may be manifested by strange dress, such as wearing unmatched socks or sneakers, by gross failures in empathy, such as changing the subject when another person is relating a traumatic experience, or by insistence on keeping the group's meeting room excessively dark so as to enjoy the "womblike" atmosphere.

Kohut (1984) explains such behavior as due to the lack of healthy internalized selfobject structures. Thus the self becomes fragmented with the result that aggressive and sexual drives no longer operate within a relationship matrix. Needs then tend to be expressed in ways that are divorced from the awareness of others, and the focus becomes solely on immediate gratification and tension reduction. In Kernberg's (1984) view, borderline patients have failed to integrate good and bad self and object representations associated with a fixation at the rapprochement phase of development, resulting in nonspecific ego weakness, primary process intrusions, and identity diffusion. Any or all of these deficits may combine to produce maladaptive deviant behavior.

Yalom and Leszcz (2005) emphasize the contraindication to including such people in a psychotherapy group, since the deviancy often interferes with the work of the group. These patients tend to become the object of ridicule, are easy targets for scapegoating, and may foist undue pressures and strains on the group. Without denying the validity of such concerns, I would suggest that group treatment also has the potential for toning down such maladaptive behavior. If other redeeming qualities make the deviant individual sufficiently acceptable to the group, then the combination of group acceptance and empathic confrontation has the potential for ameliorative effects. When the offending patient begins to permit awareness of the need for a good mutual relationship with other group members, he or she will gradually modify abrasive characteristics. Cohesive psychotherapy groups, like strong families that offer a proper balance of love and discipline, are capable of producing a civilizing and socializing influence on their members. Pathological narcissism and acceptable group behavior are in a constant state of tension, much like the common human dilemma of wanting to get close to another person without losing one's personal identity.

A highly narcissistic man who tended to monopolize, felt entitled to an extra share of the group's time, and who easily lost control of his temper when confronted by the group, was a candidate for scapegoating and ostracism by other members. But he also had the saving grace of being able to apologize in the next session for his nasty outbursts and eventually became a valued group member as he toned down his neediness and volatility.

Summary

The group psychotherapy literature contains many cautions regarding placing some self-disordered patients into group. In addition to proceeding with care, the use of individual treatment as a supportive adjunct permits a broad range of such patients to use group constructively. But one should also recognize that certain borderline and narcissistic characteristics such as demandingness, egocentrism, social isolation, and socially deviant behavior could be positive indications for group psychotherapy. These characteristics represent a "double-edged paradox" in that they may be either indications or contraindications, depending on the intensity and rigidity of the characteristic and the total personality context in which they are embedded. The group situation highlights pathological demandingness, with the group typically exerting pressure on the patient to reduce such behavior. Similarly, an egocentric person who experiences difficulty listening and responding to others is quickly confronted in the group setting with the fact that the group task involves not only self-disclosure but also attending and reacting to others as well. The socially isolated individual, fearful of exposing his emotional needs, finds multiple identification opportunities and encouragement within the group for taking such risks. And finally, the socially deviant patient who manifests strange and abrasive behavior will find himself under the civilizing and socializing influences of a cohesive, accepting group once he has become sufficiently integrated into it. While patients with these characteristics may place a strain on the group members and the therapist, efforts on their behalf are often rewarded.

CHAPTER ELEVEN

Group psychotherapy of the borderline patient

eginning in the 1970s, the borderline patient became a focus of
interest for mental health professionals. This phenomenon is
related to the empirical and theoretical advances in this area
which occurred under the leadership of Grinker, Kernberg, Mahler, and
others. Previously, there were early reports of group therapy with these
patients based on a limited theoretical formulation in contrast to later
advances in understanding their developmental defects. In recent years
there have been numerous research studies and clinical reports on the
group treatment of borderline patients which I shall first review and
then offer my personal perspective on the special advantages as well as
limitations of group treatment for this population.

As a starting point, let me clarify my orientation to the main characteristics of the borderline patient. I see it as a diagnosis of ego capacity
and weakness. Borderline patients, like the rest of us, come in many
psychological sizes and shapes and manifest multiple varieties of
characterological features, personality attitudes, and behavioral dispo-
sitions. They may be histrionic or inhibited, passively withdrawn or
aggressive, grandiose or humble, paranoid or masochistic. In fact, more
than most other types, they often present erratically fluctuating behavioral pictures, a variability that is based mainly on poor reality testing

and identity diffusion. In a quite comprehensive survey of empirical observations and research findings, Lenzenweger (2010) observed that borderline patients comprise one of the most heterogeneous forms of psychopathology.

The term borderline refers to a range of ego functions and object-relations patterns which are more defective than in neurosis but more intact than in psychosis, using Kernberg's conception of the personality organization of these patients (1984). The borderline syndrome embraces a wide range of pathology, with some patients falling closer to the neurotic end of the boundary, while others function closer to psychosis. With regard to their ego functions, these patients manifest a chronic instability as well as vulnerable reality testing and a low tolerance for disturbing affects. From the object-relations standpoint, they are given to splitting in all aspects of self and object integration with resulting identity diffusion and unstable relatedness. Meissner, in his book *The Borderline Spectrum* (1984), elaborates on the range of ego functioning from high level (close to neurosis) to low level (close to psychosis) that characterizes this syndrome. That formulation was also the theoretical undergirding of the research study on the individual treatment of the borderline patient performed by this writer and his colleagues at the Menninger Clinic (Horwitz et al., 1996).

Since the appearance of group psychotherapy as a significant treatment method in the 1940s, borderline patients have been treated in many different settings and in groups of varying composition: outpatients and inpatients, homogeneous and mixed, combined with individual treatment, and solely in group. A common denominator in many of the reports in the literature is that certain borderline patients may fail to progress in individual psychotherapy but respond well to group treatment, sometimes alone and sometimes in conjunction with individual treatment. No one is able to say with precision which kind of patient, combined with which kind of group, offers the best prognosis. On the other hand, the literature is fairly clear that there are special features of group treatment which make it both indicated, as well as especially contra-indicated, for certain borderline patients.

A number of authors cite the special advantages of group treatment for borderline patients: Groups, particularly supportive ones, tend to limit regressive pressures insofar as they present a social context and can be viewed as a holding environment (Kibel, 1991). Groups present multiple opportunities for healthy identifications with peers and with the therapist without putting excessive demands on the patient to be an active participant (Pines, 1990). For patients who tend to be threatened by the closeness of the dyad and view the therapist as a potentially powerful and threatening figure, observations by peers are often more acceptable (Tuttman, 1990). And the supportive group atmosphere permits the borderline's aggression to be modulated by libidinal attachments to the group and thus contributes to the healing of defensive splitting (Kibel, 1991).

Homogeneous versus mixed groups

A few early workers have described successful experiences with groups composed entirely of borderline patients. Most were outpatient groups where the patients were also seen individually, at least in the initial phases of treatment. Each of the therapists stressed the importance of supportive measures, such as increased therapist transparency and activity, encouragement of socialization among members, symbolic as well as actual feeding of patients. On the other hand, others encountered major difficulties in attempting to form an alliance with a homogeneous group of borderline patents and recommended strongly against attempting to deal with a homogeneous group of borderlines.

There is a fairly consistent recommendation by most writers that borderline patients are best treated in groups of neurotics and character disorders, provided they are carefully selected and do not exceed "more than one or two" in number (Pines, 1990; Rutan, Stone, & Shay, 2007). These cautions are introduced both because of the potential stress on the patient, as well as the strain such patients place upon the group and the therapist. Since their pathology is of a more profound nature than the usual neurotic and they are clearly more handicapped than others in the group, they run the risk of being scape-goated or alienated from their more competent peers. By the same token, neurotic patients often find it difficult to tolerate a fellow patient whose behavior is widely deviant from their own. The therapist runs the risk that his better integrated patients may drop out if the borderline patient is not admitted carefully and sparingly.

Concomitant or combined individual treatment

Individual treatment for borderlines, either prior to or during the group experience, is recommended by most writers on this topic (Rutan &

Alonso 1982; Rutan, Stone, & Shay, 2007). Some authors recommend combined group and individual therapy for the majority of borderline patients taken into a group in which the same therapist does both treatments, because of the proneness of borderline patients to engage in defensive splitting. According to Rutan and Alonso (1982) the dropout rate in groups is significantly reduced when patients are in a concurrent individual process. There appears to be a consensus among most writers that some form of combined or concomitant individual treatment should be made available to the borderline patient.

Supportive vs. expressive technique

Another point of general agreement in the field is the necessity for special techniques with these patients, whether they are treated in homogeneous or mixed groups. There appears to be a consensus that a therapeutic attitude, which may best be described as active friendliness, should be maintained in order to afford patients the kind of emotional nourishment they need to maintain their membership and participation.

Considerable research has been done on various models of individual psychotherapy with borderlines and all report medium to large effect sizes. The most interpretive of these is Transference Focused Psychotherapy devised by Kernberg and colleagues (2008) and they report somewhat better results when compared with both Linehan's Dialecticical Behavioral Therapy and psychoanalytically oriented supportive psychotherapy. The issue of how expressive *vs.* supportive one's therapeutic interventions should be was directly examined in a study of individual psychotherapy with borderlines by this writer and his colleagues (Horwitz et al., 1996). The conclusion of that research, an intensive study of a small N, was that a higher level borderline was able to tolerate an expressive-uncovering procedure, while a lower level patient required a primarily supportive approach. We observed that the lower level patient tended to respond to confrontation and interpretation with marked paranoid reactions.

Another recent contribution from the individual therapy field is the article by Caligor, Diamond, Yeomans, and Kernberg (2009) who suggested that in order for a borderline patient to utilize Kernberg's transference-focused psychotherapy, they must be helped gradually and in stages to overcome their tendency to be flooded by affect, to become more reflective, and to abandon their tendencies toward concrete thinking. The implication of this finding is that at least with lower level borderline patients, an interpretive approach might be contraindicated in a group setting.

Most group therapists believe that borderline patients require more protection by the group therapist than their neurotic peers because of their fragility and tendency to be narcissistically injured (Rutan, Stone, & Shay, 2007). Kibel (1991) recommends the use of a supportive, group centered method which emphasizes the commonality among the patients. He also adds that active guiding of borderline patients toward helping their peers is a valuable ego-building tool.

With regard to the special problems of the borderline patient in a predominantly neurotic group, Leszcz (1992) emphasizes that such patients need protection by the therapist against premature confrontations and against becoming the target of scape-goating. As the most fragile and vulnerable members of a group, those borderlines who are provocative and masochistic, require special care and attention by the therapist. This issue will be further elaborated below in the section on technique.

The appropriate patient

Assuming the proper kind of group, preferably mixed rather than homogeneous, and the addition of both combined individual treatment as well as supportive interventions, what are the special indications and contraindications for the patient falling under the broad rubric of borderline disorder? We still lack exact criteria for inclusion or exclusion, although certain general considerations have been noted by several writers. Obviously the patient should be able to "stand the group", and be capable of sticking with the treatment despite the special strains and anxieties that are likely to occur particularly in the early stages of membership. The borderline patient is characteristically plagued with those defects of ego and object relatedness that tend to make her a high-risk patient in terms of her potential for dropping out—hence the universal caution in the literature for special care in selection and preparation.

Frequently such patients are characterized by qualities that tend to merit exclusion. They show poor tolerance for unpleasant affects; they have difficulty in permitting themselves to become attached to others; they have problems controlling hostility; and are susceptible to paranoid anxieties and reactions. Most writers believe that patients should be excluded from a group when they manifest excessive narcissism, poorly controlled hostility, and excessive levels of anxiety. Leszcz (1992) emphasizes that patients with a propensity to develop paranoid reactions should be excluded and, in addition, asserts that the level of the patient's ego functioning should be assessed before admission to an ongoing group.

A low-level borderline patient was referred to my group by her individual therapist on the grounds that she needed additional support that he thought the group might provide. When I saw her initially, I developed great misgivings about her suitability based upon her insatiable need for attention and affirmation combined with a deep-seated bitterness toward significant figures in her life who, she believed, had deprived her of the care which she deserved. My impression was that she needed some kind of structured environment, like a hospital or partial hospitalization to contain her neediness. After much deliberation, I decided to admit her to my group with the idea that her alliance developed during three years with her individual therapist would be a significant support. Soon after she arrived it became clear that she viewed the setting as a potential smorgasbord for gratifying her sense of deprivation and an opportunity to devour all of the time and attention that was available. The negative feedback she began to receive from the group exacerbated her poorly controlled self-destructive acting-out (self-mutilation and suicidal threats). The gamble did not pay off and everyone involved, including the patient, agreed that group therapy was inappropriate for her.

In a personal communication, Kibel (2011) emphasized the need to exclude patients with long standing anti-social features. These patients typically derive gratification from sadistic and manipulative behaviors toward others and are capable of inflicting traumatic effects on others in the group, particularly vulnerable and fragile individuals.

Given the ego weaknesses that characterize many of these patients that militate against acceptable functioning in the group, why introduce a group modality at all? Paradoxically, as with the narcissistic patient, the very qualities and defects that make the borderline patient a problematic group member are the same qualities that are often best treated in a group setting. Groups are a medium par excellence for highlighting difficulties in relationships; and they are frequently the ideal setting in which to resolve or attenuate angry, self-defeating behavior, based on a positive, supportive environment. When the patient's ego defects are sufficiently modulated both by his own capacities and by the application of appropriate treatment parameters, there are special features in group psychotherapy which hold particular promise for this type of patient.

Dilution of transference

All of the writers on group treatment of borderline patients agree that the dilution of the transference, and of affects generally, is an important feature of a group for the treatment of the borderline patient (Chapter Eight) and underlies the successful use of groups, particularly those who experience a dyadic relation as too stressful. Writers on the special indications for groups have emphasized that many patients with chaotic, amorphous, and fragile egos do especially well in group treatment because the group situation modulates affective outbursts and helps to prevent unwanted regressive reactions (Kibel, 1991).

Leszcz (1992) has presented a summary of the potential advantages of group psychotherapy for some, but not all, borderline patients: "it appears that the particular difficulties presented by BPD that get activated in individual therapy may, in some instances, be better illuminated, contained, and treated in the group psychotherapy setting". (p. 436). Similarly, Rutan, Sone, and Shay (2007) believe that borderline patients engage in self-defeating defenses in their effort to form and maintain relationships and then add "Groups provide unparalleled opportunities for observing this defensive operation at work ..." (p. 321). There are multiple reasons for this advantage, the primary one being the dilution of the transference.

There are opportunities for diffusing transference reactions upon the multiple targets present in the group so that negative feelings toward parental introjects, for example, may be directed toward one or more peers in addition to, or instead of, the therapist. Group treatment, as opposed to individual treatment, affords the patient more opportunities for social and emotional distance, which may be necessary for the patient at a given time. He is less pressured to participate and this gives the opportunity to regulate, when necessary, the intensity of his emotional involvement. One patient, for example, fell asleep when his particularly conflictual issue, the wish to return to one's parental home for nurturance, was being discussed.

There is greater reality orientation in group as opposed to individual treatment. A group more closely simulates a social interaction and hence produces a greater pull toward appropriate social responses. Marginally functioning psychotic patients are able to maintain a much higher level of functioning in a group, in contrast to regressive behavior in individual therapy.

While these factors are indeed valid, they represent only one side of a coin which includes pressures toward emotional intensification (Chapter Eight). We must not forget the contagion and resonance phenomena which tend to enhance emotional responsiveness in group members. Nor must we overlook the dynamics of competition and sibling rivalry which heighten emotional intensity in a group. These factors are especially pronounced in groups employing a group centered orientation which usually works in the direction of interpretive-uncovering and therapeutic regression. The point I wish to emphasize is that the group therapist must recognize tendencies toward both dilution and intensification and, as in individual therapy, he may attempt to exploit one set of factors over another when the clinical situation warrants it.

Activation

Group interaction stimulates or activates patients who would otherwise tend to be passive and withdrawn. One type of borderline patient is characterized by schizoid withdrawal, weak in verbal participation, maintains distance from others, and rarely initiates contact spontaneously. They usually assume the role of observer in a group and, as such, may be quite perceptive and insightful. When they do engage, they are inclined to participate around the problems presented by others rather than disclose intimate facets of their own lives.

Such patients often experience difficulty in communicating in individual treatment because of their difficulties in tolerating personal closeness. The paucity of real relationships in their lives is a further deterrent to therapeutic work and thus a group provides the activation and stimulation such people may find useful. There is common agreement that the supportive setting of a group permits withdrawn or paranoid patients to participate at their own pace and hence may contribute to drawing such people out of their protective shells. For such patients a group experience may indeed be their first opportunity to participate with others on an emotional level.

Emotional gratification

Although groups have built-in frustrations, they also provide a wide variety of gratifications which make them attractive and pleasurable despite the anxieties of participation. More often than not these gratifications may be ego building in themselves and may contribute silently and unobtrusively to significant personality change in a borderline patient. A cohesive group whose members experience feelings of acceptance helps to bolster self-esteem and gratify dependency needs.

Another important form of gratification especially characteristic of groups is the positive reinforcement which often flows from member to member. Feelings of acceptance and affection constitute a warm matrix within which patients may make significant gains in self-esteem and self-acceptance. This is not to overlook the opposite force that may operate as well, the multiple negative affects that may arise, such as paranoid anxieties, the fear of being dominated or overlooked, or the conviction that the treatment will not be helpful. These reactions are explicated by Nitsun (1996) in his work on the "anti-group", and present a challenge to the therapist, particularly with regard to his more vulnerable patients.

Expression of hostility

The dilution of transference is especially helpful in regard to borderline patients' acute difficulties in dealing with hostility and aggression. There is a general consensus that a central problem for these patients is their difficulty in dealing with vast amounts of latent destructive energy, partly based upon excessive early oral frustration and inability to integrate good and bad internalized objects, as well as constitutional predisposition to poor impulse control (Kernberg, 1984). The clinical picture presented by these patients consists either of weak impulse control, immobilized passivity, or a fluctuation between these two extremes.

For the passive inhibited patient, the group provides an "unfreezing" experience, especially in the early stages, by permitting vicarious identification with both aggressor and victim in hostile exchanges transpiring in the group. She is likely to witness angry confrontations as well as attacks and counterattacks that usually occur without permanent damage to either party or to the relationship. Later, with the support of the group, the patient may permit herself to express her anger toward other patients or toward the therapist.

With regard to the patient gaining a better appreciation of his distorted attitudes, confrontation by peers or the group's consensual validation is often more effective than a similar observation by the individual therapist who tends to be seen as either a malevolent or over-idealized figure. The literature provides examples of borderline patients in a dyadic relationship who were unable to make satisfactory progress because they were immobilized by fear of their hostility (Leszcz, 1992). When placed in a group, this fear was gradually attenuated, particularly by witnessing others express hostility toward their peers or to the therapist without destructive results.

Multiple identifications

A commonly recognized mechanism of change in individual psychotherapy is identification with, and internalization of, the therapist's attitudes and values, thus strengthening the therapeutic alliance. This process has often been referred to in the individual psychotherapy literature as borrowing the therapist's ego strength and is related to a corrective emotional experience. The identification process has tended to be depreciated by some analytic therapists as merely an educational process, rather than one involving conflict resolution and structural change. But for patients with significant ego weakness, the ego strengthening of identification with healthier ego attitudes and behaviors is commonly regarded as both desirable and frequently durable. Group psychotherapy not only affords a patient the opportunity to identify himself with the therapist, but also with a variety of patients in the group.

Many group therapists stress the opportunities for finding identification models in a group. For example, a patient who clung masochistically to a destructive, unfulfilling marriage because of her fears of loneliness was supported by another patient with similar issues who was nevertheless able to separate successfully.

Modification of character armor

The group is an especially good medium for the exploration and alteration of maladaptive character defenses. The group setting provides a multiplicity of stimuli and consequently elicits a wide range of affects and behaviors. Not only does it bring out attitudes toward authority figures, but also feelings of sibling rivalry, feelings about sharing a parent figure with others, reactions to hostile exchanges, demands by others for participation, and reactions to displays of positive feelings. In other words, many behaviors, which in individual therapy tend to get described by the patient rather than enacted, are seen in a group in vivo—hence the emphasis in the group therapy literature on the numerous here-and-now opportunities to experience and modify maladaptive behaviors.

The more severe the character disorder, or the more prominent the ego weakness within which the character defenses are embedded, the more likely the patient will regard his character traits as ego-syntonic. As mentioned earlier, some severe character disorders are able to accept confrontations from other group members more easily than from a therapist alone because the therapist often tends to be viewed as either idealized, devalued, or threatening. In addition, there is the phenomenon of the "mirror reaction" in a group, viewing one's own behaviors enacted by one's peers, in helping a patient to loosen his hold upon repressed, ego-syntonic traits. Whether it be excessive narcissism, tenacious masochism, clinging dependency, or infantile rage, their blindness to these characteristics in themselves tends to abate when seeing these characteristics in others. They may at first be repulsed and alienated by what they see, but this may be the beginning step in helping them to recognize these self-same maladaptive defenses in themselves.

Character problems associated with orality are particularly well suited for treatment in groups. Because of the borderline patient's fixation at the level of oral deprivation and aggression, one would expect many such patients to be characterized by difficulties in tolerating the frustration of dependency needs, the necessity to share the time and attention of the group with others, and feelings of envy and disappointment in witnessing the successes of others. These wishes and the variety of responses to them tend to be markedly highlighted in a therapeutic group. Provided such patients have the necessary minimum tolerance for frustration, and when adequate adjuncts to group treatment are available, such as combined individual therapy, these infantile and narcissistic strivings emerge readily and become opportunities for therapeutic work. The patient is not only confronted by the group with his excessive greed, but he must cope with the task of dealing with it more adaptively.

Countertransference dilution

Borderline patients present a special challenge to all psychotherapists by virtue of the strong affective responses they evoke in the therapist. They have the capacity to create anger, disappointment, frustration, and feelings of inadequacy. Therapists must constantly cope with these feelings within themselves in order to be optimally therapeutic. The greater the patient's pathology, the more intense the counter-transference reactions. Kleinian therapists have elaborated on the primitive defense of projective identification (Chapter Seven) in which unwanted affects and unwanted part objects are projected into others and the patient then strives to manipulate and control the malevolent impulses he perceives in the other person. A similar phenomenon occurs as a complementary reaction in the counter-transference, in which the patient's distorted perceptions of the therapist tend to elicit feelings which complement what the patient is experiencing.

The earlier observations in Chapter Eight about dilution and intensification of transference apply equally to the phenomenon of counter-transference. Group psychotherapists have often observed that the intensity of their reactions to patients in a group tends to be somewhat muted when compared with their reactions to the same patient in a dyadic situation. In part, this observation may be based on the dilution of the patient's transference in a group, as well as on the as the use of combined or concurrent individual therapy. Just as group psychotherapy promotes multiple targets of transference, so does the presence of patients who may act as therapist-surrogates help to defuse counter-transference reactions.

One young adult patient in group psychotherapy was in a concomitant day hospital treatment program as well as an individual therapy process. He presented himself as disinterested in taking any initiative in either going to school or seeking a job and saw no reason to do so as long as his over-indulgent mother was willing to support him. This seeming apathy actually masked a deep-seated fear of being assaulted by more powerful males toward whom he felt vulnerable. Both his individual therapist and his hospital coordinator slowly became irritated with his seeming lack of motivation and eventually "fired" him, while his group therapist, although occasionally reacting similarly to his slow rate of change, was much better able to tolerate his more diluted counter-transference reactions. Eventually, the patient's underlying fears were uncovered in the group treatment and he slowly began taking on adult responsibility.

On the other hand, there is sometimes an intensification of counter-transference toward the entire group when the cumulative affects of individual members resonate to produce a powerful impact upon the therapist. Whether it is anger, sadness, or demands for dependency gratification in the group, the therapist may be pulled strongly into the group's affective life, sometimes more intensely than occurs in individual therapy.

In enumerating the special advantages of group psychotherapy for the borderline patient, we must not overlook the equally important special risks mentioned earlier. A borderline patient in a neurotic group may be an easy target for scape-goating by virtue of his greater difficulties in living and his tendency to experience more alienation and inadequacy. He is also a candidate for decompensation and increased regression when the group is undergoing stress in reaction to the vicissitudes of group life, such as the entry or departure of members, expressions of successes and failures, or the inevitable interruptions of scheduled meetings.

As has been mentioned, a borderline patient may alienate the better-integrated members of a group by his difficulties with commitment to relationships and by his occasional deviant behavior. Some writers (Yalom & Leszcz, 2005) have described how the poor choice of patients in an ongoing group can produce a virtual dissolution of a therapy group. Less emphasized, however, are the special contributions that borderline patients make to the functioning of a predominantly neurotic group. Others have stressed the value such patients have by virtue of their easy access to unconscious thoughts and feelings. Because of their relatively weak capacity for repression of unconscious material, they tend to be in greater touch with primitive impulses and fears and hence are able to facilitate a group's coming to grips with such content.

Supportive measures

The borderline patient typically suffers from a deep-seated sense of unacceptability, basic mistrust of others, and an inability to sustain satisfactory relationships. All writers consider it essential that the group therapist take active measures to counteract the patient's tendency to feel unaccepted, unloved, and even attacked. Warmth, friendliness, empathy, and active demonstrations of the desire to help are common prescriptions. This approach is easier in an all-borderline group than it is in a predominantly neurotic group. Even though it is possible for the therapist to offer differing treatment to his group patients depending on their individual needs, these differential attitudes must be offered with sensitivity and discrimination.

In one group with a single borderline individual, I became increasingly comfortable with providing supportive measures to this man which I did not provide to the other patients. One of his patterns was to find it difficult to control his excessive obsessiveness and as a result he would often hold the floor without end, a form of monopolizing that required special attention. My typical method of handling this problem was to interrupt him with the observation that he was becoming "too detailed", as opposed to an interpretive or confrontive intervention, and fortunately he usually responded positively to this kind of structuring. The other patients were sensitive to the fact that he needed this kind of ego supportive intervention that I did not use with the others.

Other kinds of supportive measures include the necessity to protect the patient against being scape-goated, particularly when he attempts to provoke other members into hostile reactions. Also emphasized is the therapist's need to acknowledge the patient's achievements or efforts without at the same time attempting to pressure the patient into certain desired behaviors to which he is not yet committed. Some writers discuss the importance of ego strengthening in the early phase of therapy (raising self-esteem, overcoming mistrust, decreasing feelings of isolation) before the more definitive tasks of ego repair and integration can occur (Leszcz, 1992).

A more specific kind of support is emphasized by Kibel (1991) in his recommendation of a supportive group centered approach which underlines the commonality among patients. Whenever possible, he attempts to comment on the shared concerns, preoccupations, and defenses manifested by his patients. Such a technique helps to foster greater cohesiveness in the group, a greater sense of belonging, and helps to neutralize feelings of being different and an outsider. This approach tends to be keep peer transferences more fluid. As a consequence of their splitting defense, borderline persons tend to view others in black-and-white terms, as good or bad, friend or foe; but when patients begin to perceive similarities between themselves and those whom they initially regarded as unacceptable or unfriendly, their extreme attitudes become less pronounced.

Confrontation

Most authors agree that one must go beyond mere friendliness and encouragement in order to be therapeutic. But the challenge to the group therapist and to the other members is how to confront the patient in a way that is tactful and empathic and makes it possible for the patient to hear the message and use it.

In a survey of a number of therapists as to their observations of borderline patients in a group, Colson (1974) reported considerable variability in the reactions of such patients to confrontations regarding their behavior or defenses. Some observed a tendency for these patients to profit from confrontation, whether from peers or therapist, while others reported the opposite tendency of angry, defensive, and even disorganized, reactions. These differences may be understood in terms of the observation that some of these patients may be thin-skinned while others are thick-skinned (Bateman, 1998). Certainly the use of confrontation also depends on the nature of the relation already established with the therapist and the group, as well as the rigidity of the particular behavior or defense in question.

Most therapists believe that one has to take special care with the kind of observations and confrontations that one presents to the borderline patient because of their fragility, paranoia, and sensitivity. Various recommendations include "special treatment" such as answering direct questions, offering empathic responses when they have been injured, protecting them from scape-goating, and deflecting the group's focus on the patient's difficulties to an examination of their own affective reactions.

Uncovering and interpretation

The trend within the group psychotherapy literature is best characterized by the tendency to refrain from exploration and uncovering. For the most part, group therapists believe that therapeutic change in borderline patients may best occur by means of strengthened identifications, increased awareness of their maladaptive behaviors, and help in correcting their reality-distorting tendencies. But, the uncovering of unconscious wishes and fears is usually not recommended for borderline patients for two reasons: the patient is already too much in contact with his unconscious fantasies and hence needs help in repressing them; and an uncovering procedure runs the risk of being understood as criticism and rejection.

Some clinicians point out that borderline patients in a mixed group are able to tolerate greater exploration and interpretation in depth than they can in an individual therapy setting. The explanation for this phenomenon is based on the "multiple identifications" or the supportive effect of a group setting in which the interpretation often pertains to more than one person, particularly when the therapist works with the group-as-a-whole. In another context I have referred to this phenomenon as the "protection of the group theme" (Chapter Six).

In general, the context of the group appears to make a critical difference in determining how amenable the group is to using active interventions like uncovering defenses as well as confrontations. A contribution by Macaskill (1980) contended that the therapist's focus upon the group's narcissistic defenses against underlying fears is capable of bringing about an acceptance in the group of their shameful and anxiety-laden concerns. His in-patient group initially rejected the idea that leaving the hospital was an issue for them, and in fact often expressed the idea that once they were discharged all of their problems would be solved. When the therapist persisted in challenging their denials, the group began to acknowledge their underlying fear of reentering their communities. This uncovering process was clearly facilitated by the structure of a hospital setting.

Research perspectives on technique

While most clinicians clearly gravitate toward a mainly supportive approach with borderlines, some research findings indicate the usefulness of interpretive work.

A research study by McCallum and Piper (1999) points in the direction of the usefulness of intensive dynamically oriented group psychotherapy with personality disorders, including borderline, paranoid, and dependent patients. These were individuals in an eighteen week evening treatment program (five evenings per week, for four hour sessions) where the major treatment modality was an insight oriented small group. A large percentage of their patients were able to engage in psychodynamic work and begin to engage in self-reflection, assume responsibility for contributing to their own difficulties, and were able to be helpful to others.

Similarly, a randomly controlled study in a day hospital setting by Bateman and Fonagy (2001) reported on their successful use of analytically oriented interpretive techniques with borderlines. They studied forty-four borderline patients randomly assigned to either partial hospitalization including individual and group psychotherapy or a control group which received standard out-patient psychiatric care consisting of case management and medication. Both were in treatment for eighteen months and were evaluated at termination followed by an eighteen month follow-up study. The partial hospitalization group significantly improved to a greater extent than the control group in practically every dimension studied, including symptoms, self-mutilation, suicide attempts, and readmission to the hospital. In addition, the intensive treatment group showed continuing improvement during the post-treatment period. Even more impressive were the results of their five year follow-up study of these patients in which they found all of the advantages of their mentalization based treatment not only stablilizing but actually continuing to improve.

Wilberg et al. (2003) studied 187 poorly functioning personality disordered patients who were treated with Foulkesian group psychotherapy for twenty weeks in a day hospital setting followed by two years of once-a-week outpatient group therapy. They found relatively modest improvement in these patients, compared to the Bateman and Fonagy results and speculated that the less lengthy in-patient treatment might explain the difference.

Marziali and Munroe-Blum (1994) compared a group of some forty patients who received interpersonal group psychotherapy with a matched group who received psychodynamic individual therapy. Both groups received twelve months of treatment and were seen at a twelve month follow-up period. Interpersonal group therapy combines some features of structured, behavioral treatment with a psychodynamic approach. They found that both the group therapy patients and the controls showed similar "significant change". Marsha Linehan and her colleagues (Dimieff & Koerner) (2007), using dialectical behavior therapy in groups have reported significant change in their active, structured treatment of borderline patients.

In summary, it appears that both supportive and expressive methods offer promise for the treatment of borderlines in groups. The use of partial hospitalization with this population seems to be especially useful in conducting successful intensive psychodynamic group treatment. On the other hand, the more supportive and structured approach offered by behavioral approaches also was helpful. There are suggestions, however, that intensive analytic treatment offers the additional bonus of continuing improvement after the treatment has terminated.

Conclusions

The literature points to many characteristics of groups which make them particularly suited for treating borderline patients. I would like to underline my agreement with certain points mentioned above and then introduce some additional perspectives.

First, I concur with other clinicians that most borderline patients in groups also need a combined individual therapy relationship, preferably on a regular basis. The weight is on the side of having the same therapist doing both treatments insofar as separate therapists lend themselves to the complication of splitting. The individual therapy usually serves a supportive function. Many borderline individuals experience periodic flare-ups of extreme anxiety accompanied by some degree of disorganization and one can more effectively and flexibly deal with these reactions on a one-to-one basis. My own experience has been that failure to provide such patients with a regular supportive individual contact makes it difficult for these patients to maintain their membership and participation in the therapy group. This is particularly true in the early stages of membership in the group before they have become integrated into the group.

Second, group treatment is likely to be helpful with borderline patients in using careful, well-timed confrontations to help them overcome egocentric and abrasive character traits. While the diagnosis of BPD does not imply a particular character diagnosis, it is no surprise that many of these patients show narcissistic disturbances associated with their early fixations and defenses. They are the group members who monopolize, alienate, and antagonize more frequently than the group's better-integrated patients. If their narcissistic pathology is severe and their needs and demands are insatiable, they should be excluded from a group as should the patient with anti-social personality who is likely to inflict uncontrolled sadism upon others. On the other hand if these questionable patients show some control over their abrasive behavior and especially if they have some redeeming characteristics (like the patient who was able to apologize to the group after an unseemly outburst), they can achieve a satisfactory degree of acceptance. And of course, only after the borderline patient has become integrated in the group and has developed a stable therapeutic alliance, may the therapist or group members begin to confront him with his provocative, self-defeating behavior.

Groups are especially suitable for these problems because the group setting illuminates such behaviors in bold relief. Group patients necessarily compete with each other for time and attention. They must tolerate the frustration of not having their problems immediately and fully attended to. They are asked to listen to, explore, and try to understand the communications of their fellow patients. Small wonder, then, that problems of greed, vying for attention, and other competitive behaviors become highlighted, especially among patients with a strong sense of deprivation. And confrontation about an undesirable characteristic or behavior is more effectively heard when a "jury" of one's peers passes judgment as opposed to the more ambivalently held therapist.

A difficult issue is how much can group treatment contribute to the attenuation of splitting in borderlines. These patients are deficient in integrating their primitive good and bad, self and object representations, and have resorted to the use of splitting to prevent the infiltration of aggression into their over-idealized images of self and significant others. There is a fairly good consensus that the need to rely on the primitive defense of splitting is due to the infant's experience of rage at a depriving mother and his need to protect the image of the good mother, albeit at a considerable psychic cost.

Borderline patients are notoriously prone to narcissistic injury from comments that point out their infantile wishes, their strivings for special or exclusive attention, or their inordinate demands. In an individual psychotherapy setting, such interpretations tend to be received as a total assault upon the person's acceptability and a condemnation of his nonhuman qualities. In my work on the Menninger Foundation Psychotherapy Research Project, I observed (1974) that a number of patients in dyadic treatment, many of whom were borderline, showed substantial improvement in treatment that was not mainly exploratory and uncovering. Rather, these patients were able to achieve significant and stable change through a variety of supportive methods emphasizing the consolidation of a therapeutic alliance, rather than the interpretation of the transference. Although several good neurotics profited considerably from psychoanalysis, a few borderline patients, who were mistakenly diagnosed as healthier than they actually were, did poorly in an uncovering procedure. These observations are consistent with Rockland's (1992) use of supportive methods with borderlines in individual treatment. On the other hand, Kernberg, Yeomans, Clarkin, and Levy (2008) compared their transference-focused psychotherapy (TFP) with dialectical behavior therapy and supportive psychotherapy and found that their tratment was more effective in a number ofdimentsions.

Within limits, I concur with those who have observed that some borderline patients are able to accept both confrontations and interpretations more readily in groups than in individual therapy. The group setting offers certain safeguards for these patients, provided they function at the upper level of the borderline spectrum and have had the opportunity to develop a good alliance with the group. First, they have the possibility of regulating the intensity of their reactions. Insofar as group-wide interpretations are offered to the entire group, individual members are considerably freer to accept or reject the therapist's comments as applicable to themselves. Second, since other people are being addressed as well as themselves, particularly in a group centered interpretation, the borderline individual is afforded the "protection of the group theme". He finds it more difficult to react to the interpretation as a devastating criticism insofar as several others, if not the entire group, are simultaneously being told similar things about themselves.

Working with borderline patients in a predominantly neurotic group of course makes an expressive-uncovering approach difficult to implement, since the thrust of an analytic-expressive treatment effort is to interpret the transference and to impart insight into unconscious motivations and defenses. Wide variations among the group members in tolerating interpretations place a special burden on the group therapist and make it especially necessary for him to exercise tact and sound clinical judgment in gauging how "deep" his interpretations should be to the more vulnerable borderline person.

And finally, a theoretical consideration which requires further examination and study. Most writers agree that the borderline's fixation point of developmental arrest is at the rapprochement phase, where the infant has begun, but has not achieved, separation and individuation from his mother. In order to successfully renegotiate this process, it makes theoretical sense that a dyad is the best crucible in which to re-experience these pre-oedipal, two-person struggles and conflicts. It is likely that a period of group psychotherapy with the same therapist could help the patient gain some distance, some breathing space, in the course of the struggle to separate from the individual therapist-mother. But the eventual resolution of the paranoid anxieties should ideally be done within the individual setting which most closely approximates the patient's conflictual life situation, that is, the mother-infant dyad.

My belief is that group psychotherapy primarily helps to attenuate abrasive, maladaptive behavior. It also provides the opportunity to deal with conflicts and defenses in a supportive, nurturant, and non-regressive setting which may contribute to the reduction of defensive splitting. Such treatment is particularly helpful where the closeness of individual treatment has proved too stressful for the patient. This does not gainsay the use of long-term individual psychotherapy to provide both supportive and expressive help in raising the ego functioning of these individuals.

CHAPTER TWELVE

Group psychotherapy with narcissistic patients

M y belief is that group psychotherapy is usually the treatment of choice for narcissistic pathology, often when combined with individual treatment. Of course the patient needs to be carefully selected since some patients who are especially prone to narcissistic injury, usually the "thin-skinned" ones, and are unable to tolerate the stresses associated with group membership: the need to share the time and attention of the group and the possibility of being criticized by one or more peers. The other contraindication would be the severe narcissist whose behavior is intolerable to the group and is likely to be extruded by the group members. Succinctly, the group may be contraindicated when the patient is unable to tolerate the group and the group is unable to tolerate the patient.

However, most patients with narcissistic pathology are likely to benefit from group therapy because this modality highlights the patient's pathology and affords the patient an opportunity to change or modify his or her most self-defeating pathology. The major task of a group patient is two-fold: (a) to disclose the experiences in his life that are causing difficulty and (b) to listen to others in the group attentively with the intention of understanding and being helpful. Self-disclosure is a significant difficulty for patients who are fearful of criticism or attack. And a glaring problem for narcissistic people is their difficulty in becoming interested in other people and empathizing with the emotional struggles that others present. The experience of being in a group permits the narcissistic patient to become more aware of these deficits and to begin attempting a new kind of behavior in a setting that is nonpunitive and encouraging.

I believe that the theoretical and technical advances during the past few decades have helped practitioners immensely both in understanding narcissistic pathology and in treating this widespread problem. A major contributor in this area was Heinz Kohut (1984) who introduced the idea that narcissism is not simply a troublesome reaction that needs to be brushed aside but requires the therapist both to understand the sources in the individual's development that have lead to such behavior and to respond with a consistent empathic stance. And Otto Kernberg (1984), with his integration of Kleinian and ego psychology concepts has contributed to the further understanding of the conflict based defenses such as splitting and idealization/devaluation, which characterize the narcissistic person.

The theories of early development embodied in object relations theory and attachment theory represent a significant shift in the evolution of psychoanalytic theory in broadening the diagnostic understanding and treatment of all patients, including the well- functioning neurotic. Freud's early studies of hysteria led not only to enhanced understanding of the neuroses but to insights into both normal and abnormal functioning generally. Similarly, the early phases of development which have been so important in understanding narcissistic phenomena are beginning to penetrate the area of normal and neurotic functioning.

Ronald Fairbairn (1952), writing in the 1940s and 1950s, was the first to introduce the notion that very early developmental fixations and conflicts, which he termed "schizoid", left indelible marks upon the psyches of all people and, to a greater or lesser extent, should be attended to in all psychotherapies. My own analytic work with well-functioning neurotic people has been enriched by my knowledge of object relations theory learned in the context of treating narcissistic patients. I am considerably more attentive to problems relating to the development of the self stemming from early experiences in which the "true self' had to be submerged because of the patient's need to maintain a stable bond with a threatening or rejecting parent who was perceived as not accepting the infant or child as a separate individual in his own right (Winnicott, 1965). The marked growth of interest in the topic of narcissism largely stems from the incorporation in our field of major advances in psychoanalysis of object relations theory, self psychology, and attachment theory.

Some diagnostic considerations

There is a general consensus among many writers that narcissistic patients, while basically struggling with the same underlying issues, may show either overt or covert symptoms of their pathology. Thus, Gabbard (1989) describes the hypervigilant narcissist who adopts a silent observing role while anticipating signs of being frustrated or ignored; in contrast there is the oblivious narcissist who is intent on gratifying her own needs for attention and applause with little appreciation for the impact her behavior may be having on others. The hypervigilant view is not too different from Masterson's (1983) concept of the closet narcissist whose grandiose and idealizing self is carefully hidden from view in contrast to the overt narcissist who clamors for attention. Similarly, Akhtar (1992) describes the narcissist's self-concept as shifting between the poles of grandiosity and inferiority while Burstein and Beale (1976) have proposed a subtyping of the narcissistic character on the basis of a grandiose *vs*. inadequate classification, which they characterize as two sides of the same coin. Basically, both types are dealing with fear and rage concerning frustrated dependency wishes, but take rather different stances around this conflict. And finally, Rosenfeld (1987) originated the dichotomy between the thin-skinned and thick-skinned narcissist where the thin-skinned person tends to be fragile and vulnerable, while the thick-skinned individual is defensively aggressive and oblivious. All of these dichotomies focus on similar underlying structures that tend to be manifested by opposite overt behavior.

Adjunctive supports

There is probably one point of consensus among group therapists, learned through experience in therapy groups, that many narcissistic patients require some degree of adjunctive support in addition to group psychotherapy. Many narcissistic patients tend to experience intense needs for time and attention, for magical solutions, for dramatic demonstrations of love, and basically exhibit an incessant search for a good mother. Concomitantly, they have to cope with large doses of anger and frustration, feelings of being unloved and unlovable, not to speak of distorted paranoid perceptions of the attitudes of others. The press of these strong instinctual, person-oriented needs within a personality which is self-disordered often makes it difficult for the usual outpatient, expressive psychotherapy group to provide the kind of "holding environment" which can keep internal pressures from producing anxiety and possibly decompensation. The major vehicle of treatment should be only one expressive modality, whether group or individual, while the adjunctive treatment should be conceptualized as the structure necessary to make this expressive treatment possible.

Group therapists are familiar with the complaint from many patients at some point that individual psychotherapy is what they really need. For the most part, these are transference manifestations which surface especially when the group is dealing with its rivalry struggles and the patient experiences a sense of frustration of dependency needs, or the wish to be the therapist's favorite. Such expressions by patients are the bread-and-butter experience of the group therapist and usually need only to be interpreted, not acted on. However, like the case of the borderline patient who often needs adjunctive support, these wishes are not only transference manifestations but may also express an important reality need to permit the patient to tolerate the group. In my experience, a frequent reason for treatment failure of narcissistic patients in group psychotherapy is the therapist's omission of adjunctive individual treatment.

Sequential group and individual therapy

There are times when both individual and group treatment are used, not as concomitant or combined therapies as described above, but as separate therapies where each modality may be preparation for the other, depending on the special needs of the patient. Under certain circumstances, the narcissistic patient may move into an intensive individual psychotherapy after he has completed reasonable growth in his group treatment and is now better prepared to deal with the intimacy of an individual relationship. The greater closeness of one-to-one therapy will activate the patient's core problems such as the fear of intimacy and thus permit a further working through of the underlying conflicts. On the other hand, the converse may sometimes be true where individual therapy is desirable first in order to prepare certain patients for the vicissitudes of a group experience. Some narcissistic patients fear the consequences of entering a group and anticipate attacks from peers or frustration of deeply ingrained wishes to be the exclusive object of the therapist's attention. Kosseff (1975) proposed that following a period of individual psychotherapy, a patient with problems of separation should be transferred into combined group psychotherapy with the same therapist. This experience could contribute to helping the patient gain distance and "breathing space" in his struggle to separate from the individual therapist/mother. But he also recommends that the eventual resolution of the patient's paranoid anxiety should ideally be done within the individual setting which most closely approximates the conflict laden developmental situation, that is, the mother-infant dyad.

Intensity of primitive wishes

Like the borderline patient, the narcissistic patient typically places inordinate demands upon the therapist. He often has the fantasy of a magical cure, that it will be immediate and total, but in addition is fearful that the whole experience will turn to ashes. Insofar as he thinks of himself as a very special person, he may feel entitled to special consideration, to be the recipient of privileges which others do not get, and to receive a greater share than all the rest since he was deprived early in life.

On the surface it would appear that a group would only rub salt in the wound of an individual with a sense of entitlement and a need to be special. Such needs are inevitably frustrated in an individual relationship but even more so in a group. More than any other factor, this craving provides the rationale for providing such patients with the gratification of an individual relationship. But the counterpoise to the patient's experience of frustration is the opportunity the group provides to begin appreciating the necessity to consider the presence and the rights of others. Under ideal circumstances, many narcissistic patients will gradually begin to appreciate the inappropriateness of their expectations and be able to tone down their rage at being frustrated. Of course, if their tolerance for frustration is severely compromised, they may angrily withdraw, act out, or even quit treatment. But being afforded the opportunity to hear about the inner lives of their fellow patients in a way which was relatively unavailable to them prior to their group experience, contributes to their ability to see their fellow patients more as whole persons, rather than as part objects whose presence only signifies the opportunity for exploitation and gratification.

Working with patients who have eating disorders or problems with addiction, Battegay (1991) found that they showed improvement while in group treatment but lost most of their gains at follow-up. Most of these patients suffered from narcissistic personality disorder and he explained their progress mainly on the basis of the group gratifying frustrated dependency needs but they were not able to internalize these positive experiences. He observed that many of these patients need long-term group treatment, often life-long.

A positive therapeutic gain is best illustrated by a narcissistic patient who made unusually good use of her three-year-long group experience, along with concomitant hospitalization at the outset of treatment, described in detail in the next chapter. At the end of her first year in the group she achieved her first important insight, that she needed to learn that the world does not revolve around her alone. This awareness began to dawn on her as we tried to explore her tendency to sit silently in the group, expecting others to take the initiative in drawing her out or that others would know when she was distressed without their being told. Much of her remaining group experience consisted of successfully assimilating that important insight and gaining gratification from attempting to help others.

Erotization

An especially difficult kind of transference manifestation of some narcissistic patients is the tendency to erotize the relationship. Almost invariably such reactions are a genital expression of infantile needs to be nurtured, soothed, and comforted. The special difficulty presented by these reactions is the narcissistic patient's tendency to project, and sometimes projectively identify, her instinctual wishes onto the therapist so that the patient may develop a highly distorted view of the real relationship. In a dyad, as opposed to a group situation, the privacy of the setting not only stimulates such fantasies but in some instances may contribute to the expectation that these wishes may indeed get gratified.

A female patient whom I treated individually for over a year before she terminated against advice developed an intensely erotized relationship which she expected to be gratified. Because she considered her husband an inept lover who left her sexually dissatisfied, she believed she had a right to expect the therapist to take care of such needs. Furthermore, she perceived the therapist as inviting her into a situation in which such fantasies were fostered and, like Eliza Doolittle, expected more than just words. Despite my interpretive efforts, the patient was unable to alter her expectations and her mounting frustration and anger led her to terminate the relationship.

Sometime afterward, and now in a hospital setting, the patient started a three-year period of group psychotherapy with another therapist which was quite helpful to her. Her erotization of the transference continued in the group but in a much more modulated form. During the first year of treatment, the group therapist wrote, "She makes it clear she would be only too glad to erotize the treatment situation and make the relationship with the therapist the end rather than a means. She makes no bones that this is difficult to do in the group and that this is a frustration for her. She makes veiled threats that she might be able to get her hospital doctor to yield to her entreaties and then she will have finished with me". In the course of a relatively long period of treatment, the patient was gradually able to experience less peremptory sexual demands and, when they did occur, she viewed them as embarrassing and depressing rather than as needs which should be fulfilled.

Overidealization and devaluation

Splitting is the underlying basis for many transference reactions in the narcissistic patient, as it is in the borderline patient, and the alternation between overidealization and devaluation is directly linked to the patient's oscillation between disparate ego states. A group provides the opportunity for the patient to correct these distortions and to limit the breadth of these pendulum-like oscillations. To the extent that such corrections occur, the patient's integrative capacities are strengthened.

Narcissistic patients typically view the therapist as an all-powerful figure who either is their savior or, at other times, is the reverse—callous, cold, and destructive. The presence of other patients in the group who have different perceptions frequently offers a corrective antidote. This factor is especially significant in a predominantly neurotic group where the group's collective capacity for reality testing is often enhanced. In other words, the dyadic situation depends solely upon interpretations or confrontations from an already distorted appearing therapist while the group context provides multiple clarifying pressures from one's peers.

Similar factors operate with regard to unrealistic perceptions of one's fellow patients. The additional corrective factor is that insofar as the other participants are able to be considerably more transparent and self-disclosing than the therapist usually can be, this additional information helps to attenuate the peer transferences and distortions. For example, a male narcissistic patient with very strong tendencies to idealize others, not only elevated the therapist to the status of "giant" but viewed a seriously incapacitated woman in the group as enviously competent and creative. As others, including the idealized patient herself, shared their perceptions of her real handicaps, he was able to tone down his view of her capacities and this corrective experience contributed a quantum of needed reality testing.

Narcissistic rage

Most writers agree that a central problem for these patients is their difficulty in dealing with vast amounts of latent destructive energy based developmentally on excessive degrees of early frustration. Furthermore, their inability to integrate good and bad internalized objects deprives them of the capacity to neutralize their hostility with quantities of positive, libidinal impulses. The clinical picture presented by these patients consists either of markedly poor impulse control on the one hand or immobilized passivity on the other and often a brittle fluctuation between these two extremes.

A group setting is particularly helpful in facilitating the expression of disagreements, criticisms, and anger, especially towards authority figures. As mentioned earlier, the famous pediatician Dr. Benjamin Spock once observed the striking difference between private consultations with parents regarding their children and those which he did with parents in small groups. In a one-to-one setting, parents rarely disagreed or argued with the expert's advice, while in a group there was considerably more questioning and doubt expressed. Also, a group provides an "unfreezing" experience for the passive, inhibited patient, particularly in the early stages, by permitting her to identify herself vicariously with both aggressor and victim in hostile exchanges which she witnesses. The patient observes that angry confrontations, attacks and counterattacks most often occur in the group without permanent damage to either party, and eventually the patient may begin to permit herself to express anger towards other patients or the therapist.

Vulnerable self esteem

Pines (1978) has aptly compared the borderline patient to the hemophiliac whose capacity for self-healing and repairs after narcissistic injury are prominently defective: "... they bleed at slight traumas that do not affect the more robust characters, and they are deficient in essential inner qualities necessary for normal self-healing" (p. 115). These hypersensitive reactions equally apply to some narcissistic patients, the thin-skinned ones, and may be understood in terms of the patient's impaired sense of self. Her view of herself as a loving and lovable person is constantly being battered by feelings of deprivation, envy, ingratitude, and the wish to retaliate. Good feelings about herself in relation to others are highly unstable and self-esteem is quite vulnerable.

The factors which contribute to neutralizing these reactions consist first of the predominance of positive responses which group patients usually receive from their peers for their contributions to the group, their efforts to improve, and their real achievements. Unless a patient becomes the victim of scape-goating, which the therapist can usually control, most patients find the group experience a positive "holding environment", a supportive refuge from the stresses of everyday life, once they have become integrated into a cohesive group. But even more sustaining is the patient's experience of being a significant figure in the life of another person. Unless he is obnoxious and excessively difficult, his presence is usually desired, his contributions valued, and he has the growth experience of being able to provide help to others.

The transference reactions of these patients constitute a profound challenge for individual and group therapist alike and may often be handled more effectively in a group as opposed to an individual setting because of the more controlled therapeutic regression which the group may provide. The actual presence of others besides the therapist introduces the significant factor of social reality which may contribute to attenuating unrealistic expectations. Intense narcissistic beliefs of entitlement and of being special will often get muted in a group situation. Second, the reactions of the peer group contribute to diminishing the reality distortions that impair the patient's perceptions and functioning. Phenomena like over-idealization or devaluation, particularly of the therapist, get dampened more readily in the group situation because of the input of the other patients in addition to that of the therapist. Third, the multiple identifications and behavioral models to which a narcissistic patient is exposed facilitates new, improved behaviors such as the appropriate expression of anger and self-assertiveness. And finally, not only does the group provide the patient with the opportunity for greater detachment and limited involvement when she needs the distance, but the therapist likewise may retain greater neutrality and be less prone to counter-transference pulls in a group as opposed to the dyadic situation. These favorable therapeutic influences contribute significantly to the major therapeutic task of integrating the split between the disparate good and bad self and object representations, and thus strengthen self-esteem.

One patient with marked inability to take on adult responsibility as well as denial of need from others, announced in the group that he had dropped the only college course he was taking. The group was irritated that he had failed to tell them that he had even enrolled in college some two months earlier. He confessed that he felt inferior because everyone in the group had finished college and he doubted that he could carry even a light load. He was informed by the group that he discourages exploration of his problems by often retreating into "I really don't want to go into it". The session helped to convince him that the group was truly interested in helping and this session was the beginning of a greater openness in dealing with his serious life issues.

Reducing narcissistic and abrasive behavior

In addition to multiple reality inputs, there is a second mechanism of change consisting of awareness, control, and reduction of abrasive and narcissistic behavior. Such change may be less structural and intrapsychic as opposed to more interpersonal but nevertheless can contribute immensely to significant improvements in the patient's relationships. Unquestionably, a group provides a setting par excellence for the opportunity to make the patient more aware of her inappropriate behavior.

A group setting has the distinct advantage of being able to highlight in the here-and-now the patient's egocentric, often repugnant, behavioral tendencies. The patients' need to be special, their excessive demandingness, their view of the therapist or peers as important only insofar as they gratify their needs—are characteristics that are likely to be relatively unnoticed for a long period of time in individual therapy because the therapist gratifies these needs by paying undivided attention to the patient. In a group, however, not only is the patient unable to be the center of attention at all times, but he is even asked to listen to others and to respond to them in helpful ways.

A twenty-three-year-old college student, diagnosed as a narcissistic and borderline personality, was hospitalized for drug addiction and manic episodes. In group psychotherapy he was a flamboyant raconteur, interesting and engaging, but tending to monopolize the group's time. He had some awareness of his greed in the group and rationalized that no one else was talking so he might as well take the floor. However, he had the tendency to fall asleep when he was not in the center of the stage. His difficulty in listening to and in becoming interested in the problems of other patients exactly paralleled his relationships outside the group, in particular with women, who only interested him insofar as they were an applauding and appreciative audience. Being confronted by the group with his egocentrism gave him a better appreciation of the impact of such behavior, and made him begin to view it as an ego-dystonic aspect of his character, and afforded him an opportunity to modify it first within the group, and later in his social relationships.

There are the patients whose measuring rod of therapeutic help is based upon the amount of time the group was focused upon them. They typically object to being included in the therapist's interventions about the whole group since they view such comments as compromising their sense of specialness. Usually, they attempt to monopolize the group's time and attention and the therapist has the special task of protecting the group from being manipulated and exploited by them while at the same time protecting the offending patient from being scape-goated. The major help for these highly egocentric people usually comes from their peers whose confrontations, offered in a context of a basically helping attitude, have the possibility of enhancing the patient's appreciation for their abrasive behavior.

At the other end of the pole is the silent narcissistic patient who often taxes the group's forbearance and the therapist's skills. A patient's silence has multiple sources and may communicate a variety of meanings in the same way that a group silence needs to be diagnosed. The narcissistic aspect of silence may convey the attitude of superiority, that one does not belong with this horde of barbarians, or more egocentrically, that others need the help more than you do. Another basis for silence is the self-absorption of the narcissistic character who has a limited capacity for becoming engaged in the matters which preoccupy others and who therefore listens poorly or is unable to empathize with the pains or joys which others experience. Silence is not infrequently employed by a patient to call attention to himself, to test the interest of the group in whether his non- participation will be noticed. Such narcissistic motivations, when uncovered, can be quite helpful to the patient in attempting to become more attentive to others. A frequent comment by successfully treated group patients is that they are now considerably more comfortable about participating in social groups, an outcome which is at least partly an effect of decreased narcissism.

Sometimes the major learning experience in a group consists of working through primitive envy and greed so that feelings of intense deprivation are no longer a primary theme in the patient's life. The group patient is implicitly asked to share the oral supplies available to the group with her fellow participants. Insofar as she is able to overcome frustration and rage surrounding these deprivations, she reaches a higher level of maturity, much as the infant must gradually give up the expectation of getting mother's breast whenever she wants it. Winnicott (1975) describes this stage of development as a period of gradual disillusionment, referring to the infant's initial illusion that she is the center of mother's universe. Confrontation with her unreasonable demands and her anger at not being immediately gratified is potentially a most useful group experience. Put in another way, an intensive analytic long-term group experience ideally provides narcissistic patients with the opportunity to learn about their maladaptive infantile behavior and helps them experiment with new and more mature response patterns.

Self psychology perspectives

The growth of self psychology as a significant branch of psychoanalysis has encouraged a number of group therapists to apply and build on Kohut's insights. Several writers (Harwood, 1992; Bacal, 1991; Segalla, 1998; Stone, 2009) have emphasized the ready availability of selfobjects in a group setting. The group setting provides patients with selfobject responses not only from the therapist but from other members and from the experience of the group-as-a-whole. Members can experience the group fulfilling idealizing, mirroring, or alter-ego transferences. (Stone, 2005).

Stone (2009) emphasizes the cultivation of empathic responsiveness toward the narcissistic patient. Not only do these patients need to experience the empathic responses of the therapist and other patients, but they profit by observing and identifying with the empathic responses displayed by their peers and the therapist. Furthermore the therapist needs to focus on the patient's resistance to seeking out his repressed, unconsciously desired affirmation from others in the group. The self psychology notion of resistance is based on fears of being traumatized. Bacal (1991) departs to some extent from Kohut's primary emphasis on empathy by speaking of the necessity to strike a balance between reactiveness (the spontaneous view of the patient as a separate other) and responsiveness (the empathic response to the patient's selfobject needs). Segalla (1998) introduces a concept parallel to Kohut's selfobject, but specific to being in a group setting. She contends that humans are hardwired to be a part of groups, and coins the concept of "groupobject" as a potential source of fulfillment of the need to be a part of a group, analogous to the need for attachment and affiliation as described by Lichtenberg (1998).

Karterud and Stone's concept of the "groupself" (2003) has some similarities to Segalla's groupobject. They define the groupself as a "project", an ongoing process which may be enhanced or diminished depending on the positive or negative events transpiring in the group. When individuals come together in a group they share conscious and unconscious wishes concerning what they desire from the group and when these common wishes are to be gratified. They strive for positive developments such as an enhanced alliance with the therapist, visible progress of one or more patients, feelings of pride in the group and in oneself as a member of the group—these are the essence of the groupself. On the other hand, negative events result in feelings of depletion of the self. Further, although Stone subscribes to the view that group-as-a-whole interpretations may contribute to helping patients with inner conflicts, his main emphasis, following Kohut, is upon empathic interpretations which contribute to stabilizing a disrupted fragmented self and helps to link disrupted states to developmental trauma. He emphasizes offering understanding and explaining (interpretations) from an empathic position rather than from the perspective of an external observer. He endorses this writer's recommendation that individual interventions should ideally precede comments about the whole group.

Internalization of new representations

First, one method of integrating ego splits consists of using transference interpretation, insight, and working through, thus leading to conflict resolution. Second, the reduction of pathological narcissistic behavior in a group often involves something closer to social learning in which defensive patterns become better appreciated as adaptive failures and are ultimately reduced or given up. A third curative process is best described as internalization of new self and object representations.

My work on The Menninger Foundation Psychotherapy Research Project, a study of forty-two cases of individual psychotherapy and psychoanalysis, suggested the importance of internalization in leading to both intrapsychic and interpersonal change (Horwitz, 1974). In individual treatment, the internalization process may partly consist of an introjection of the therapist's attitudes, ideals, and behavior patterns and is fostered by the therapist being perceived as a role model for his patient. This kind of internalization involves the acquisition of a new self and object representation, by means of assimilating the gradually developing therapeutic alliance. These occurrences are highly significant, particularly for the self-disordered patient, even though they characteristically develop without being noticed or verbalized. Internalization undoubtedly occurs in group treatment as well, especially given the multiple opportunities for introjecting peers as well as the therapist.

With regard to the patient's internalization of the therapist's attitudes and behavior, the group patient has the opportunity to see the therapist in a somewhat more detached way than in individual treatment. He witnesses the therapist engaging in a wider repertoire of behaviors and, in particular, is able to assume the role of spectator while the therapist is either interacting with another patient or even dealing with the group-as-a-whole. Sometimes patients will discuss their impressions of observing the therapist's behavior and may report on their efforts to incorporate some aspect of the therapist into their ego ideal. A narcissistic man, for example, became aware of his weak involvement in the lives of his family and reported with some pleasure on his beginning to behave more like the therapist during the family's dinner hour, in listening to and drawing out family members.

The internalization of the therapist's attitudes toward the group and toward individual patients not only contributes to improved interpersonal behavior outside the group, but the group itself is a setting par excellence for such skills to be practiced and learned. The patient is asked to become something of a therapist's assistant as one of his roles in the group. The term generally has a pejorative connotation insofar as it is usually applied to those patients who use the role to defensively resist engaging in self-disclosure and spontaneous interactions with peers. But if it does not become a rigidly exclusive role, it helps the patient give up his egocentrism. Thus, a narcissistic woman with a serious difficulty in assuming a maternal role with her own children and who struggled with a strong wish to give up her parental responsibilities, developed a genuine interest in helping a younger female patient in the group who was clearly more handicapped and disorganized than herself. In part, it was a healthy identification with the therapist's helping role and the gratification from this experience contributed to her marked improvement. The group not only fostered this identification but encouraged its implementation within the group setting.

In addition to the internalization of the therapist, there are both peer alliances as well as relationships to the group-as-a-whole, which are capable of becoming internalized. As the patient progresses in therapy and develops an increasing bond with the therapist and the group, the expectation of being treated with respect and acceptance predominates over the fear of being manipulated for the benefit of others. This significant corrective experience becomes internalized as it does in individual therapy. In addition, the multiple relationships with one's peers as they evolve into increasing feelings of mutual regard, of being able to resolve interpersonal misunderstandings and conflicts with peers, of efforts to empathize and help others—are new kinds of relationships which the narcissistic patient may begin to incorporate into his behavioral repertoire. Thus, the alliance with both the therapist and one's peers is a potential curative factor in a group.

Difficulties and opportunities

The hazard of describing the special advantages of group treatment is the tendency to be carried away by one's own theoretical formulations. As I have reminded the reader on a few occasions (and quietly reminded myself), a narcissistic patient is extremely difficult to treat whether the setting be group or individual treatment. I have mentioned the paradox in all psychotherapy that the very patient characteristics which make treatment indicated are also the ones, like self-destructive or masochistic behavior, which often lead to treatment failure. This paradox is even more pertinent to a group setting in which the presence of a peer group presents special challenges. The narcissist's abrasive characteristics will inevitably produce friction and dissatisfaction among members. Monopolizing, lack of empathy, and the propensity for destructive acting-out are characteristics which need treatment but may also place a heavy burden upon the whole group. Such patients are usually the prime targets for scape-goating by virtue of their insensitivity and provocativeness as well as their deviancy.

On the other hand, some of these individuals are capable of loosening up group norms by their tendency to think and act in unconventional ways. As mentioned earlier, both Shields (2000) and Gans and Alonso (1998) emphasize how the troublesome narcissistic patient may become a real asset to the group. Their rebellion against group norms, their efforts to extort the attention of the group and other irritating behavior, in contrast to the compulsive compliance of their more proper peers, provides an opportunity for constructive results for the entire group. The therapist has the opportunity to confront the group's frequent ostracism of the troublesome patient with the possibility that such reactions may be motivated by repressed wishes in oneself that are similar to what the offender is presenting.

On the other hand, rigidity of defensive and behavioral patterns, particularly those which antagonize and alienate others, should be carefully scrutinized when the patient is being screened for admission. The rigidly grandiose patient who needs to be smugly superior, contemptuous, and haughtily disdainful is unlikely to have a bright future in a group. Unless he also presents some redeeming qualities such as insight into, and discomfort with, his behavior, he would either best stick to a dyadic format or would need to make considerable progress in an individual setting before being considered for a group.

Narcissistic patients tend to show nonspecific ego weakness characterized by a low tolerance for anxiety and frustration. The challenges consist of the patient's capacity to undergo the stress of not having his infantile needs immediately gratified, of having to set them aside in deference to another member, or of not being awarded top prize in his competitive strivings with the other patients. If the prospective patient does not have the capacity to tolerate minimal amounts of frustration without resorting to angry withdrawal or serious acting-out, he is unlikely to have a successful group experience. One index of these characteristics may be a very erratic work record or history of transitory relationships. The patient who consistently finds his life situation ungratifying or intolerable and quickly seeks out greener pastures is likely to behave similarly in a group.

Matching the patient to a particular group primarily involves the dimension of deviancy. To what extent will the patient's unusual behavior make him stand out as odd, strange, and a potential object of ridicule: For example, the extremely schizoid patient whose language is stilted and cryptic, whose attitudes are excessively puritanical and rigid, and whose non-verbal mannerisms (like poor eye contact) will make him a deviant member. Also, the narcissistic patient's limited capacity to take on responsibility in his life compared to the fuller lives of his neurotic peers may also emphasize the patient's conspicuous difference. Deviancy is usually the prime contributor to premature termination and is likely to be anti-therapeutic for both patient and group (Yalom & Lescz, 2004).

There is a phenomenon in groups to which narcissistic patients are particularly susceptible and which may best be described as the "six-month crisis". At about this time, group patients begin to perceive with greater accuracy what the eventual fate of their pathology is likely to be in the group. Their expectations of magical cure, the need to give up destructive passivity, the pressure on them to alter their grandiose stance towards others—all tend to come more sharply into focus as the new patient observes the working of the group and the fate of such issues in other patients. Depending on the patient's level of motivation as well as her ego strength, she may opt at this point to take her pathology and run. This crisis may occur sooner and sometimes later but it often tends to peak around the six-month point.

Summary

Group psychotherapy is often the treatment of choice for narcissitic pathology and is frequently used concomitantly with supportive individual treatment, preferably with the same therapist. The rule of thumb is that group treatment should be used when the patient can tolerate being in a group and the group can tolerate the patient, since such patients are frequently self-absorbed, demanding, and troublesome.

Within limits troublesome narcissistic patients may be an asset to the group insofar as they model "true self" behavior for patients who tend to be excessively compliant and submissive. Narcissistic patients' proneness to infantile demands and outbursts, their sense of entitlement and disregard of the needs of others become exposed more clearly in a group than in an individual process. If they are able to tolerate the frustrations and negative feedback that is often elicited, they have the opportunity to begin modifying their self-defeating behavior. Also, as pointed out by the self psychologists, the group provides multiple opportunities for gratifying selfobject needs and experiences. Another type of change process is afforded by the multiple opportunities to identify with the adaptive behaviors of both therapist and peers. Finally, counter-transference reactions to these difficult patients will often be more muted than in individual treatment because the therapist's expectations for change in one particular patient tend to be more attenuated by the presence of a group.

CHAPTER THIRTEEN

The treatment of a narcissistic patient

In the preceding chapter I indicated that group psychotherapy is the treatment of choice for many narcissistic patients, often accompanied by some form of concomitant treatment. The rationale for this point of view is twofold. First, group psychotherapy presents patients with the dual task of not only disclosing their own personal struggles but also requires them to devote an interest in the struggles of others in the group. Second, the group situation challenges patients' needs to be the center of attention and expects them to share the attention of the group and the therapist. Thus the group highlights some of the major character defects of narcissistic persons and provides them with an opportunity to understand better the nature of their own pathology as a first step towards making significant behavior change.

This chapter will be devoted to a detailed description of the group treatment of a narcissistic personality, a married woman in her mid-thirties who was admitted to the hospital after a suicide attempt. The treatment occurred during a bygone era in which long term hospitalization consisted of more than a month or two and this woman was an in-patient for well over a year while she was attending a twice-a-week group. The other five patients in the group, three men and two women, also started their group treatment as in-patients. Unlike many groups that take place in a hospital, these patients were not all on the same unit and hence their extra-group contacts were not extensive or frequent.

In the case presentation which follows, not only will the emergence and treatment of narcissistic problems be illustrated, but the special advantages of an inductive group centered approach will also be demonstrated. Throughout the process, the patient being focused on was seen as participating in a group-wide conflict, that is, she was not the only one in the group afflicted with the wishes and conflicts being addressed—a fact which made it somewhat easier and more palatable for the patient to accept her own egocentrism that began to take on an ego-alien quality.

Treatment process

Marcia began her group treatment in a manner that had characterized her entire thirty-five years of existence: she was a silent observer of the passing scene. A petite and shapely woman who was casually but carefully groomed in slacks and blouse, she sat erectly and impassively in her chair. She seemed to be listening attentively, although one could occasionally detect a slightly haughty, contemptuous smile when another member disclosed a weakness or human frailty The other five patients in the group were all inpatients as she was, and were all more talkative and assertive than she. After the first few sessions of this new group, the patients began to pressure her to join them in sharing her life problems. Politely and quietly, she demurred explaining that she was too anxious and uncomfortable to talk in the group. She added that she was only comfortable in one-to-one relationships and was attending the group only because her hospital doctor had prescribed it. She made it clear that she had minimal expectations from the group and implied that she would be happy to reverse her attitude if we could prove we had something to offer her.

The group members were not put off by her refusal to participate and within the first few weeks she was drawn out about the problems that had precipitated her admission to the hospital. Married at the age of twenty-five to a rising young business man, she gave birth to three children in rapid succession. The birth of each child increased her anxiety, fears of her inadequacy as a mother and homemaker, and feelings of fatigue. Her third pregnancy was unwanted and caused an exacerbation of "queer sensations in the head and chest" and incapacitating fatigue. Convinced that these problems had a physical basis, she sought an examination at the Mayo Clinic where they told her that her problems were psychogenic. For the next three years her functioning slowly grew worse and she finally began once-a-week outpatient psychotherapy in her home town. After six months of no improvement and increasing marital tension, she made a suicide attempt, or possibly a gesture, by taking an overdose of Tylenol.

A few months after her admission to the hospital, she entered the group. She had achieved some symptomatic relief but was still having difficulty in mustering enough energy to carry on her hospital schedule. The group devoted much of one session listening to her eventual account of her marital difficulties in which she described her husband as a well-meaning, energetic, and successful business executive who was unable to tolerate her proneness to fatigue and need for rest. He seemed to love her, but did not fully appreciate her wishes for tenderness and affection.

After a few more interactions with the group, she appeared more interested in greater participation. But we were soon to learn that it was more than just peer pressure that motivated her disclosures. Shortly after an early session when her husband had visited her, she not only frustrated him by not spending the night together at a motel but she informed him of her discussion of their marital difficulties in the group which further incensed him. This was the first of numerous incidents during her first year of therapy when it was necessary to point out her efforts to damage her marriage as well as her treatment. We learned that her wish to regress into a passive state, free of responsibility, was so great that she often had become neglectful of her husband and children. She longed to return to her carefree college days when she was actively courted by many beaus but never seriously involved with anyone. She had serious doubts about her capacity to fulfill the demands of wife and mother.

Within the first two months, the patient's core pathology emerged with considerable clarity. The members were going through its first group-wide sense of frustration about having to share the therapist's time and interest with each other. They felt that their investment had to be split six ways and that their progress could be six times as fast if they had private sessions. Marcia took her usual spectator role but there was little doubt that her silence gave assent to this group theme. Of course, these feelings did not emerge as directly as I describe them.

For example, the group had encouraged one of the male members, Ray, to monopolize a session with a boring recital of the early genesis of his inferiority feelings starting with age three. The therapist interrupted this tiresome monologue and inquired into the group's collusion in keeping Ray talking, even though everyone was obviously bored and uninterested. What emerged was a silent, perhaps unconscious, compact that because of the scarcity of time available to each one and the possibility of being squeezed out, each member was entitled to one full session all to himself. They then vented their frustration and anger at having to be in a group and having to share the therapist's time. This theme of oral deprivation was to recur on several occasions during the life of the group.

At the end of the above session Marcia lingered behind and requested a private interview with the therapist. I told her it would be better if she brought up whatever matter was on her mind in the group. She grimaced angrily and strode off with no further response True to form, during the first fifteen to twenty minutes of the following session she sat quietly, though perhaps more withdrawn than usual. When I was convinced that she was not likely to make a move, I reminded her and the group of her request and wondered why she was not clarifying what she had had in mind. Rather curtly she told me that she had forgotten all about it and, in fact, could not remember what she had wanted to discuss with me. She was clearly dismissing me and the group as utterly useless and insignificant. I told her that her attitude very clearly depicted an important problem: when her demands are not gratified, she not only withdraws in anger but she also conveys "You are beneath my contempt". I speculated aloud that this dismissal may be similar to what occurs between her and her husband that leads to the wall of anger between them and to her frequent and dramatic retreats to her locked bedroom.

I was encouraged by her non-verbal response to my comments. She neither confirmed nor disputed what I had said but her haughty expression disappeared. I thought she may even have enjoyed this confrontation of a pathological pattern. At any rate, she appeared less withdrawn and I felt, correctly, that a beginning exploration of the patient's primary narcissistic conflict was occurring in this hour.

I do not wish to convey, of course, that the group therapy was occurring in a vacuum. There were two facets of her hospital treatment which ran parallel to these group developments. Her hospital doctor was wisely enforcing a program of requiring that she not lie down during the day nor cuddle up in a chair in front of the fireplace. When she insisted on getting insight before she gave up her old ways, he replied, "Change first and we'll work on the understanding later". Second, her husband visited her once or twice a month and together with the hospital doctor and social worker, marital therapy sessions occurred in which the couple's hostile, distancing devices were examined.

During the next few months there were many observations made by the group and the therapist about Marcia's egocentrism. The most obvious was her pattern of not involving herself in the conversation when she was not the center of interest. These confrontations seemed to have some effect since the patient was beginning to regard her narcissism with some degree of distaste. She reported to the group with mixed pleasure and apprehension, some three months after starting, that she seemed to be acting differently around her husband. "I am getting away from the idea that God created the earth and Marcia G". Although no one regarded this as a solid gain, it was significant that she was beginning to view her demandingness and sense of entitlement as ego-dystonic and not as an inalienable right.

During the fifth month of treatment and on the occasion of one of her husband's visits, she reported her mixed feelings about her husband becoming resigned to her long course of treatment. She knew that she reacted adversely to his pressure but she also needed it in order to move. Then she verbalized, perhaps too glibly, her basic problem: "I don't like to share my husband with his business, his civic interests, or with the children. I resent the burdens he places on me of being the young matron who must be the charming and gracious hostess to his friends and business associates". She said she wanted to assume some of these responsibilities, but without the tension and discomfort that she experienced in the past. It was easier for her to recognize her conflict over sharing outside the group, in the "there and then", than in the here and now of the group interaction. The group once again pointed out that her reluctance to share was manifested in the group by her low level of participation when her problems were not being discussed. She made a feeble effort to defend herself which only promoted further pressure from the group about her lack of involvement in hospital activities.

During this interaction she had become decidedly livelier, and when asked if she simply looked upon the hospital as a resort, she gleefully responded that her hospital doctor had chided her in a similar way. I was able to underline the exuberance she showed when people criticized her for her inactivity in the group and in the hospital—a living-out in the group of the gratification she experienced when her husband put pressure on her. Thus, an important facet of her silence in the group was the secondary gain of getting pressured by the therapist or group members to be more active. Being the target of criticism obviously had its narcissistic and possibly masochistic rewards.

About a month after the above session, Don, one of the male members, had to terminate the group because of a move to another city where he was to begin individual treatment. The group now consisted of two men and three women. Among the many reactions to this event was the group's envy of this patient (partly because he was going into individual therapy) as well as a concern about the therapist's fantasied over-readiness to let one of his "brood" depart from the fold before he was ready. Concomitantly there was an unconscious concern that premature departure might occur for any of them if they did not make sufficient progress. In the session following Don's departure, Elsa described how inconvenient it would be for her to return early from an out of town visit with her parents in order to get to the group next time, and wondered about not coming to the group on that day. Bert described how his hospital doctor suddenly shifted an early morning appointment to an inconvenient hour in the late afternoon, and he had a good mind not to show but he guessed he needed the appointment. Marcia took issue with Elsa's attitude, stating that her children were visiting and she would have enjoyed spending the morning with them but felt a responsibility to be here because "the group functions best when everyone is here". She described how well the visit with her children was going. In contrast to the last visit when she was a "quivering mess", unable to do anything with or for her children, she was now genuinely enjoying their company and could interact easily with them. She was delighted this morning when they came running into their bedroom at the motel and she took real pleasure in seeing their happy faces. But, she lamented that her husband is depressed about her slow progress and is tired of being home alone.

I was able to point out the common group theme that one has to subject oneself to all kinds of indignities from the therapist in order to get a few little crumbs of help. Marcia, for example, was overtly expressing a favorable attitude toward the therapy but covertly was denigrating it. I said that her positive feelings towards her children were understandably encouraging to her but for some reason she is not willing to convey this change to her husband. Instead there seemed to be some resentment toward her husband (and probably toward me) about having to make this progress; hence, her difficulty in making clear the progress she is achieving. She then recalled that her husband had very much favored her hospitalization after her suicide attempt and she recalled thinking at the time that his decision to send her far from home meant a wish to get rid of her, and she still harbored angry feelings about it. At any rate, she began to understand her irritation over the external pressure that she grow up, get well, and act like an adult. This interpretation of Marcia's resentment was made in the context of a common group feeling of anger about having to comply with the therapist's demand that they work hard lest they be "kicked out", the way they fantasized Don had been.

The group continued to work on their inordinate expectations of me and others, their angry reactions to frustration, and their special ways of dealing with this anger. Related to this were their fears of closeness. On a meeting following a cancelled session, there were a number of reports of success and accomplishment. Bert had received a raise at work, Ray was successful in his dieting and had lost forty-eight pounds since starting in the group, and Elsa was complimented by her hospital doctor for her initiative in taking on more responsibility. I noted this theme of success and also drew attention to Elsa's change from her usual seat to taking the chair next to mine but she denied that she might be expressing some wish to get closer to me. Marcia stated that sexual thoughts about me were disturbing her. Although she did not elaborate her transference feelings at the moment, she described considerable feelings of rebelliousness against meeting the demands of her husband and hospital doctor. It made her feel good to tell herself that she could keep engaging in her old way of doing things if she so desired: if she wanted an afternoon nap, her husband was not going to make her feel guilty. On the other hand, she said, she knows that she gives her husband double messages. She had spent a very good day with him last weekend and he wanted to discuss his concerns about their eight-year-old daughter whose frequent headaches worried him, but she felt too tired. Instead of telling him she would prefer to do that some other time, she blurted out that she didn't want to have anything to do with him or the children now or in the future. Fortunately she was able to retrieve the situation the next morning and explain that she really didn't mean it. Somehow, she said, she has the need to push people away and pull them towards her at the same time.

I told the group that a cancelled session had stirred growing feelings of missing me and of closeness to me that created some discomfort for them, and that Marcia's sexual feelings, for example, were producing fears of enforced submission and hence rebelliousness. This led to a number of statements about having missed the last session, about liking the group and the therapist, accompanied by considerable uneasiness. The men discussed fears of homosexuality and a generalized concern was expressed about losing their feelings of individuality. Marcia wanted to know why they couldn't just say they liked me without going through these intricate maneuvers. She was able to get a glimpse in this hour of why she had to rebel, argue and attack men when she was beginning to experience feelings of affection.

Towards the end of the first year the group began to work on their feelings about the therapist's impending summer vacation. But this time the group had become comfortable enough to disclose some of their unpleasant secrets: homosexual fears, anti-Semitic attitudes, and one man's history of physical assault on his mother. Marcia began to acknowledge her distaste for her femininity. She envied her two older brothers who were more successful than she, and she envied the two male members of the group who were both well on their way to being discharged from the hospital. She acknowledged feelings of resentment as she listened to them relate successful experiences and was convinced that the therapist must be more proud of their accomplishments than hers.

Within this context, Marcia began working on what she regarded as her hospital doctor's "unfair accusation" that she was sexually seductive. She found little comfort from the group, especially from the men, who thought the observation was indeed correct. They pointed to her quiet come-hither glances, her tendency to play one man off against another (mainly therapist against male members but also hospital doctor *vs.* therapist), and her readiness to cut people off when they got too friendly. Whereas the others in the group expressed more direct anger about my upcoming vacation, Marcia was clearly dealing with such feelings through an aggressive use of sexuality which mainly took the form of conveying her preference for her hospital doctor.

It was somewhat of an improvement over her previous symptoms of fatigue, body-pains, and retreat to bed. She made invidious comparisons between her now-favored hospital doctor and her depreciated group therapist which I interpreted as her reaction to being left. A relevant bit of history emerged when she related that her husband's decision to attend a business convention without her because she was not up to it, was the event which triggered her suicide attempt leading to hospitalization.

By the end of the first year, Marcia was still the quietest person in the group, but she was no longer the silent member. She had become more involved in the lives of the others, more interested in their problems, and could occasionally take the initiative in attempting to draw them out. The special feature of the group, especially for a self-centered, demanding person like Marcia, was the opportunity to observe in vivo the vicissitudes of her pathological problems. As mentioned earlier, the explicit task for the members was not only to report on their own experiences, both outside the group and within it, but also to become engaged in understanding and helping the other group members. She indicated she had begun to modify her excessive preoccupation with herself and she also had a clearer picture of her competitive attitudes with men which contributed to her passivity as a way of dealing with bottled up rage. She was distinctly less satisfied with her demandingness and had made progress in the group in overcoming her passivity.

During the second year of treatment the patient's struggles with her passive demanding wishes continued to be a major focus of her psychotherapy. She began making plans to move into the Topeka community and with each step forward, there were doubts and vacillations, and a resurgence of the wish to retreat to safer positions. The group maintained a steady pressure on her as did her hospital doctor. We frequently challenged her assumption that she had to move out of her comfort zone before taking a new step, that her conscious goal to change frequently got lost in her effort to find comfort. The fact that three of the five patients in the group were already out of the hospital at the beginning of the second year, of course, added to the pressure.

During this second year she was able to maintain and expand her active participation in the group. She became more open in expressing anger and irritation with other members and with the therapist. With considerable fear and reluctance she rented an apartment in town, furnished and decorated it, and began spending nights there by herself. Each move was taken with much trepidation and the wish to find a comfortable nest in a childish relationship with her hospital doctor. When her children visited for the first time in the new apartment, she became more quiet and withdrawn in the group, and attempted to hold on more tightly to the hospital and hospital doctor.

She became the spokesperson in the group for the attitude that one must be cautious about expressing one's feelings because of hypercritical reactions and retaliations from fellow members. Such ideas were mainly associated with real, but also projected (superego), criticism because of persisting wishes to avoid the responsibility to her marriage and children. At the same time, she was repeatedly confronted with the secondary gain of her passivity: the criticism, prodding, and pushing which such behavior engendered provided her with the sense of security that the group members and therapist were really concerned about her.

As Marcia became more active, her aggressive use of sexuality came into greater focus. During a week that I was away, I had encouraged the members to meet without me which they did. As they recounted their experiences afterwards with the leaderless meeting, Bert said he could not understand Marcia's anger at me for being gone inasmuch as they were well prepared for my absence. He became increasingly irritated as Marcia taunted him for acting as though my absence had no effect. Bert then acknowledged being out of sorts today because an attractive woman at work had put him down for no apparent reason. Significantly, Marcia suggested that she might have been flirting with him. Then she talked at some length about having gone to dinner with two men who were "old friends" and she couldn't understand why she was so uneasy. It was the first time she had gone out with anybody beside her husband since coming to the hospital. She was skeptical when I mentioned the possibility of some relationship of this event to my absence. Sex was in the air and Elsa spoke of sitting in the hospital lounge with two men and another woman and they began to engage in heavy petting with the result that they were asked to break it up and one of them got restricted. I commented on the increased sexual feelings in the group when they met without me. Marcia acknowledged that her sexual feelings about me interfered with being able to fully enjoy sexual relations with her husband. It was not long before the two men confessed their strong attraction to Marcia which had grown to uncomfortable proportions in the past week. From here it was not too difficult to establish that Marcia's reaction to my absence (mainly anger) had led to retaliative flirtatious behavior both within and outside the group. She was beginning to see more clearly how she consistently used sex as a weapon against me as well as her husband.

At the start of the third year the group lost Elsa who was continuing treatment at another hospital, thus reducing the membership to two men and two women. (Because of the likelihood that Marcia and Ray would be leaving Topeka during the next year, I decided against adding new members at this time.) Marcia was manifesting increased feelings of confidence in her ability to manage her life. She had successfully weathered the summer with her children in her apartment and was spending less time at the Day Hospital and more time as a volunteer worker at a school for crippled children. Her activity in the group increased concomitantly. She reported that a dramatic reversal of roles had begun to occur in the joint interviews with the husband. She now assumed the active, questioning role in their interaction instead of the reverse. In turn he was becoming more depressed as he was now being faced with a more energetic wife who needed him less to bolster and encourage her. While consciously concerned about him, she was sorely tempted on many occasions to lord her new strength over him, to berate him for his declining sexual powers in contrast to her increased sexual interest. Her awareness of her own tendency to use her seductiveness with other men helped her to control such behavior, particularly when her husband was feeling so vulnerable. There were several instances in the group of more open competitive struggles with men: her feelings of anger and defeat when the men in the group were succeeding or when the therapist made a correct and telling observation about her. She would explain these by saying that she didn't like to hear the truth. But the truth was that she didn't like to hear the therapist.

In the final months of her treatment the remaining four members began to work on termination of the group. Marcia now showed a healthy sense of urgency to return home to be with her children and husband. She was also quite intimately involved and concerned about the lives of the other members. This was especially true in relation to the other female member who was not only some ten years younger but also considerably sicker and for whom she developed a genuinely maternal attitude. She began recognizing and appreciating her husband as a warm, well-intentioned man and tended to dwell less on his insecurities and his occasional insensitivities. She recognized that her need for pampering, compliments, and special attention was unrealistic and excessive and although such wishes had not completely disappeared, they were under much better control. She could now accept warmth from him without starting an argument to create distance.

Despite these significant gains, her need to maintain contact two or three times a week with her hospital doctor throughout the period of her group psychotherapy indicated that she was by no means ready to return home without some continuing help. She was referred to a therapist in her home town and she left with confidence, both hers and ours, that she could maintain her gains.

Discussion

This was a patient with a pronounced narcissistic personality disorder which left her ill-equipped to deal with adult responsibilities. A spoiled, pampered child, she had never learned to achieve gratification by effort or accomplishment. Her relationships were characterized by quietly waiting for others to pay her homage or to prove their love by large doses of attention and concern. Her capacity to invest interest in others was sadly lacking. Confronted with the demands of marriage and children, her strong infantile needs could no longer be satisfied. She wished to have unending attention from her husband, even to the point of his neglecting his business, and she regarded each successive child as another competitor for his affection.

During her three years of treatment, she made very significant strides in overcoming her life-long personality defects. The contribution of her in-patient and Day Hospital treatment which ran concomitantly during most of her group therapy undoubtedly also played an important role in her change. The hospital doctor's firmness in insisting upon her adherence to a work schedule was a necessary part of the treatment structure. Unquestionably the good relationship she maintained with him and her desire to please him helped her to strive for and consolidate adaptive movement instead of lapsing so easily into tempting regressive positions. The joint interviews with her husband helped them both to see how each manipulated and antagonized the other. I believe that no psychotherapy, individual or group, could have succeeded in the beginning without the support of the hospital. She was too hungry for nurturance and too needy for affection to have been able to tolerate one or two hourly appointments per week offered by an out-patient therapist.

What changes occurred in the patient which might be attributed primarily to the group? All of the evidence points to a significant attenuation of her self-centered, demanding strivings. From an ego-syntonic attitude of wishes to be given unending supplies of love and attention without effort, she began slowly to question the justification of her position. She gradually permitted herself to share in the help available in the group without feeling angry and deprived and then finally went on to experience satisfaction in being interested and concerned about the needs of others. In the group we saw a dramatic change in the level and quality of her participation. She moved successively from initial silence and inactivity, then to participation only in terms of her own problems, and from there to a capacity to share the group's time with others without feeling cheated. Furthermore, she became actively concerned about the life problems of the other members. She encouraged the male members in their hesitant and tentative steps towards closer relationships with women. She took a clearly maternal attitude toward a younger woman in the group who was often lonely and confused.

Outside the group, she had begun to change her attitudes towards her husband and children. Mainly, she reported new-found gratification in being a mother to her young children. She was less demanding of her husband's time and attention and was not so ready to view her children as competitors. She was able to become more appreciative of her husband's needs, particularly during his depressed periods. She saw him more realistically as a person who was not able to manage angry feelings easily but she could also recognize and appreciate better his warmth and humor.

Her increased activity in the group was more than simply a manifestation of an attenuation of intense oral needs. She had made a decisive change in her view of herself. This shy, quiet, retiring woman became a person who could assert her own ideas and opinions because of an elevated sense of her own worth. She no longer was plagued with a sense of guilt as an inadequate, unloving mother and hence her self-esteem was significantly raised. She was much less frightened of her angry feelings, particularly since she had some confidence that not all of her dissatisfactions were unwarranted.

There is always the temptation for a therapist to exaggerate his role in a successful patient's gains. We indeed saw some clear-cut changes in her behavior both within and outside the group. But these advances were in the context of support from both the therapist and the hospital doctor. The stability of these changes without such ongoing support is, of course, an open question without a full follow-up study which unfortunately is not available. Furthermore, the patient's need to hold on to her hospital doctor throughout the course of her treatment certainly suggests that the resolution of her neediness was far from complete. But her behavioral changes both within the group and outside of it are more than merely suggestive evidence that she achieved a significant attenuation of her disabling narcissistic behaviors.

To return to the original thesis of this chapter, group psychotherapy was, in my opinion, the treatment of choice for this particular problem. The group presented the patient with the task of sharing the attention of the therapist and the other members. The patient not only had the task of coming to terms with a number of "competitors", but she also needed to develop an interest and concern for the lives of her peers. Thus this task of a willingness to share in the time and attention of the group and to participate in the discussion and understanding of the lives of others hits the narcissistic person directly where she lives. Patients who are unable to tolerate the frustration of the group, as our patient could not do at first, require either individual treatment or, as in the case of Marcia, the adjunctive support of a hospital. However, alteration in the structure of the group like granting her private sessions with the group therapist as she initially requested would probably have been anti-therapeutic. It would have gratified the very wishes to be special that one was attempting to highlight and work out. The frustration of her infantile demands was the motor which drove the treatment. While individual treatment could have eventually gotten to the patient's neediness, it would probably have taken a far longer time. Most patients with this problem in individual psychotherapy experience the gratification of being the sole object of attention in the one-to-one situation. Secondly, the task of developing a concern for others, so lacking in such people, can only be examined in individual therapy from the patient's reports of his current life situation, not in the lively drama of the here-and-now of a group where the patient has to share time and attention.

All people must tame their primitive, infantile urges and find fulfillment while concerning themselves not only with their own needs but also with the needs of others. Group psychotherapy is a modality uniquely suited for helping persons modify earlier patterns of egocentrism, demandingness, and greed in favor of a capacity to give as well as receive. Those individuals who failed to develop the mature patterns necessary for adult living in their original nuclear family are provided a second chance in this family-like experience.

CHAPTER FOURTEEN

The self in groups

In a well-known Woody Allen film, the central character, Zelig, learns early in life that his survival depends on his imitating the characteristics of those around him. Zelig is a caricature of a person. He lacks a solid core of identity and, like a chameleon, assumes the physical characteristics and behavioral mannerisms of people in his immediate environment. While being interviewed by a psychiatrist, for example, he became a mirror image of the thoughtful, attentive therapist. The film may be regarded as a metaphor about social pressures toward conformity with its loss of autonomy and individual freedom, but we may also view the character of Zelig as an example of a severe personality disorder, a man who suffers from an underdeveloped and distorted sense of self. Even more significant is the possibility that this particular developmental defect is evidence for the centrality of the concept of the self. How else might one describe this condition than to assume that what Zelig lacks is the stable organizing mechanism that we call "the self"?

What we learn from this and other fictional works is that a major challenge to all human beings is to form and maintain a definition of one's self, a sense of identity that is continuous with one's past, that provides for stable, predictable behavior, and that is a satisfactory base for future growth. We are rediscovering that an organized sense of self, which includes both conscious and unconscious aspects and subsumes dominant as well as hidden aspects, is basic to personality functioning, and this view has gained increasing recognition mainly as a result of the contributions of object relations theorists and self psychologists.

Psychoanalysis continues to seek a proper place for a concept of self in its structural theory. A major theoretical question is whether the early view of subsuming the concept of self under the rubric of the ego as one of many ego functions or whether it best considered a superordinate concept that transcends the ego, as suggested by recent theorists (Kernberg, 2006). The evolving definitions seem to be, first, that the self is a hierarchical organization of self and object representations, which is more or less stable and cohesive; and second, that it includes the experience of being a separate, defined individual with a sense of identity and continuity.

As the mental health field has given more prominence to some form of self psychology, it behooves group therapists to learn about and contribute to these questions with our own special perspective. Individual psychotherapy has much to teach via the deep exploration of developmental and motivational factors. What therapy groups may lack in providing historical detail, they more than compensate with their attention to the breadth of a patient's reactions to multiple inputs from a variety of personalities. The complex layering of selves which characterizes a single person is richly displayed in a group psychotherapy setting. A group is a laboratory par excellence for observing relationships that derive from various self-organizations, and it has much to teach about how self structures may be modified.

In this chapter, I shall first examine the current theoretical issues regarding the concept of the self. Next, I shall propose some ideas about the specific effect of therapeutic groups on the self and I shall illustrate these views with a clinical example of a group patient whom I treated for over four years.

The self in psychoanalytic theory

The earliest approach to the concept of self was the pioneering contribution of Erik Erikson (1950) when he described the central importance of the development of a sense of identity. He viewed identity as an overall synthesis of ego functions as well a sense of solidarity with group ideals and group identity, the latter being of special importance to group therapists. Thus, he described the onset of an identity crisis in adolescence as occurring when the teenager fails to receive confirmation from significant persons of appreciation of his changing self definition.

Perhaps the most vocal challenge to traditional psychoanalytic theory has come from our British colleagues, whose ideas were not very closely heeded in this country until the seventies. Thanks largely to Otto Kernberg's writings about object relations theory as well as an important article by J. D. Sutherland (1980) on the British object relation theorists we have become more aware of the importance of a theory of the self. Sutherland pulls together the ideas of Balint, Guntrip, Winnicott and Fairbairn, and emphasizes that, despite their highly individual viewpoints, they have in common their belief that a superordinate concept of the self is a necessary addition to existing analytic theory.

These British theorists all stress the first several months of life as a crucial period for establishing a relationship matrix, which organizes and colors subsequent life experiences. When the infant feels valued and accepted for his or her own self by an "ordinary good enough mother", it is being launched onto a developmental path that contains the foundation of basic trust and a sense of harmony with its environment. According to these observers, this all-important, experiencing self was insufficiently represented in traditional ego psychology. Winnicott (1965), for example, believed that a person's view of himself as a unitary being with a sense of his value as a person, and indeed, a reason for wanting to live—are dimensions that are frequently neglected in clinical work and in our theories as well. His formulation of the development of a false self to comply with the demands of an environment that conflicts with the person's evolving true self, expressed in its extreme form by Zelig, conveyed Winnicott's recognition of the central importance of the experiencing self.

To return to our own shores, there are a number of self theorists who have similarly emphasized the early maternal environment as the starting point of their theories. Hans Loewald's (1960) classic paper on the therapeutic action of psychoanalysis emphasized the similarities of a child's earliest experiences and the curative effects of the patient-therapist relationship. The paradigm he uses is the infant's response to the ministrations of the mother: "The bodily handling of the child, the manner in which the child is fed, touched, cleaned, the way it is looked at, talked to, called by name, recognized and re-recognized—all these, and many other ways of communicating to him his identity, sameness, unity, and individuality, shape and mould him so that he can begin to feel and recognize himself as a distinct individual, as separate from others yet with others. The child begins to experience himself as a centered unit by being centered upon" (p. 230). This was written long before self theory became an accepted framework of theory and clinical practice.

A major contributor has been Heinz Kohut (1977) and his formulations on self psychology. Kohut, like Fairbairn (1952) about twenty years earlier, has questioned the basic tenet of the dual instinct theory and has asserted that man is primarily object-seeking as opposed to seeking gratification of drives. According to this view, aggression is not instinctive but a result of the frustrated wish for what Kohut calls an "empathic selfobject". The superordinate role of the self is implied in his concept of the bipolar self, which he defines as the "tension arc" between mastery on one side and ideals on the other.

Kernberg (2006) also proposes a superordinate concept of self as a basic construct. He disavows any connection with the Fairbairn notion of relationship-seeking as a primary motive, and disagrees with both Fairbairn and Kohut on their rejection of the dual instinct theory, but he does view the self as a mediator of numerous ego functions. Kernberg believes that the concept of self is a central structure in that it integrates the self-representations at various stages of development and is "the superordinate organizer of key ego functions such as reality testing, ego synthesis, and above all, a consistent and integrated concept of the self and of significant others" (p. 914).

Jon Allen (2012), an important contributor to attachment theory, posits the development of a secure self based on empathic and responsive parenting which forms the basis for the capacity to mentalize and to establish warm and gratifying relationships in later life. He cites a number of studies that point to the consistency of attachment modes from infancy to adulthood.

Westen and Wilkinson-Ryan (2000) offer a fairly comprehensive summary of the components of identity and self as follows:

> A sense of continuity over time; emotional commitment to a set of self-defining representations of self, role relationships, and core values of ideal self standards; development or acceptance of a world view that gives life meaning; and some recognition of one's place in the world of significant others. (p. 529)

Thus, a superordinate concept of the self has emerged from many sources within psychoanalysis. The arguments in its behalf have been, first, that a concept of experiential self is needed that contains both conscious and unconscious elements, organizes one's primary identity as well as hidden selves and sub-selves, and provides a sense of continuity and stability. Second, it provides emphasis on the self as agent, as integrator of diverse internal motives with a long-range perspective of the past and the probable future. Third, a concept of self permits a greater recognition of the primacy of the early maternal matrix, which gives a stable shape and patterning to later life experiences. And finally, there is an emphasis on the importance of the person's need for and recognition of input from significant others in reinforcing one's self-definition.

The self in therapy groups

Kohut's contributions to self psychology were first applied to therapy groups by Stone and Whitman (1977), who emphasized that group therapists need to recognize the presence of narcissistic transferences and should create an accepting atmosphere for expressing narcissistic needs and wishes for selfobjects in the group. They correctly observed that a therapist's group-wide interventions are usually rejected by the narcissistic patient on the grounds that it violates his sense of being special.

Self psychologists in the group setting recognize the importance of both insight-giving as well as the silent gratification of selfobject needs that often transpire in a group. With regard to the former, Baker and Baker (1993) emphasize helping patients understand their self object needs and how they respond to both gratification and frustration of these needs. At the same time they also stress the necessity to provide a "selfobject surround" that affords gratification of narcissistic needs and strengthens selfobject bonds.

Harwood (1992) views a special advantage of the group setting as providing multiple opportunities for the experience of empathy and acceptance, particularly where rejection or criticism may occur from either a peer or the therapist. The group-as-a-whole often provides a buffer against the negative experience and loss of self-esteem which inevitably occurs in the course of group interactions. Rutan, Stone, and Shay (2007) point to the opportunities presented in a group, particularly for patients whose capacity for empathy is impaired, for them to observe the empathic behavior of others and to begin to identify with these adaptive responses. And Segalla (1998) presents the interesting concept of groupobject, in parallel to the selfobject, which potentially supplies gratification for the "group self". Her idea is that we are hard-wired for attachment, not only to significant individuals, but to groups as well, based on our earliest experiences in being members of family groups. To the extent that such early memories were pleasurable, there developed a need to find such group affiliations.

Thus, for the most part, groups provide patients with numerous opportunities for growth in self-esteem, developing the capacity for empathy, gratifying the need for affirmation of one's identity, and pro-viding the individual with gratifying affiliations with a family type group. At the same time there are inevitable hurtful and negative expe-riences that will occur that hopefully will be used by the therapist and the group to promote learning and growth.

Case illustration

Even though the patient, Gary, had come from a family of professional people, he dropped out of college rather early and became a skilled mechanic. His marriage at age twenty-one was quickly beset by ten-sion and disagreement, and the couple separated five years later after he decided to return to college and pursue professional training. By the time Gary sought psychiatric treatment at the age of twenty-eight, he and his wife had been separated for about two years but were maintain-ing fairly close contact, especially around their five year-old daughter. He was then in his second year of graduate school, depressed to the point of finding it difficult to study, and becoming concerned about doing poorly in school even though he was still in the top ten percent of his class.

Superficially, Gary was a pleasant, likable young man, eager to please and intent on getting a prescribed set of guidelines from the therapist to relieve his depression. For many months he referred to the group as "the class". Behind his friendly exterior was a conviction that people found him unpleasant to be around, although without any clear idea about what they found objectionable. He was quite sensitive to being ignored by others and frequently felt that women found him unattractive once they got to know him. In the group he was indeed capable of infuriating women with his need to subtly depreciate them, but he mainly elicited negative reactions for his inability to fully commit himself to the group. The discrepancy between his overt self and his hidden self, from the point of view both of understanding and treatment, became a major focus of his treatment.

Much of the behavior that Gary showed in his relationships, inside and outside of the group, consisted of a dominant self that was primarily "false". He presented himself as a student, ready and eager to learn whatever lessons the therapist and group members would present in order to help with his depression and his relationships. His presenting problems were his difficulties in reciting in class, and later, his disturbed relationships with women. He presented only enough of his life experiences to convey that he needed help and then expected others to offer advice and rules for better living. He was consciously and unconsciously filled with the conviction that if he revealed his inner self, his sense of weakness and neediness, he would surely be shunned. That hidden self gradually surfaced but only slowly and painfully over a period of years.

The importance of his earliest interaction with his mother was suggested by his highly vulnerable self-esteem, a great reluctance to share his innermost thoughts, and a readiness to assume that others preferred not to be in his company. Despite prominent oedipal problems contributing to this, the severity of these reactions suggested an early sense of unacceptability. I shall describe the patient's treatment under three main rubrics that eventually modified his fragile sense of self: (1) mirroring (2) peer relationships and (3) a sense of belonging.

The mirrored self

Group therapists have long recognized that a group may be thought of as a "hall of mirrors", to use Foulkes and Anthony's (1973) felicitous term, in which the images of each patient's self, sometimes valid and sometimes distorted, get reflected back to the patient from his peers. Pines (1982) made an extensive study of mirroring in groups and emphasized its significant function in providing insight, particularly via "benign mirroring".

One kind of mirroring, reflections and input from the group, affords both the positive responses that provide a necessary holding environment and therapeutic alliance, while also offering the feedback essential for growth and therapeutic movement. Gary, was rather quickly integrated into the therapy group. He was a good listener, asked many questions of others, but presented himself as naive and helpless in the ways of the world. He quickly found nurturance and acceptance within the group but behind his superficial amiability was an unwillingness and inability to commit himself to full affiliation, either with the group or to a female partner. On occasion he would absent himself without notice for one or more group sessions, with the rationalization that his demanding professional work had earned him a much needed rest or vacation. He found it difficult to understand that such behavior was offensive, in part because he needed to see himself as invisible and insignificant in the lives of others. The repeated confrontations by the group of their unwillingness to tolerate his neglect and exploitation gradually validated his sense of importance to his peers, and was the first step in uncovering his need to ward off his feelings of dependency on others.

Gary's dependent self, hidden behind a facade of self-sufficiency, and bolstered by his selecting female partners who pursued him, required a long period of working through before he truly recognized its importance in his life. The therapist was able to confront his counter-dependent reactions both in the transference and in his external life. However, his constant exposure to other patients in the group who wore their dependency on their sleeves, who bemoaned the absence of the therapist during interruptions, and who clearly expressed their anger and depression on these occasions, contributed to his greater appreciation of dependency as a universal wish and gradually lowered his defenses against recognizing his own inner neediness. In the latter phases of his treatment, he was among the first in the group to appreciate his own and others' reactions to object loss. One might say that the group's expressions of their dependency strivings constituted a mirror for him in which to observe his denials of his inner needs.

A second mirroring function, that of providing feedback to others, is often more revealing than the first. It is a commonplace finding that our perception of others is colored by our image of ourselves. We both project and projectively identify in our relationships, and there is at least a little of ourselves in how we see others. Those perceptions then become the source of increased understanding and, hopefully integration, of our unwanted selves.

What is instructive about our patient is the long period of time that elapsed during treatment—over three years—before his reactions to others became significant indicators of internal conflict. During this time he was defensively distant, unable to become truly involved, and notably lacking in empathy and depth of understanding. There were occasions when I believed that his emotional illiteracy was an example of alexithymia, a constitutional inability to make contact with feelings. However, gradually the hoped-for relaxation of defenses did indeed occur, and the patient became a more fully functioning person in the group.

Gary's comments to and about others began to reflect his need for nurturance combined with a profound fear that disappointment was inevitable. For example, in a heated exchange within the group, one of the other men had become incensed at a woman who was complaining about her feelings of having lost the therapist's interest and concern. The male member berated this woman for the repetitive nature of her complaint and for her greed and selfishness. Gary was surprisingly understanding of the other man's internal struggles with unacceptable feelings of being cheated of time and attention. Gary gently confronted this man with his need to criticize the female patient in the service of denying his own sense of neediness which he was projecting onto her. This helpful interpretation could never have occurred without his having made contact with his own frustrated dependency needs.

Peer relatedness

All writers recognize the importance of the so-called "peer transference". Yalom and Lescz (2005) put a major emphasis on the interpersonal learning that is derived from inter-member interactions. Early writers have tended to view peer interactions as an important stage in the development of a group once the group has come to terms with its dependent and counter-dependent transferences toward the therapist. Grunebaum and Solomon (1980) proposed that group psychotherapy be reconceptualized so that the primary task of the therapist is that of fostering an atmosphere in which fruitful inter-member interactions occur. Indeed, this is the model used by Yalom and Leszcz (2005) in promoting insight into members' self-defeating behaviors, primarily based on feedback by their peers.

Gary's typical response to males was to be conciliatory and deferential, seeking above all to gain approval from a paternal imago who he expected not to be readily pleased with him. It required many months before he could question any of my interventions. Even more striking was his masochistic attitude toward another male member who consistently taunted him with his passivity and his inarticulateness about feelings. In the course of his exposure to these criticisms, and as his self-esteem began to grow mainly based on feelings of acceptance in the group, Gary clearly shifted in his ability to protect himself, both inside and outside the group, and no longer remained a defenseless victim. He gradually began to manifest a sense of being this man's equal and clearly showed that he no longer was intimidated by sarcastic attacks. The group's positive feedback for his new, more mature responses reinforced this pattern.

Beginning evidence of his assertiveness occurred in the context of a group-wide feeling that their contributions to the group were unwelcome which occurred after a vacation interruption. The male member, John, who often criticized Gary for his passivity observed that Gary was being intimidated by the fear of his (John's) aggressiveness. Their exchange became somewhat testy with Gary saying that undoubtedly John would like to see him take a back seat in the group and then asserted that his problem in talking in the group had nothing to do with him. Rather, it was a transitory feeling he was experiencing in the context of what was transpiring in the group. This exchange was the start of his self-assertion in the group.

Sense of belonging

Most writers agree that the treatment relationship in itself, whether individual or group, has an inherently therapeutic effect. Within individual psychotherapy there has been increasing emphasis on the importance of the relationship to the therapist, as well as the acquisition of insight, in producing change. The new experience of the patient finding another person who remains interested and committed despite being exposed to the darker, less pleasant sides of the patient's personality contributes to a sense of greater self-acceptance. Often referred to as a "corrective emotional experience", it is recognized by most group therapists as a major contributor to patient change.

Harwood (1983) stresses the strengthening effect of becoming integrated into a group. The process of assimilating a new member is always fraught with uncertainty for the therapist, new patient, and group. However, once a member has passed the initiation rites, the supportive aspect of being valued, found needed and desirable by others, and being capable of contributing to others leads to a considerable rise in self-esteem. In addition, group members, unlike the therapist, are not being paid for their interest and commitment. Depending on his personal style and treatment philosophy, the group therapist will usually react in a somewhat more muted way than will the patients. Hence, group members individually and as an entity are capable of supplying highly positive and validating input.

Scheidlinger (1980) observed that the strengthened feeling of identity associated with the sense of belonging is a necessary first step for a patient beginning to work in a group. He cited Erikson's idea that identity is not only a subjective sense of the self but includes as well a synchronization with a group identity, "a social collective with a sense of shared human qualities, a commonality with others, an ideology, goals, and a group's basic ways of organizing experience" (p. 222). To the extent that the individual is able to integrate his sense of individuality and uniqueness with a group's norms, his sense of identity is enhanced.

At one point, the entire group was involved in heightened anxiety and tension around the possibility that one of the patients, a woman struggling with the crisis of being discharged after a long-term hospitalization, would consume all of its available time. These feelings were hidden behind objective appreciation of the woman's real needs and reaction formations that even exaggerated her distress. As the group's fear of deprivation and loss because of this patient's special needs were gradually acknowledged, the patients could permit their own needs to be expressed clearly and intensely. Whereas in the beginning Gary tended to exclude himself from these group emotions, they became a clear part of his experience of himself.

During Gary's tenure in the group, he had three serious relationships with women, each of which lasted almost a year and, despite exciting and optimistic beginnings, they ultimately failed. When the initial infatuations with these women wore off, there was a gradual loss of interest and, eventually, an alienation. "We have nothing to talk about" was his frequent refrain. Initially, there were inhibiting oedipal factors that interfered, and later the fear of exposing his neediness and dependency deterred his commitment to these women. The main cause of the problem, which became more apparent over time, was his expectation of being viewed as unlovable. Whenever his current girlfriend became preoccupied with her own inner struggles, he experienced an overwhelming sense of rejection and angrily wished to retreat. He became convinced that she had seen a defect in him associated with his weak and dependent hidden self and therefore was shifting her romantic interests elsewhere. The all-important change that occurred was his active perseverance in the relationship. He began sharing his feelings with his partner and made encouraging strides in giving up his need for constant reassurance.

This positive change occurred mainly because of the patient's gradual assimilation of the conviction that exposing his childish, needy self does not automatically mean he will be abandoned. I believe it was his experience of becoming even more accepted and integrated in the group following a significant self-exposure that was mainly responsible for his progress. The group insisted that he not withdraw from them, that he not withhold information about his relationships until it is too late, and that he do more than fend off their questions when he seeks to get help. Moreover, they and the therapist gave him positive recognition when he was able to modify his characteristic self-defeating patterns.

Gary changed significantly both outside and within the group. There was a clear difference in the quality of his relationship with the woman with whom he ultimately formed a stable relationship, particularly in his capacity to work with her on his feelings about their interaction. Even more striking was the fact that he selected someone quite different from his past romantic choices. She was an accomplished woman with a clear investment in her own career and, most important, was not in hot pursuit of him, a pattern based on his easily threatened sense of acceptability. His current friend is clearly devoted to him and he has become better able to tolerate greater mutuality in the give-and-take of a more mature relationship.

The parallel change within the group was his ability to initiate communication about his experiences and needs. In the past he exhibited an exasperating inarticulateness and inability to reveal more than the tip of the iceberg about his inner life. In the final stages of treatment, he was willing to expose hidden aspects of himself, and understanding his difficulties became possible.

The prolonged period required for this effect to occur was both typical and atypical. We know that structures laid down over many years should not be expected to change over a weekend. But Gary's pattern of defenses, particularly his passivity and withdrawal, contributed to slowing the process of change. During the course of his four years of treatment, he had seriously considered terminating at certain points, particularly when his presenting problems of depression and work inhibition had subsided. However, with the encouragement of the group and the therapist, he persisted, and has been able to reach his new goal of finding a gratifying love relationship.

In summary, the concept of self has been claiming increasing attention of psychotherapists for several decades. Both within and outside of self psychology, there is increasing recognition that a super-ordinate self, a hierarchical organization of self- and object-representations, is necessary in order to: (1) incorporate the existence of an experiential self which acts, plans, and takes initiative; and (2) integrate the diverse and often hidden sub-selves that develop during one's development. There are special features of group psychotherapy that particularly contribute to the emergence, growth, and integration of this basic structure of the human psyche. Of particular importance are the effects of being mirrored by others as well as offering mirroring to others; the opportunity to experience more mature and gratifying peer relationships; and heightened self-esteem bolstered by a sense of belonging and acceptance by one's peers.

CHAPTER FIFTEEN

Narcissistic leadership in groups

Narcissistic leaders in groups are capable of impeding progress of their patients and, at worst, can produce iatrogenic effects. Significant interferences may occur when the therapists are unable to tolerate the expression of negative transferences and when they need to be idealized by their patients. The rare therapist who is a malignant narcissist is capable of inflicting severe damage by sadistically exploiting the group to satisfy his own pathological needs. Less severe interferences consist of inhibition in making transference interpretations, reluctance to seek out training or supervision, and a difficulty in protecting patients against being scapegoated. All therapists have some degree of proneness to these problems although hopefully to a minimal degree.

The effect of the therapist's personality on the psychotherapy process has become a subject of increasing interest and study by dynamic therapists. With the growing acceptance of both object relations theory and relational psychology, particularly in dyadic treatment, a decided shift has taken place from a predominant focus on the pathology of the patient to an emphasis on the interaction between the personalities of both patient and therapist. This shift has variously been referred to as a move from a one-person to a two-person psychology and as a focus on intersubjectivity or the mutual effect of one psyche upon another, and the "analytic third" (Ogden, 1994) growing out of the interaction of the two participants. No longer is it sufficient to examine the contribution of the therapist's personality solely in terms of his or her countertransference; rather there is an increasing emphasis on how the character, attitudes, and personalities of the two participants mutually influence each other and thus impact both the process and the outcome of the treatment.

In the early days of psychoanalysis narcissism was a pejorative term because it indicated that libidinal energy was being directed toward the self rather than towards others. But as the concept has become less instinctually based and is now understood mainly in terms of relational factors, there has been a growing recognition that narcissism is a necessary constituent in all personality functioning, shared by all humans, and is involved in the need for the regulation of self-esteem. This function is as vital psychologically as are the physiological functions of the regulation of temperature, respiration, and heartbeat. The nine items listed in DSM-IV under narcissistic personality disorder— including grandiosity, need for admiration, sense of entitlement, lack of empathy—may all be sub-headed under the heading of pathological mechanisms or defenses in attempting to regulate one's self-esteem.

The negative aspect of the term refers to pathological methods of regulating self-esteem, but there are also healthy and normal means of exercising that function. Pathological narcissism manifests itself in self-absorption, difficulties with empathy, excessive need for admiration, rage reactions and a host of other characteristics that in a therapist would at best interfere with, or at worst, be destructive to a therapy process. Healthy narcissism, on the other hand, is reflected in a stable sense of one's worth based on realistic achievement, the ability to recover quickly from disappointment or failure, and finding reassurance and support in one's relationships when needed—personality traits in a therapist that would facilitate the therapy process.

In the same way that there are forces in a group psychotherapy situation that tend towards both dilution as well as intensification of the transference (Chapter Eight), there are similar forces in a group that tend to either exacerbate or minimize the therapist's counter-transference reactions in general and narcissism in particular. The presence of a group of patient "observers" who witness the therapist's interaction with other group members, and the influence of the contagion effect in which patients' negative transferences are augmented by mutual stimulation, are some of the pressures that increase the therapist's narcissistic vulnerability. On the other hand, patients in a group are capable of imposing a dose of reality upon distorted perceptions of other patients, and not infrequently members are capable of supplying needed support to therapists when pressures on them are intensified.

The object of this paper is to examine the effects of the group therapist's narcissism, both pathological and benign, on the functioning of the therapy group. Since there is a dearth of material on this topic in the group psychotherapy literature and since the issues are actually quite similar in other areas, I shall be referring to contributions from individual treatment as well as narcissistic leadership in larger systems like organizations and national groups.

Literature review

Winnicott's (1965) seminal formulation on the true self—false self dichotomy is particularly relevant to our topic. He observed that the parents' own pathological needs are to a greater or lesser extent imposed upon their children. As a result, the development of the child sometimes becomes distorted in the direction of complying with parental demands at the expense of being in touch with her own true self, that is, the spontaneous and free expression of interests, ambition, and talent. The more negative outcomes of such parental pressures eventuate in offspring with "as if" personalities. Winnicott observed that those individuals who themselves have developed into such false self personalities are usually ill equipped to become psychotherapists because their limited awareness of their own emotional lives and their need to keep authentic, spontaneous impulses under marked repression make it difficult for them to permit their patients to move in the direction of discovering their true selves.

Based on his observation of former psychoanalytic candidates whose psychoanalytic treatment failed to resolve their narcissistic resistances, Kernberg (1975) emphasized the frequent feeling of boredom and disillusionment with doing intensive therapeutic work exhibited by such professionals. They often seek to do brief intense treatment, characterized by "instant intimacy" rather than become involved in a lengthy, in-depth relationship with a patient. In selecting prospective therapists he stressed the importance of evaluating the quality of their object relationships, that is, the depth of their personal relationships with others. He made the astute observation that object relations in depth involve not only libidinal investments but aggressive investments as well and "they involve the capacity to love well and to hate well ..." (p. 237). Therapists who have not modulated their own narcissistic defenses will find it difficult to experience the empathy and commitment necessary for working effectively with their patients.

Saretsky (1980) emphasized that analysts with over-idealized self images place expectations upon themselves that are impossible to achieve and this unconscious pursuit of perfection prevents them from experiencing the full range of drives and affects in their interaction with patients that are necessary in order to respond appropriately to the patient's behavior. Such therapists may expect themselves to understand their patients fully and immediately, believe they should never feel angry or have any other negative emotion, should never be bored or intolerant, and never experience despair or hopelessness. These excessive self expectations not only hamper the functioning of the therapist but inevitably place undue burdens upon the patient, much like the insecure mother who requires her baby to be happy and responsive at all times.

Welt and Herron (1990) in their book *Narcissism and the Psychotherapist* treat this topic in considerable detail. Like Saretsky they observe that most therapists find it difficult to examine their own egocentric propensities on the grounds that their most desired self-image is that of the "selfless helper". Insofar as therapists need to nurture that illusion, they shortchange both themselves and their patients. To the extent that therapists can pay attention not only to the needs of their patients but to their own self interest as well, they are presenting a model of healthy narcissism for their patients to emulate. Therapists who are not unduly self-sacrificing, who attend to their own personal lives as well as to those of their patients, who do not feel that they must be available to their patients no matter what the cost to themselves—provide their patients with a good role model and the best treatment experience.

Observations by psychotherapists who study the personality of leaders in organizations as well as nations offer additional insight into the effect of narcissistic leadership on these systems. Kernberg (1985) believes that the most serious and damaging type of pathological character structure in a leader of an organization is that of the narcissistic personality disorder. Not infrequently such people are strongly motivated to attain positions of power and prestige, not because of their interest in improving the institution, but rather to achieve control over others and to seek the adulation and idealization of their staffs. Typical pathological reactions consist of conscious and unconscious envy of the success of others, the difficulty in accepting capable, autonomous work from one's subordinates, envy of the strength of the professional identity and convictions of one's staff, and the need to cultivate a group of devalued "yes men". The staff is often called upon to expend much energy in bolstering the leader's self-esteem, which places a significant drain on their creative resources.

Both Jerold Post (1993) and Vamik Volkan (1980) deal with the psychology of political leaders who manifest pathological narcissism. Post emphasizes that the mirror hungry personality of the leader nicely complements the idealization hunger of his followers. As in organizations, the major psychological functions of individuals who surround the narcissistic leader are to maintain the self-esteem of the authority figure. At the same time because of the leader's sense of entitlement, he is given to self-righteous outbursts of rage when his ambitions are thwarted.

Volkan distinguishes between the narcissistic national leader who is reparative as opposed to destructive. The former strengthens the cohesiveness and stability of his own grandiose self by idealizing a group of followers whom he then includes in an idealized extension of himself. In contrast, the destructive leader engages in a splitting operation in which he attacks a segment of the population who represent disowned and devalued aspects of himself and thus reinforces his split-off grandiose self. In most instances there is a mixture of the two styles and very rarely can the reparative style be maintained over any significant period. Both approaches tend to induce a collective regression among the followers.

Turning now to the research literature, Lieberman, Yalom, and Miles (1973) made an extensive study of seventeen encounter groups and paid particular attention to ferreting out casualties, that is, regressions that were serious, not transient, and were related to the group experience. They made the interesting discovery that three of the group leaders (less than twenty percent) produced six of the sixteen casualties (almost forty percent) and the six casualties all reported the experience of being cruelly attacked by the leader. These leaders tended to be charismatic, intrusive, and confrontive. They could be quite supportive if the members progressed at the leader-prescribed rate but those who failed to meet his standards were treated in a derogatory, demeaning way. These high-risk leaders were reacting to their participants based on whether the member was performing in a way that would reflect favorably upon the leader, especially since their work was being carefully scrutinized by a research group. Those participants who were unable to meet the leader's narcissistic needs were summarily dismissed as being of no value.

The present writer (1985), using the data of the Menninger Psychotherapy Research Project, made a special study of the differences between six therapists who were rated by the researchers as showing a low level of skill in contrast to seven therapists who fell into the high skill category. I did an impressionistic study of the extensive observations offered by the researchers in describing the strengths and weaknesses of each therapist. On the basis of this data I observed certain expectable differences insofar as the "highs" were better able to convey warmth and acceptance towards their patients, were less over controlled and inhibited in the treatment setting, and were less prone to reacting in an impulsive, often thoughtless, manner.

However, the overriding factor differentiating the "highs" and "lows" fell under the syndrome of narcissism. The low-skilled therapists frequently applied techniques in which they had a special interest rather than the treatment that was most appropriate to the patient. One analyst failed to reverse a downward spiral induced by the intensive uncovering method of analysis that the patient could clearly not tolerate and his excessively long persistence in his mistake was based on an unrealistic and exaggerated sense of his therapeutic prowess. The "highs" were capable of finding gratification in their work through a steady and consistent application of their approach determined by the needs of the patient in contrast to the "lows" who were frequently unable or unwilling to engage in that kind of steady commitment. My conclusion in this study was the following: "The lows often showed an insufficient capacity for concern and empathy, were easily frustrated when gratification was not readily forthcoming, and often became authoritarian and controlling. They tended to care more about their own performance than about the plight of the patient and were hampered by an attitude of therapeutic omnipotence" (p. 18). These findings, based upon an extensive study of these therapists and their treatment, are consistent with the clinical and theoretical expectations reported by other writers.

Manifestations of pathological narcissism

Since narcissistic defenses exist in all individuals on a continuum, ranging from the adaptive to the mildly pathological to the malignant, I shall first present the grossest manifestations of narcissistic leadership and later describe more benign reactions to which all therapists are prone to some degree.

Encouraging a false self

Winnicott's important contribution regarding the development of the true and false self has sensitized us not only to how parental demands and expectations have a negative effect on a child's development but we are now more aware of how therapists' neurotic needs, particularly their narcissism, produce significant inhibitions in the therapeutic process. Therapists with marked narcissistic vulnerabilities find it difficult to tolerate negative transferences, criticisms and devaluations, and will usually communicate their unhappiness with such reactions. Sometimes such communications take the form of the therapist being unduly nurturing, failing to confront the patient with acting out or other significant resistances, and in general trying to avoid any behavior toward the patient that could elicit a negative response.

Among the special prerogatives that group therapists possess, and one which has the potential for considerable abuse, is the possibility of encouraging the group to scapegoat an offending member. In one group, for example, where the therapist had great difficulty in tolerating any criticism toward himself, a patient consistently and with increasing vehemence pointed to the flaws in the therapist's leadership. The therapist failed to recognize that this individual was the spokesman for the negative pole of the group and rather than interpret this group transference, the therapist indicated by his silence and the tightening of his facial muscles that he was displeased with these attacks. As a result, the group felt encouraged to scapegoat the offending individual and eventually this patient was extruded from the group. One of the most important maintenance functions of the group therapist is to prevent such scapegoating but in this instance the therapist, because of his own narcissistic vulnerability, made no effort to interpret the scapegoating of the member who carried the negative affect for the group. Such a weapon is readily available to the group therapist and sophisticated group therapists are wary of falling into this counter-transference trap.

An even more extreme manifestation of the same tendency may be seen in those therapists who consciously or unconsciously encourage their patients to flatter or otherwise idealize them. I recall attending a professional program in which a group therapist unabashedly read a number of letters from his group therapy patients offering testimonials to his wonderful qualities as a clinician and as a human being. The therapist's grandiosity was exceeded only by his insensitivity to the difficulties he was perpetrating.

The need to see progress

An important facet of the grandiosity of narcissistic therapists is to see themselves as perfect in every way, talented, and highly effective. Likewise, their patients are expected to comply with this self-image, to perform in a manner befitting an ideal patient, and show results consistent with the therapist's view of himself. When patients comply with these expectations and manifest the "as-if personality" dictated by the therapist's self-image, they are more than likely to develop a tenuous outcome that is maintained only as long as they are receiving some kind of positive reinforcement from the therapist.

As demonstrated by Lieberman, Yalom and Miles (1973), woe unto the patient who either is unable or unwilling to play the game according to a narcissistic therapist's expectations. These are the people who get ignored, are dismissed, or worse still, are openly attacked for their ineptitude or obstreperousness in doing the work.

It is not long before a therapist learns that the work of helping people change using talking treatment is usually not characterized by easy successes or immediate gratification. Particularly in the field of treating personality disorders, small gains are not readily achieved and usually require long term commitment by both therapist and patient. Most narcissistic therapists either leave the field entirely or begin a long search for new methods that offer the promise of a quick fix and vainly chase after each new fad appearing on the horizon. They are the people who are most prone to professional burnout and often feel quite disillusioned about their careers.

Malignant narcissism

Kernberg (1989) has proposed a diagnostic category for those patients who show characteristics of the narcissistic personality disorder that are accompanied by antisocial behavior. He assigns the apt label of malignant narcissist to these individuals and views them as holding an intermediate position on the continuum from narcissistic personality at one extreme and antisocial personality disorder on the other. Malignant narcissists display ego-syntonic sadism and a paranoid orientation, although a few may have the capacity for concern for others as well as the capacity to experience guilt.

They are people whose pathological grandiosity has been infiltrated by "the earliest sadistic superego pre-cursors" and hence a largely ego-syntonic sadism exists alongside a paranoid orientation. Fortunately, such people usually do not gravitate towards the mental health professions but tend to become members of violent fringe groups or terrorist organizations.

A respected senior group therapist presented a paper at an AGPA conference on the iatrogenic effects of group psychotherapy and courageously disclosed his experience over many years in a group conducted by a charismatic, but evil group therapist. This former patient described the therapist as having developed an "abusive, cult-like practice". The treatment started as conventional group therapy but evolved into a destructive and abusive pattern which included the following: the therapist had sex with most of his female patients within the group session itself; charged fees as high as $150 per patient per ninety-minute group session; humiliated patients by having them stand naked in front of the group with demeaning signs around their necks; fined patients exorbitant amounts for even minor lateness which he then pocketed. This therapist has long since fled the country and a few years ago a few of his former patients banded together and lodged a formal complaint against him. The head of the ethics committee of his national professional association was quoted as saying that it was the worst case he had heard of in the twenty years that he has been investigating professional misconduct. One is hard pressed to fathom why these high functioning professionals tolerated such flagrant abuse for this long a period.

The conventional wisdom regarding abusive behavior by therapists, particularly sexual abuse, is that it is much less likely to occur when a patient is a member of a therapy group than in a one-to-one treatment. Only a malignant narcissist or antisocial personality is capable of flagrantly breaking all the taboos. While this case was certainly extraordinary, I have little doubt that less extreme forms of abuse get perpetrated in groups in which ethical and legal standards are flouted by individuals with defective superegos. Therapists, whether individual or group, frequently are granted immense trust and power by their patients that occasionally get exploited by therapists to gratify their own pathological needs—to exercise power, to sadistically abuse others, to pursue greedy, acquisitive aims, and strive for sexual domination. The power to heal is always exercised in the shadow of the power to harm.

Benign manifestations of therapists' narcissism

There are a variety of relatively common difficulties that therapists manifest which interfere to a greater or lesser extent in treatment. But one must also remember that some mild or benign narcissistic character-istics could be useful in furthering the therapeutic process. Permitting oneself to become the target of a patient's transferences often involves translating metaphors about other significant figures in the patient's life and applying them to yourself, often a threat to novice therapists who must not allow themselves to be that important. Likewise, accepting the idea that you may be the most important figure in a patient's life, at least for a certain period of time, stimulates some degree of grandiosity in the therapist. If the grandiosity neither needs to be suppressed nor threatens to get out of control, the therapist can be reasonably comfort-able in dealing with the transferences, both positive and negative, in a constructive way. This benign narcissism is particularly challenged in a group situation where the transferences from several patients, fre-quently in tandem with each other, impinge upon the therapist.

Inhibition in interpreting

There was a disagreement in the literature regarding a therapist's most likely counter-transference response to the idealizing transference of the patient. Kohut (1984) believed that premature interpretations of ide-alization result from discomfort of therapists with the patient's praise and adulation and hence they encourage the patient to take back the projection prematurely by means of confrontation or interpretation. On the other hand Kernberg (1984) contended that therapists more often than not enjoy the compliments attributed to them and sometimes even believe them, with the result that the patient's transference idealiza-tion may go un-interpreted. My observation in the supervision of group therapists is that the majority of them in the early phases of their work experience a significant difficulty in recognizing latent transferences, both positive and negative. The idea that one might be the center of the group's attention feels excessively self-centered especially to the novice therapist. In the usual social situation it is considered poor form to think of yourself as having a special and dominant influence upon a group of which you are a part. The difference between therapy groups and an ordinary social group or work group is that the therapist assumes a special transference-inducing role by virtue of having a unique status. Also since the therapist is usually less transparent than any of her patients, she becomes the target of the patients' projections. Also, thinking of oneself as the central person in the group may constitute a threat to an unconscious and unacceptable wish to be the center of attention.

A corollary of the same reaction is the therapist's fear of ridicule and humiliation by group members when she makes an interpretation of the transference to the leader. When group therapists begin interpreting the group's transference to them, it is not uncommon for their patients to declare "what makes you think you're that important?" or "why do you always believe that we are thinking about you?" The fear of such a reaction or the difficulty in dealing with it, even when it is clearly a manifestation of group resistance, is consistent with the therapists' own self-critical tendencies about attributing too much importance to themselves. Adding to this anxiety is the treaters' unconscious concern that their patients may discover a hidden and unacceptable grandiosity in their therapist.

On the other hand, there is also the tendency on the part of some narcissistic therapists to pull for a focus on themselves from the patient group, even when there is scant evidence for such interpretations. These individuals are not only comfortable with their need for attention, and probably oblivious to it, but they permit their craving for such reactions to override the needs of their patients. It is possible that one of the unconscious motives for group therapists to gravitate toward group work is the opportunity to exhibit one's skills in front of an audience. Such wishes are not pathological in themselves, and may even be adaptive, provided they do not interfere with an optimal responsiveness to one's patients.

The challenges faced by therapists' narcissism are illustrated in the following vignette. A narcissistic male patient appeared in a group session and with great satisfaction told the group that he had met a mental health professional who had referred to their leader as a "world class therapist". The group therapist was momentarily flattered and tempted to accept this idealization as factual, but quickly regained his bearings and encouraged, first the patient and then the group, to elaborate their reactions to this exalted evaluation. The patient was a spokesman in the group for defensive over-idealization and was gradually able to understand better how placing others on a pedestal helps him to avoid the fear that people on whom he depends may have clay feet.

The effect of the therapist's grandiosity

There is a fairly general agreement in our field that many professionals who practice group therapy are inadequately trained in this modality. There may be several reasons for this state of affairs including the sense that training in individual therapy provides one with license to practice all of the sub-specialties, a fallacy that the group psychotherapy field needs to challenge whenever possible. But another contributing factor may be the grandiosity of some therapists who believe that their benevolent presence in a group will have a curative effect on their patients. These people are imbued with a sense that they have special therapeutic powers and their mere presence is capable of producing a desired effect. These are the therapists who do not seek out the training, supervision, and consultation that could enhance their skill in dealing with their group patients.

There are a variety of subtle manifestations of grandiosity that often appear in the therapeutic setting that are mainly associated with a sense of omniscience. One is the tendency that some therapists exhibit by delivering oracular pronouncements, which invite unquestioning acceptance. Such therapists present themselves as not only experts in the field of human behavior but as individuals endowed with infallibility. One of the problems with the original, now defunct Tavistock method of group psychotherapy (Chapter Six) was that the interpretive paradigm consisted of delivering long lecturettes after the therapist had diagnosed the common group tension and each individual's mode of dealing with it, which enhanced the therapist's appearance of being all-knowing.

Ideally, therapists should approach the task of treatment with a sense of being engaged in a voyage of discovery in which they use their expertise to add new perspectives to the patient's view of his life and relationships. There is a need for the therapist, not only to tolerate ambiguity, but also to be aware that she need not have all the answers at her fingertips. Narcissistic therapists have difficulty in disclosing their own doubts or uncertainty about their understanding. For example, these therapists often have a problem in encouraging the patient to elaborate a statement that appears important but which is patently incomplete. The patient may be reluctant to go into detail for defensive reasons, and the therapist colludes by having to appear omniscient. Such therapists have to convey to their patients that nothing ever takes them by surprise and that whatever unfolds in treatment is completely expected. The all-knowing therapist may provide a measure of comfort to the idealizing patient, but also impedes personal growth and development.

Finally, some therapists are prone to subtle and unnecessary boasting about occurrences in their personal lives. A therapist who changed his office within an organization was asked about the reason for the office change. The therapist found it necessary to provide the patient with the knowledge that he had received a promotion, a fact that was entirely gratuitous and unnecessary. Such boasting sends a message to the patient that the therapist needs to be mirrored.

Negative transferences in groups

Therapists with relatively mild narcissistic vulnerabilities may function well until the group begins to cast doubts on the therapist's competence, thus threatening his self-esteem. In general this occurs when there is a build-up in the group of negative transference. Such reactions are not uncommon and are most often seen in response to interruptions, bringing in new members, frustration of dependency needs, etc. Frequently anger and hostility are expressed indirectly by acting-out or by displacement of affect from the therapist to a peer and it often requires interpretive work to redirect such feelings toward the therapist.

When such a development occurs, the group's anger, criticism, and attacks produce a special strain on all therapists but particularly on therapists with deep seated doubts about their own adequacy as treaters. Such attacks mobilize fears of failure, concerns about humiliation, and may even elicit anxiety about one's negative counter-transference reactions. These dynamics are common to both individual and group psychotherapists but they are more accentuated in a group situation for two reasons. First, a group-wide frustration and anger may appear to the group therapist as a valid and realistically justified reaction simply because of the number of individuals who are manifesting it. The transference component of the group's attacks and criticism are more difficult to recognize when they come from more than one person since we are accustomed to gauging the reality of an event in terms of consensual validation. "Fifty million Frenchmen can't be wrong". The therapists' capacity to assess the validity of the group's criticisms tends to be compromised by the confluence of the number of voices and the therapists' readiness to find themselves lacking.

A second special stressor is the fact that the therapist is performing in a public arena. Insofar as therapists have an exhibitionistic need to demonstrate their excellence, their benevolence, and their curative powers—negative responses by their patients may indeed strain their fragile self-images. As demonstrated by Lieberman, Yalom, and Miles (1973), narcissistic therapists tended to counterattack and demean their patients when the latter did not behave in accordance with their self-image needs. Other defensive reactions may consist of the therapist taking flight by withdrawing emotionally from the group or possibly not hearing the negative communication. When group therapists are attacked or criticized in this kind of public setting, whether the negative expressions are justified or not, there is an increased pressure on their narcissistic vulnerability.

Overreaction to a patient's narcissism

One of the most useful features of group psychotherapy is that it highlights the patient's egocentrism and self-absorption. Under ideal circumstances, narcissistic patients begin to observe such behavior in themselves or other members and are able to gently and supportively confront their fellow members with such manifestations as failures of empathy, their lack of commitment to the group, or tendencies to monopolize. The therapist has a key role in attempting to model the tact and timing necessary to deal with such behavior that is often irritating and even disruptive. However, insofar as the group therapist struggles with her own narcissistic issues and, in particular, experiences unconscious conflicts and defenses in this area, she will be prone to be excessively critical and prematurely confrontive of the patient's defects.

An example was the occurrence of an excessively early confrontation of a highly narcissistic man who was a newcomer to the group. He introduced himself by relating that, now in his third marriage, his wife was beginning to complain about his neglect of her, much as his previous spouses had done. He callously described his enjoyment of drinking with the boys after work and how much he needed his golf game for relaxation, finding it difficult to understand why his wife wished to deprive him of such innocent pleasures. The therapist's obvious counter-transference irritation with this man led him to the un-empathic intervention of requesting that the women in the group let him know about how it would feel to be married to him. Assuming that most therapists would understand that active interventions of this sort needed to be postponed until a therapeutic alliance has been established, one may wonder whether the therapist's personal issues were interfering.

Coping with one's narcissism

There is increasing acknowledgment in the field that the way thera-pists regulate their self-esteem is of great importance in the therapeutic relationship. Not infrequently the analyst permits the patient's aggres-sion to get displaced onto outside targets and fails to handle it within the treatment relationship. In analytic institutes, for example, there are always ready-made opportunities to find external bad objects, often persons with different theoretical approaches. When the training ana-lyst colludes with his patient in displacing the negative transference onto others, a symbiotic, mutually gratifying relationship may ensue. The narcissistic tendency towards splitting and idealization is a com-mon pitfall not solely confined to the patient population. Finnell (1985) states that diagnosing a patient as a narcissistic personality disorder provides professionals with the opportunity to project their own narcis-sistic tendencies and thus defensively disavow them by finding them in one's patients. She noted that we often refer to patients as suffering from pathological narcissism and a grandiose self while professionals refer to themselves and fellow professionals as showing "residues" of narcissism, a minimization of the problem. She argues for the conscious recognition of the universality of these problems including among men-tal health professionals.

Alice Miller (1979) carries the Winnicottian idea of the etiology of the "as-if" personality one step further as it applies to psychotherapists. She believes that persons who are drawn to the profession of psycho-therapy usually have cultivated their talents for sensitivity and empa-thy to the problems of others in an effort to be especially attuned to the feelings and needs of their parents. As a result, she believes that the development of a true self tends to be compromised to some extent and psychotherapists in general need to come to terms with the early trauma by parents who were not available to fulfill their primary narcissistic needs. In addition, they should ideally experience the resulting narcissistic rage at having been so deprived. Otherwise, she says, they will tend to force their patients into delivering "as if" productions in order to assure that their therapist will be an understanding and empathic mother. Both Miller and Finnell stress the need for psychotherapists to recognize the pervasive presence of these issues.

If these problems are indeed as universal as they seem to be and a personal analysis is no guarantee that they are always reasonably resolved, wherein lies the hope for promoting not only increased acceptance of their presence in therapists but also of overcoming their negative effects on therapeutic work? There is no single solution and certainly no panacea in view. In addition to personal therapy, both individual and group, some therapists have availed themselves of long-term peer group supervision throughout most of their careers, and this method offers promise of helping with counter-transference generally, and narcissistic issues in particular. When functioning optimally, such groups provide the opportunity to expose one's anxieties and self-doubts to a few trusted colleagues, ideally in a secure, non-threatening setting. Narcissistic personality characteristics, often unconscious, are never easy to confront whether in a patient, supervisee, friend, or a spouse. Under optimal circumstances, and in the course of building trust in a stable peer group, the collective observations of friendly colleagues may contribute to the enhanced maturation and skill of psychotherapists.

Summary

Insofar as the egocentric needs of a therapist find their way into the treatment relationship, a patient's growth and potential for change may become compromised. Significant interferences occur in the work of therapists who encourage suppression of negative feelings and those who have to bolster their sense of perfection by needing to see progress in their patients. The most harmful effects on patients are inflicted by the malignant narcissists who are prone to sadistically exploiting the group to gratify their own pathological needs. More benign manifestations of a therapist's narcissism consist of such things as an inhibition in making transference interpretations associated with the fear of being seen as self-centered. Some therapists have the inflated belief that their mere presence in the group facilitates a benign effect and magical change, thus foreclosing the need for training and honing of skills. A group therapist's difficulty in dealing with negative transference in the form of devaluation or criticism may lead to efforts to suppress such expressions and, even worse, colluding with a group's scape-goating and extrusion of members who become spokespersons for these affects. When group therapists fail to see the kind of progress in their patients that fits their grandiose self-image, they are likely to withdraw from or criticize the patient. The universality of narcissistic issues as an impediment to the work of therapists is increasingly recognized in our field. One suggested approach to this problem is the increased use of long-term peer group supervision.

PART IV

TRAINING

Teaching, training, and supervising are frequently a part of a professional's responsibility as he begins to master his craft. Since the Menninger Clinic was a major teaching institution with training programs in all of the mental health specialties, it was natural that our staff soon embarked upon the teaching of our growing expertise in group therapy.

All of the chapters in this section are organized around the theme of the unstructured small group or the experiential group which is the workhorse training event most similar to a psychotherapy group. Chapter Sixteen deals with a wide variety of issues concerning group psychotherapy training within an organization, including the essential element of the attitude of the administration toward the practice of group treatment. The inclusion of a therapy-like group in the curriculum requires the administration to understand the difference between this event and the typical didactic course. Chapter Seventeen focuses upon the expected developments in an experiential group and the leader's techniques in dealing with the group. Chapter Eighteen describes a model for a three day workshop offered by the Menninger group therapy staff and the rationale for the various events, the original version having been written in collaboration with Harriet Lerner and Esther Burstein.

Even before offering didactic courses in group psychotherapy, we introduced experiential groups, first for psychiatric residents and later for other professionals, largely due to the efforts of a National Training

Laboratories trained staff member. These groups turned out to be very popular with our trainees, in part because they provided a quasi-therapeutic and supportive experience, especially helpful to young professionals embarking upon a new and challenging career. On the other hand, the administration was decidedly less enthusiastic about this new venture since we attempted to make it an elective course and, even more strangely to them, we insisted on not recording attendance and not offering grades or evaluations of the student's performance. Much communication with the school authorities was necessary to persuade them that these procedures were desirable. They were much relieved when we began didactic teaching of group psychotherapy and did not make similar requests to depart from the usual classroom protocols

We began to offer workshops in the early 1970s as a continuing education offering to a nation-wide audience. The workshops were partly based on the staff's exposure to the human relations training sponsored by the A. K. Rice Institute but modified to emphasize group therapy as opposed to their effort to teach group dynamics primarily applied to organizational life. For the most part our continuing education participants had very positive experiences, often based on their first exposure to a psychodynamic process. The workshops also had some unintended positive consequences for the staff. It was an important collegial experience in which we all had an intensive exposure to each other's clinical thinking since the staff met regularly over the three day period to discuss their groups. I believe the workshops also contributed to increased morale among the group therapy staff insofar as each of these events created a welcome sense of collegiality.

A further development was the staff's interest in starting a leaderless therapy group composed of group psychotherapy staff members. Partly it was a reflection of the growing popularity of such groups nationally and internationally, but I also suspect that the faculty experienced some envy of the participants in their workshop groups who seemed to profit and even enjoy the excitement of intensive and probing group interaction.

Finally Chapter Nineteen is the keynote speech I delivered at the opening of an AGPA two day institute featuring an unstructured small group experience for the participants. Having been a participant as well as a leader of many of such groups, it was an excellent opportunity to reminisce about my own experiences as a participant and hopefully encourage the attendees to engage as actively as they could in this forthcoming event.

CHAPTER SIXTEEN

Training programs within organizations

Aprogram of training within an institution for the practice of group psychotherapy is conditioned by two main factors. One is the overall educational orientation of the institution, in particular its attitude toward cognitive *vs.* experiential learning. The second factor relates to the specific features of group psychotherapy: the model or models being taught, its relationship to other treatment modalities, and its status as a therapeutic method in the institution. Both topics will be discussed in this chapter.

Group psychotherapy vs. *other therapy groups*

In order to establish guidelines and policies for group psychotherapy training, it is necessary to differentiate this endeavor from a number of other group activities in which the trainee may become involved. For instance, he may be called upon to conduct a ward meeting, lead a committee of patients planning social or recreational activities, advise patient government meetings, etc. These are only a few of the patient groups which have a therapeutic intent but which must be distinguished from group psychotherapy. What distinguishes group psychotherapy from other group treatment? In group psychotherapy (1) a relatively small number of patients are involved, the maximum being eight to ten; (2) the mode of interaction comes as close as possible to being solely verbal, as opposed to various kinds of recreational or other activities; (3) structuring and agenda setting are kept to a minimum by the therapist, in contrast to current event groups or other discussion groups; (4) the therapist, with training in psychopathology, psychodynamics, and the techniques of both individual and group psychotherapy, is capable of recognizing and interpreting transference phenomena; (5) an objective in all psychotherapy groups is to enhance the patient's self-awareness, particularly his patterns of interacting with others; this aim contrasts with group counseling which emphasizes solutions for specific reality problems.

It is most important for the young professional to learn that there are many different kinds of helpful approaches to patients, especially hospitalized patients. Group psychotherapy shares a number of features and characteristics which are common to other group therapeutic activities such as community meetings and patient government groups which foster the feeling of belonging, opportunity for socialization and group interaction. Group psychotherapy is a method with specific psychotherapeutic features including the use of transference and counter-transference phenomena, which differentiate it from other group methods.

Institutional attitudes

The importance of considering the attitudes of the organization as a whole toward this work—particularly those of its key policy-making figures—cannot be stressed too much. It is an axiom in organizational theory that the success of any enterprise depends upon the attitudes of persons at the top levels of the organization whose views are often crucial in shaping the success or failure of a program. These considerations are especially pertinent to the activity of group psychotherapy because even into the present twenty-first century when the modality has achieved considerable acceptance, it is a less well-established treatment modality compared to individual psychotherapy. Even though group psychotherapy has flourished over the past half century and has become a valued activity in numerous clinical settings, many staff members and faculty members in psychiatric institutions are still relatively uninformed about it. Group treatment has thrived in institutions where an unfavorable patient-doctor ratio prevailed and where economic necessity encouraged its growth. In these settings, group psychotherapy has achieved goals similar to those achieved by intensive individual psychotherapy and in some instances, its special virtues may make it the treatment of choice: with adolescents, infantile personalities, and narcissistic personalities. Positive views about group treatment develop from direct personal experience combined with an institutional setting where the modality is respected and utilized.

In the not too distant past, the attitude of many psychoanalysts toward group therapy was often that of parental indulgence; they looked the other way while students sowed their wild therapeutic oats, waiting patiently for them to return to the family fold and a life of therapeutic propriety. Thankfully the days are gone when psychoanalytic training programs regard group psychotherapy as anti-analytic and discouraged students from engaging in such activity.

Ideally, the senior faculty should become directly involved in working with therapeutic groups. Short of this ideal, they must be kept closely informed and should be exposed to the thinking of the group psychotherapy teachers. Their questions, doubts, and concerns should be openly discussed. Without the active support of these key figures, group psychotherapy is likely to remain the special interest of a few with its practice and teaching hampered by exclusion from the mainstream of therapeutic activity.

Currently, group psychotherapy has achieved considerable acceptance, interest, and support. In the past, however, group therapists had to surmount a good many handicaps to organize and conduct a group. We had to seek out, or more accurately, "scrounge" for referrals from our colleagues. More often than not, these referrals turned out to be the least promising patients, the rejects for whom other therapies had not gone well. When an ongoing group needed replenishing, once again the therapist had to engage in cajolery to find additional patients.

To a large extent, these handicaps and obstacles are disappearing in most clinical settings where a group psychotherapy program has been integrated into the ongoing diagnostic and therapeutic work. Thus, group psychotherapy has taken its place in the array of modalities which most clinicians now consider an option. If group treatment is indicated, it must be discussed with the patient with sufficient care to deal with his initial reservations, resistances, and misunderstandings before a final decision is made. When a clinical program lacks whole-hearted support by the administration, the method is automatically downgraded in the eyes of staff, students, and patients alike.

In order to achieve such an integrated program, one must engage in a wide dissemination of knowledge about this form of treatment among all staff levels of the institution. Only in this way will the therapist experience the moral support from the institution and his colleagues, a factor important to veteran therapists and beginners alike. And institutional support is necessary for patients to overcome the haunting feeling that they may be getting something which is less than the best. Likewise, the evaluating teams must be able to make referrals with confidence and conviction. The endorsement of the organization in all phases of the clinical operation ideally should be established for optimal treatment and training.

In the early days of my effort to establish a group psychotherapy program at the Menninger Clinic, I experienced understandable skepticism about the validity of this modality. I was told by Dr. Karl Menninger, the chief of staff, that my initial efforts should be tried first at a neighboring state hospital with "non-paying" patients. On another occasion a patient in my group was seen by a consultant for a regular evaluation of her progress and was asked whether she might be interested in having psychotherapy. She reported this experience back to the group with mischievous delight, knowing that I would greet such a comment with considerable irritation.

Principles of training

The foremost principle of group psychotherapy training in an institution with a psychodynamic orientation is that it should be based upon and utilize accepted principles of psychotherapy. As a result of my early exposure, I learned the importance of attending to the dynamics of the whole group in addition to the special concerns of each patient. The productions of the group taken as a whole can be understood in a manner similar to the free associations of the psychoanalytic patient. Also, the therapeutic method used with the individual patient has similarities as well as differences from that used in groups. In particular, a number of group dynamic principles must be kept in mind to supplement the understanding derived from the one-to-one situation. One must be aware that quiet patients often subtly encourage the more vocal ones to express feelings that the former find difficult to articulate, that displacement and projection in the form of scapegoating is quite common in a group situation and in addition, it is necessary to understand that the group's need to fill certain roles contributes to the understanding of an individual's behavior. I believe that most individual therapists can become competent group therapists with sufficient training and supervision although some find the transition to working in a group setting too discomfiting and remote from their comfort zone.

A second principle of group psychotherapy, in contrast to individual treatment, is that the therapist is presented with a more complex set of phenomena to understand and deal with; therefore, it should ideally be introduced after she has acquired some experience in doing individual treatment. The neophyte individual psychotherapist is first confronted with the task of understanding the patient's latent communications: What is the patient attempting to express, consciously or unconsciously, which he is not verbalizing directly? The art of translating the patient's metaphors, of understanding his transference reactions, requires experience under supervision. But imagine the same task compounded by the presence of several patients and complicated by more diverse channels for communicating individual needs and wishes.

Furthermore, the transference and counter-transference reactions characteristically occurring in a group sometimes may be intense and magnified. A variety of factors, including a contagion effect, may resonate throughout the group, resulting in highly regressive reactions which, in turn, may elicit equally strong emotional responses in the therapist. Prior experience in dyads with smaller doses of these emotional currents is highly desirable.

The question of the proper timing of introducing group psychotherapy training after exposure to individual psychotherapy is an open issue and is often determined by practical considerations, such as the length of the training program rather than the readiness of the individual. Also, there is some validity to the argument that the group therapist who starts his training as an individual psychotherapist must go through a period of unlearning certain techniques. The most commonly observed problem is one of focusing unduly upon individual patients and losing sight of the dynamics of the entire group.

A third assumption is that an essential part of the preparation of a group psychotherapist is the experience of being a patient in a group or at least of being a participant in a group process experience, often referred to as an experiential group. This training affords the future therapist with an opportunity to deepen and enrich his appreciation of the feelings which patients undergo in a group. Not only will she have an opportunity to observe some of her own characteristic patterns of relating herself to the leader and to her peers, but she will also attain an enhanced appreciation of a patient's anxieties and resistances. The small group experience offered as part of a training group in one's training program or in experiential groups such as those offered in professional meetings of the AGPA or IAGP, affords the trainee a patient-like experience. Some training centers have offered intensive group psychotherapy over a three-year period to their residency classes and have reported successful programs in which both therapeutic and educational goals are achieved.

Finally, I subscribe to the view that full group psychotherapy training should be an elective, just as are other subspecialties within the psychiatric field. All trainees should learn about it; not everyone should be required to practice it. Some therapists find group work quite gratifying. They enjoy the liveliness of a vivid and intense group interaction, particularly since such exchanges may be turned to therapeutic profit. But, as mentioned above, there are many capable clinicians who do not do their best work in groups and who do not find the experience gratifying. Very little is known about the personality factors in the therapist that dispose a professional to greater comfort and proficiency in one or the other modality.

Ideal sequence of training

The experiential group

As mentioned above, when offered in the first year of training, this course not only provides the student with training in the dynamics of groups, but promotes the understanding of some basic psychodynamic concepts as well. Most trainees view the course as a positive experience and as a result have often been inspired to work with groups after this introduction. The course can effectively follow the model of the Tavistock or A. K. Rice group relations conference which consists of experiences in a small group, large group, intergroup exercise, and application group. These events will be discussed below in further detail.

Recorder-observer experience

Early in his training, the trainee who so desires may become a recorder-observer, usually in a therapy group conducted by a more experienced clinician. The recorder-observer takes notes during the session, often dictates process notes afterwards, and sometimes participates in the sessions in which the leader may be supervised. The observer serves a most useful function to the therapist by contributing additional understanding of the complex processes occurring in the group. Since he is less involved personally than the therapist, he may be helpful in monitoring the therapist's counter-transference.

Didactic program

Another early phase should be a formal seminar in group psychotherapy. This course can consist of fifteen—twenty sessions organized around basic readings, a few selected films, and a group discussion of process notes ideally brought in by the students.

Treating a group under supervision

Following the above introductory offerings, the student with the above experiences may take a group of his own under the supervision of a senior therapist. Often it is desirable to be a co-therapist with a fellow trainee, since it reduces the initial anxiety of meeting with a group as a solo therapist.

The experiential group

Of the various training experiences mentioned in the preceding section, none is so difficult to describe as the experiential group or T-group (training group) as it is sometimes called. Participation in a small training group is undoubtedly highly valuable to the practitioner of group psychotherapy.

The T-group is a time-limited, unstructured group experience conducted by a senior clinician who is also acquainted with the techniques of group psychotherapy. The group's task is essentially to learn about the dynamics of groups by studying its own development. The group meets for ninety minutes once a week and usually lasts for at least fifteen sessions. The composition of the groups are ideally interdisciplinary and ought to include trainees in all of the mental health disciplines. Such heterogeneity is desirable in fostering interaction due to a diversity of backgrounds and perspectives.

The "leader" or consultant in a psychoanalytic setting may utilize the orientation that she tends to use in her clinical work, either addressing herself to group themes and conflict or focusing mainly on interpersonal behaviors. It is possible to conceptualize the distinction between the work group culture and the basic assumptions group which appears especially when a structure and agenda are removed. The primary task of the small group is to study itself, mainly its resistance to engaging in its task. Despite its usual optimistic and energetic beginning, the group will characteristically become enmeshed in strong dependency wishes resulting in a search for an omniscient leader and a lapse into becoming helpless and "deskilled". In studying how these and other emotional currents occur, the group gets a glimpse of the repressed and primitive emotions that may emerge in groups.

If one follows an interactional or interpersonal model, the focus tends to be on the patterns of behavior manifested in the peer relationships that are manifested in the here-and-now. The therapist de-emphasizes the leader transference and attempts to highlight the various patterns of relations that get played out in the group, such as: a lack of listening, inability to react with empathy, being unwilling to share significant life issues, or prematurely offering advice and counsel without truly finding out the full picture of what a fellow member is trying to convey.

However, the consultant or leader does not attend to individual or intrapersonal dynamics in these groups although the members may sometimes delve into such matters. When the group begins to engage in this kind of "therapeutic" work, the consultant must interpret the group's flight from the task of studying the dynamics of the group. He, of course, encourages the expression of feelings about various events in the group's life, but he uses such behavior to illustrate a variety of group phenomena without attending to the individual conflicts or defenses which are also in evidence.

The small group experience is an opportunity to learn about the feelings and the major processes which occur in the functioning of treatment groups. But the small group experience is also a vehicle for learning several basic psychodynamic concepts which could not be understood short of a therapy-like experience. Thus, the trainee gains some conviction about unconscious wishes and fears which he and other members of his group express, usually through a variety of metaphors and displacements. He learns about the necessity for attending not only to manifest content but also to latent meaning. The central concepts in psychodynamic treatment of transference and countertransference and their communication via metaphor are essential lessons in this course. This observation is similar to Ganzarain's finding (1989) that a group psychotherapy experience for medical students was effective in promoting a fuller understanding of the concept of transference. Students learn about the multiple and shifting meanings of a given piece of behavior by observing that the same overt manifestation is often produced by different underlying motives.

Thus, the group may hit upon certain favorite defensive maneuvers like silence, intellectualization, or avoidance, but the motive for the defense is frequently quite varied. Also, the participant has an opportunity to observe an experienced clinician dealing with a group of "patients". Basic to any educational and growth process is an identification with one's mentors; the model the students perceive unquestionably helps in their search for a professional approach in dealing with patients. Another by-product of this course is the opportunity to acquire some increased insight into one's interpersonal functioning. Insight is not one of the objectives of the course, but sometimes the group will offer "feedback" to members, and frequently participants are able to profit from self-observation of their functioning in the group.

Training issues

A number of important problems have challenged us concerning the T-group course and its role in the overall curriculum. One issue has been whether the course should properly be an elective or whether it should be compulsory for all trainees. Generally it seems more convenient administratively to make it a required course since the planning becomes simpler and the problems of coordinating the course with other classes becomes easier. On the other hand, the optimal level of motivation to participate and learn would be fostered by making the course a matter of free choice, primarily because the process involves the disclosure of feelings. Also the American Psychological Association code of ethics prescribes that any course that is therapy-like should not be compulsory.

Another factor favoring voluntarism has been the occurrence of so-called "casualties". The experience at the Menninger Clinic in Topeka with many years of training group classes has actually been quite favorable. In my opinion, the influence of the group experience in precipitating decompensations among students was minimal. Some stress and anxiety are necessary for this kind of learning, as is true for most mental health work. But, when one compares the kinds of emotional conflicts usually generated in these once-a-week groups with the strains of dealing with psychotic patients for the first time, or participating in a variety of staff groups, or beginning to acquire a new professional identity—the group experience as a source of stress seems minor.

As faculty, we have learned of the great importance of maintaining continued contact with the various educational and administrative bodies responsible for the training program. The objectives of such training and the methods used make it a unique course in the curriculum. As opposed to the didactic approaches used in lectures, reading groups, psychotherapy control groups, etc., the unstructured group is the only course that is primarily experiential. It is the one course about which considerable misunderstanding is liable to develop if not fully explained to the administration. Unless members of the faculty are actually involved in leading such groups or unless they have a special interest in group processes, staff members are unlikely to grasp the objectives and rationale of the method. We soon became aware that there has to be an ongoing dialogue between the group leaders and the administration.

A frequent concern is the question of whether or not this course is attempting to "bootleg" psychotherapy under the guise of a group process experience. The course is not advertised as treatment nor is it intended to be such. The origin of such concerns lies with issues arising out of an unstructured group and the fact that these developments may be similar to those appearing in a therapeutic group. Conflicts about authority figures—the wish to be dependent as opposed to the fear of submission, the wish to be directed as opposed to the fear of exploitation, the wish to be the leader's favorite as opposed to the fear of antagonizing one's peers—occur in all these groups and constitute the major dimensions of work. Insofar as therapy and training groups explore the feelings generated in an unstructured group, there are basic similarities in both. But the distinguishing feature lies in the attitudes toward personal insight. If a patient group avoids personal insight, it is a manifestation of resistance; if a study group focuses on providing insights to its members, it is resisting its primary task.

Finally, experiential group training for mental health professionals should be conducted by clinicians who are well experienced in the particular approach to group psychotherapy taught at the student's training site. At the Menninger Clinic we used a psychodynamic model that emphasized a group-as-a-whole approach. Yalom and Leszcz (2005) use their interactional approach in working with their trainees. Institutions which teach cognitive behavioral group, dialectical behavioral group, interpersonal group or any other form of group treatment should conduct their groups in the model that they are attempting to teach.

Future programs

Whereas the psychotherapeutic approach has the objective of achieving some kind of intrapsychic change through the medium of the patient-therapist relationship, the sociotherapeutic approach addresses itself more directly to improving interactions and transactions between the patient and significant figures in his environment. The latter groups attempt to alter the social system in which the patient finds himself, and thus promote healthier, more productive, and more fulfilling behavior. The therapeutic community, with its reliance upon promoting more open communications between patients and staff, patients and patients, patients and their families, etc., is an example of the sociotherapeutic approach. Also, family and multifamily therapy and social network therapy are a part of the same approach.

In my view, group psychotherapy is primarily a psychotherapeutic, rather than sociotherapeutic, although the dynamics of the social system are an integral part of the method and thus it appears to be close to the border between the intrapsychic and the social. The group therapist, particularly in an analytic-expressive group, attempts to encourage the development of transferences and resistances which he then uncovers and interprets. In its essential elements, group psychotherapy is most similar to the method of individual psychotherapy but in the course of implementing this approach, the therapist must use group dynamic principles, attend to the peer interactions, and partake of some sociotherapeutic methods.

Thus, the therapist must keep in mind the dynamics occurring within her group, such as the impact of the patient who has recently dropped out, or the new patient who shortly will be added to the group. She must think about the commonly shared tendency in a group to find a "messiah" who will magically remove all difficulties. She must remember the usual tendency of a group to use one of its more masochistic members to act as the recipient of the group's frustrated and aggressive feelings. She must be aware that the silent majority often agrees with the more articulate spokesman in their midst.

The various conferences on group relations provide the group therapist with an expanded view of group relationships. In addition to the small group experience, the participant is exposed to a large unstructured group of perhaps fifty to one hundred participants where members do not have face-to-face interactions and are thus subject to heightened anxiety and regressive pressure. It is highly instructive in understanding the dynamics of large groups in which we all find ourselves on occasion. And another brilliant innovation by A. K. Rice was the intergroup exercise in which members of the conference are assigned the task of joining one of three or four new groups and are then instructed to find ways to organize themselves to form relationships with the other groups in the conference. The exercise illustrates the anxieties that arise in delegating responsibility to others in one's small group and the way fantasies about stranger groups influence one's behavior.

The above experiences in human relations "laboratories" provides the student of group behavior with a broadened perspective on a variety of group behaviors in organizational settings that contribute to a richer understanding of how people function under a broad array of varied group contexts. While the small group is the basic structure for the group therapist, other group settings and tasks promote a breadth of experience that enhance the therapist's understanding of group life.

CHAPTER SEVENTEEN

Training groups for mental health professionals

Experiential groups have been widely accepted as an ideal method of training mental health professionals in a wide spectrum of skills. They offer an opportunity to understand the process of psychodynamic psychotherapy and present a model of how an experienced therapist deals with patients. In addition, they are an excellent introduction to group psychotherapy insofar as the group provides an in vivo illustration of how group dynamic processes get played out. Many training programs—in psychiatry, psychology, and social work—have adopted them as an important part of their curriculum (Gans, Rutan, & Wilcox, 1995). For many years, the American Group Psychotherapy Association as well as the International Association of Group Psychotherapy have made two day experiential groups a regular part of their annual program.

This training was first started for psychiatric residents in the early 1960s with the idea of helping them improve their skills as group leaders in the various hospital groups they lead, particularly the clinical-administrative meetings with other section personnel. As group psychotherapy programs began to grow in training institutions, the course came to be viewed more as an opportunity for trainees to be participants in a time-limited, therapy-like group and thus to learn more about the feelings of patients in psychodynamic psychotherapy, and about the major processes which occur in the functioning of therapy groups.

It has become clear during the past many years that the unstructured group—referred to variously as a group dynamics seminar, T-group, self-study group, sensitivity group, process group, or experiential group—is a microcosm or laboratory of human behavior which may be studied from several points of view. Depending on the interests and objectives of the participants and the leader, the experiential group may be used to teach participants about the dynamics of groups, illustrate a variety of clinical concepts, or it may afford an opportunity to understand the processes and techniques of individual and group psychotherapy. This chapter describes some typical events in the life of such a psychodynamic training group for mental health professions, the rationale and technique of conducting it, and the probable outcome of such an experience.

Events in the life of an experiential group

Although group dynamics classes for trainees may be conducted differently with regard to foci of interest and the kinds of interventions made by the leader, there is one uniform aspect of all these groups which produces certain predictable results. The common feature is the absence of any set structure or agenda or of clearly defined roles for participant or leader.

One of the challenges of the training group, and a major source of anxiety for the participants at the outset, are the questions of the objective of the course and what should they talk about. A group of about ten members, mental health trainees, is assembled for the first time and is given a brief orientation and "contract" by the leader. They will meet once a week for a given period of time, ranging from ten weeks to an entire academic year. Sessions will last for ninety minutes. Frequently the leader will comment about the importance of confidentiality similar to how a therapist introduces a confidentiality agreement, and he assures that no reports to the school administration would be made. Ideally the leader should not be a member of the organization's staff or faculty. The leader might say: "Our aim is to learn about group psychotherapy (or group dynamics or clinical concepts) by becoming a group and studying our process. I will make comments about my observations of the group when I feel it will be helpful. Now I will turn it over to you to get started".

Within a training program, most of the participants will usually have been together for a few weeks or months. There are usually brief introductions around the table, more notable for what is withheld than for what is told. Then what? The major initial preoccupation is with the leader and the fact that he has already indicated that his main role will be that of observer. They speculate whether he is really serious about this or is just playing a waiting game. If we are patient enough, they think, perhaps he will stop being coy and start being the real teacher that he should be. They turn to each other for help in their common misery. But their queries are almost invariably addressed to those who have some obvious differences from themselves, perhaps to find common ground, hopefully to find an ally, and often to assimilate and neutralize the threatening stranger. A native of a foreign land, or perhaps a trainee in another discipline, usually becomes the object of their interest. Typically, they ask, "What is the state of psychiatry in Argentina and did you have any experience with groups?" A pastoral counseling trainee is asked about the role of prayer in dealing with his parishioners. When the leader suggests that their questions, directed at "experts" in these unusual fields, could also be an expression of their wish to get the leader to answer questions, he is hardly heard. These interpretations are not the kind of "food" they came to get.

Resentment about being observed is another underlying theme at the outset. In one group it was expressed via the issue of whether participants should be allowed to take notes during the session. The reality objection was the reduced spontaneity of the note-takers and their unwillingness to carry their load of active participation. In one group irritation was expressed toward television camera crews who happened to be visiting the school at the time; the school authorities, the students complained, were placing public relations ahead of the main goal of teaching. Another vehicle of the same theme was a preoccupation with school examinations. The group argued that examinations were demeaning to postgraduate students, fostered unhealthy competition with peers, and created needless anxiety. When the comment was offered by the leader that they were uneasy about the kind of "rating" they might get from him, even though he had made it clear at the outset that ratings or grades would not be made, the group shifted to another topic.

After the initial fear and suspicion have subsided, the group has the task of overcoming its regressively dependent and hostile attitudes associated with having a leader who refuses to lead, a teacher who will not teach, an expert who mostly keeps his own counsel. The leader's interpretations often focused upon metaphorical feelings being expressed toward him or defenses against such feelings, both tend to promote regression yet at the same time encourage a movement toward resolution. The leader listens carefully for expressions of hostility toward him, usually spoken indirectly, and consistently interprets its presence as well as the frustrations and fears which such feelings engender. He is alert to the scape-goating of other members, both to protect individuals from being unduly victimized and to uncover anger toward himself.

As the leader encourages the verbalization of such thoughts, he is implicitly communicating an accepting attitude toward such feelings. They are at first proffered tentatively and then with greater confidence. Each experience of ventilating anger, dissatisfaction, and criticism of the leader provides the members with the conviction that retribution is not in the offing and tends to promote a feeling of safety and a more realistic perception of him.

Anger and dissatisfaction with the leader is invariably manifested by fantasies or behaviors which express rebellion against the structure or contract set by the leader, minimal though it may be. Supposedly legitimate lateness, which members may initially excuse quite readily, on closer examination often express resentment about the waste of time involved in coming to the group, the fact that the leader is not teaching anything about group dynamics, or perhaps dissatisfaction with the leader's interference in the last meeting. One member absented himself from a meeting to attend a musical comedy which had come to town and blandly explained his behavior to the group on the basis of the pleasure principle: the liveliness of the entertainment was more appealing to him than the dullness of a group meeting. The group effectively pointed out the many facets of this behavior: the patent hostility which he tended to deny, his need to avoid submitting to an inferior "patient" role, his wish to find himself in the center of controversy in order to avoid being overlooked. The group's shock and dismay were partly a reaction against their own repressed wishes to behave in the same way. Other vehicles for the expression of anger are proposals that the time of the meeting be changed or challenging the wisdom of not being given reading assignments. (The members know that the unstructured group experience is followed by a series of didactic sessions based on selections from the group psychotherapy literature.) More direct expressions of resentment against the leader consist of complaints that he says too little or, sometimes too much; frequently his interpretations are attacked as invalid or, at best, un-provable.

The middle phase and major work of the group consists of reaching some resolution of the authority problem. The polarities of dependency and counter-dependency are represented by sub-groupings and most often find expression in terms of factional disputes over the problem of structure. The dependent bloc wants more direction, perhaps an agenda, and searches desperately for someone in the group with expertise. Whoever has read a book on group behavior is elevated to the position of wise man. The dependents will find much comfort in any of the leader's contributions, even if his remarks are only prods or requests for more elaboration. The counter-dependents on the other hand resent the leader's participation and oppose the effort by anyone to impose structure. They stand for free, uninhibited, and spontaneous expression of feeling. If a more timid soul should suggest that each member give a thumbnail sketch of his background and interests, these avant-garde "abstractionists" raise their voices in protest. If there is a suggestion that the group be polled on whether or not to change the meeting time, they oppose the sterile mechanics of voting.

Movement toward resolving the group's underlying dependent wishes occurs when the members begin to find agreement about their common, shared striving for nurturance accompanied by recognition of their real capacity to utilize their own resources. To some extent they are able to give up their perception of the leader as an authoritarian person who is trying to rub their noses in the dirt and hence they do not have to be so sullen nor passively angry. The leader is now seen less as a manipulator, and they feel less like puppets of his will. Concomitantly, they become more accepting of their own responsibility to use the group for learning purposes and are less prone to discount observations made by others. One group worked on the problem of why they were so upset over a particular member's absence. They wondered whether they were like a "poker" group which can function despite absences provided there is a minimum attendance, or like a "bridge" group in which a missing member precludes the game. They came to the pithy and accurate observation that they were "a poker group with bridge group feelings". The group begins to rely upon its expertise, not born of desperation but based upon a more realistic appraisal and better utilization of their capacities.

Group dynamics or T-group meetings typically deal also with the problem of intimacy, closeness, and distance from peers. How free can we get in sharing our feelings toward each other, both positive and negative? One group found much comfort and pleasure in healing the dissensions that had been present both among themselves and with the leader. They enjoyed the camaraderie and new-found warmth, but a subsequent meeting found them discussing the problem of handling the homosexual patient who makes sexual advances to his doctor. The consensus was to "tell him to cut it out" firmly and decisively, an expression of their own struggle to take distance from threatening positive feelings toward the leader and each other.

As termination approaches, there are inevitable feelings of reluctance to disband and anger about not having learned enough. Accusations are directed toward the leader for not having directed the group more skillfully, against themselves for having been maladroit or resistant students, and against their colleagues for failing to contribute more. The question of ratings once again arises, and the fear that this group did not measure up to previous ones becomes a concern. Usually such criticisms and self-criticisms are replaced by a more realistic appraisal of the benefit derived from the group.

The leader's orientation and technique

The leader's technique in any psychodynamic unstructured group is largely determined by his teaching objectives as well as by the goals, both latent and manifest, of the group members. The primary objective of the leader is often to teach the method of psychodynamic therapy and/or group psychotherapy. One may question how it is possible to illustrate a treatment approach when treatment is not actually being offered. The course is usually described in the school's bulletin as an experiential group in which the members learn about group processes by being participant-observers in their own self-study group. The course is not advertised as treatment, nor is it intended to be such. However, it is clear that many of the trainees, particularly since the course is given at the beginning of their training when anxieties about new professional roles and experiences are at their height, regard the sessions as an opportunity to deal with anxieties about their new responsibilities and identities (Munich, 1993; Swiller, Lang, & Halperin, 1993) They appreciate the opportunity to ventilate and to share their common concerns, and hope to enhance their acquisition of that valuable commodity in mental health, personal insight. Interestingly enough, in a survey of residency programs throughout the U.S., Gans, Rutan, and Wilcox (1995) found that the participants in the programs that offered experiential groups for the most part regarded their value as both educational and therapeutic.

The issues which arise in an unstructured group are substantially the same as those which appear in any therapeutic group. The mixed feelings about authority figures—the wish to be dependent in conflict with the fear of submission, the wish to be directed as against the fear of exploitation, the wish to be the leader's favorite as against the fear of antagonizing one's peers—occur in all these groups and constitute the major dimensions of work. Insofar as therapy and training groups both explore the feelings generated in the individual by finding himself in an unstructured group, there are basic similarities between them.

The distinguishing feature between the two types of groups lies in the relative emphasis upon personal insight. If a patient in a psychotherapy group avoids reflectiveness and personal insight, it is a manifestation of resistance. But a participant in this kind of training group may occasionally dip into exploring personal issues providing it does not become the major focus. The members are free to explore only the group phenomena: group themes, group conflicts, group resistances, etc. In so doing, they may perceive, or the group may point out, individual modes of handling various kinds of affects or provide feedback to individuals, but personal dynamics should not trump the main objective of studying what is happening in the group-as-a-whole. And of course, the fact that the members have relationships outside the group, will present a limitation on how much self-disclosure will occur.

Several writers have correctly attempted to draw a clear distinction between a training group and a therapy group (Munich, 1993; Feiner, 1998). Since such groups in training programs are usually not advertised as therapy, the restrictions are clear, at least for the leader, to abstain from making personal observations about conflicts and defenses of individual members. Rather his observations must be confined to group issues, group resistances, and attitudes toward group norms that are being played out in the group. This is not to say that individual members may not experience therapeutic effects in terms of silently observing their own patterns of interaction or benefitting from feeling accepted and valued as contributing members of the group.

Since many programs recognize the potential therapeutic benefits of these groups, some writers have set out a dual contract of learning about the dynamics of groups as well as exploring personal issues. An instructive account of such a procedure was reported by Nathan and Poulsen (2004) who researched three small groups in their university in which the prescribed task was both personal development through the exploration of oneself and one's relations to others as well as the educational goal of professional learning. The authors refer to the dual goal as involving multiple foci. Their termination interviews revealed that the ambiguity of personal *vs.* professional goals left most of the participants struggling with how to deal with the dual task. They discovered that one of the groups was predominantly personal while the other two largely engaged in intellectualization. Such a finding is not too surprising insofar as the dual goal presented the participants with a ready-made defense against self-disclosure (at some level necessary even in self-study groups) and thus unwittingly encouraged defensive avoidance of either task. There is a general consensus that the ideal structure of such groups is to present the problem of learning about group dynamics through studying how a group develops and leaving the therapeutic aspects to remain in the background as a by-product of the interaction.

Faculty offering experiential groups must face the issue of the position of the leader vis-à-vis the administration of the training program. At a minimum the administration must be oriented to the special nature of such groups and the importance of making them non-evaluative and non-reporting to the training program in order that the participants have the maximum freedom to disclose personal information and reactions as well as have confidence that the leader will maintain confidentiality about what transpires in the group. Since Munich (1993) attempts to draw a strict wall against any possibility of the process group being thought of as a therapeutic endeavor, he appears not to regard confidentiality as a critical issue. He does not attempt to reassure members of his intention to avoid disclosure to the other faculty or the administration of what transpires in the group. He merely states that he permits the group to deal with the confidentiality issue. On the other hand, Swiller, Lang, and Halperin (1993) emphasize the importance of the privacy of the group and make the valid point that if the faculty is too small to find leaders who do not have other relationships with the members, an outside consultant should be sought. Not reassuring the participants of the leader's intention to maintain confidentiality or the failure to set up the parameters to reinforce such privacy would be an impediment to the group.

When the group is split about a given issue, the leader needs to bring the conflict out in the open. Thus, when the members are attempting to move in the direction of greater intimacy, they may encourage the members of minority groups to discuss the customs of their particular religious or racial groups in the hope of dissolving boundaries and finding common bonds. But despite the seeming unanimity of such a theme at the moment, there are inevitable counter-forces and thus individuals will range variously around the dimension of intimacy. Some will insist vehemently that the group should go further, perhaps wishing to go too far too fast and thus alienating members who are interested in more closeness. Some insist upon their rights to privacy and wish to remain aloof while some may seek out and exaggerate dissension and hostility as a defense against further movement toward intimacy. The leader needs to interpret the conflicting wishes within the group-as-a-whole regarding their desires to move closer to each other.

In general, the leader tends to avoid commenting on individual or intrapersonal dynamics in these groups. As mentioned above, it is a function of the contract to study group behavior and shifting the focus to providing individual insight would violate the contract. Despite the usual wish for a therapeutic experience, there is always some resistance to looking inward, particularly when the group provides the freedom not to do so. The leader, of course, encourages the expression of feelings about various events in the group's life, but he uses such behavior to illustrate a variety of group phenomena or clinical concepts without focusing on the individual dynamics which are also in evidence.

In general, these groups tend to be voluntary rather than required, in recognition of the fact that some trainees are either too uncomfortable in a group setting or are too fragile to be able to use an unstructured group modality. By the same token, participants who join such a group but begin to experience more stress than they had anticipated should be permitted to drop out without prejudice. As mentioned earlier, this policy is reinforced by the ethical code of the American Psychological Association which states that groups that are therapy-like should not be required courses in the curriculum.

What are the group processes to which the leader with a psychodynamic orientation attends? If the leader subscribes to a group-as-a-whole orientation, he will attend to the common group tension, group focal conflict, or basic assumption life illustrated in the group. This group-wide orientation lends itself to the emphasis on the study of group dynamics and helps to avoid interpretations about individual dynamics. Those therapists with a peer interaction or interpersonal focus will tend to view the group through their own special lens and behave accordingly. My own personal orientation is that practically every group session touches on one or more themes which express a common conflict, a wish countered by a fear. Ideally the group theme is developed by the verbalizations of the majority of members. But often it finds expression through one or two spokesmen who are either passively permitted or actively encouraged by the group to verbalize their feelings. A rebellious member may be subtly prodded to criticize the leader, to suggest revisions in the contract, or to absent himself from the group for invalid reasons. One of the more difficult concepts for the novice to grasp is the phenomenon of the group acting as a whole when it seems on the surface to be operating simply as an expression by one or two individuals. The emergence of a particular individual as the temporary leader of the group may often be understood as a confluence of his personal needs and the needs of the group. Too often it tends to be understood by the group in terms of the idiosyncrasies of the individual alone. Here the phenomenon of role-suction *or* the concept of the group billet is illustrated for the group to ponder.

A related group phenomenon includes scapegoating, which inevitably develops, either as a displacement from the leader onto one of the members or may result from a disowned projection of one or more members. Sometimes members form into two opposing sub-groups, often around dependency *vs.* counter-dependency wishes. But the division of the group into polarized factions or subgroups usually expresses two arms of a conflict within each individual. Other group phenomena consist of attending to the meanings of seating arrangements, body postures, and similar non-verbal expressions of feeling and conflict.

A central problem in all groups, training or therapeutic, concerns the degree of regression to be encouraged or permitted by the leader. As in individual treatment, the leader may attempt to regulate the regressive pull by the role he takes: the more silent and frustrating he is, the greater the regression. The more he limits his comments primarily to interpretations, the more frustrated the group will feel and the more preoccupied they will become with fantasies about what the leader is thinking: Does he approve of them? Does he prefer one over the others? Frequently their fantasies will take a projective turn and they will suspect, for example, that the leader's statement that he plans to miss the next meeting is some kind of trick to elicit their reactions. Conversely, if the leader's interventions are more than just interpretive, if he gratifies to some degree the members' wishes for guidance and support, if he answers some of their questions when the anxiety level is rising, the regressive reactions tend to subside. A leader may typically be asked by the group, when they introduce themselves around the table in the initial meeting, to say a few words about himself, which he usually will do quite briefly. Or when the leader announces that he plans to be absent next time, he may or may not explain the reason for his absence. The choice made in such instances will either enhance or minimize regression.

A second determinant of regressive pull is the degree to which the leader interprets leader-transference as opposed to peer-transference. The two transferences are usually related and often run parallel to each other, differing largely in intensity. A member is not only concerned about what the leader's impression of him is but about the opinions of his fellow members as well. He is not only resentful of the leader's position as an authority figure but he opposes those in the group who take on leadership positions. He is not only fearful of the leader's potential for hostile attacks but sees others in the group as similarly threatening. It is not just the leader who has obligated him to a contract; the group gradually places demands upon him as well. Authors who prefer the interpersonal model such as Aveline (1993) emphasize shared anxieties of members but avoid group-wide transference to the leader. In my view, this approach neglects a central issue in group life pertaining to the attitude toward authority figures.

Some workers believe that group classes for trainees should deal largely with the transference to the leader. In an early paper, Appelbaum (1963) conceptualized the entire process in terms of the gradual emergence of the reality principle, that is, learning to accept one's own capacities for problem-solving rather than remaining in a hostile dependent stance toward the leader who is expected to supply answers. When the group has learned to accept this responsibility, he says, it is ready to terminate.

Another model is that offered by the Bethel National Training Laboratories (NTL) which views the dependency problem as only the first of two major phases of the unstructured training group. They contend that when the group is able to assimilate the "trainer" as another member with special resources, but someone who is incapable of doing their work for them, the group moves into dealing with the problem of greater closeness to peers. They begin to have the task of sharing their observations about each other, hopefully in a constructive and helpful way, based upon their experiences together in the preceding sessions. This is the "feedback" phase which occupies a large share of NTL human relations training groups.

Whether the group remains leader-centered or becomes more peer-centered depends largely upon the leader's orientation, his goals, and the time frame of the group. After some reduction has occurred in both the exaggerated view of the leader's potency and in their hostile dependency toward him, the leader is generally faced with two alternative routes. He may be able to interpret the events in the group with a primary emphasis upon feelings toward himself, as he did earlier, or he may begin to emphasize concerns about interrelationships among members. Thus, for example, in a meeting occurring at about the midpoint of a particular group's life, the discussion centered around the feelings of comfort the members experienced in being with their confreres in the group as opposed to members of other groups. Then, in a somewhat labored way, they began to express their negative feelings about an absent member whose absence had been planned and had seemed legitimate to them. They emphasized his positive contributions to the group, and his ability to make penetrating and helpful observations about what was going on, while also expressing their criticisms of his role as leader's assistant. Insofar as the absent member was a displacement figure from the leader, they avoided negative comments which would too easily be interpreted as criticism of the leader. The leader could have emphasized the fear of expressing anger toward himself or he could have focused on their reluctance to express negative feelings about each other. The latter course would contribute to some reduction in transference feelings to the leader and encourage increased peer interaction. Focusing upon the leader, on the other hand, would lead to the further uncovering of regressive fantasies about authority figures.

The problem in conducting such groups, as in doing psychotherapy, is that of encouraging enough regression to induce tension and promote work while avoiding excessive frustration and anger. But an additional factor, where there is a time limitation, makes it necessary to help the group avoid excessive regression toward the leader since one hopes to achieve some resolution of such feelings by the end of the course.

Since this group is primarily educational in its ultimate purpose, the leader must be especially conscious of the techniques he uses. His interventions must not only help the group deal with its conflicts and resistances but also give his students a model to emulate. A frequent resistance in the early stages is the group's reluctance to deal with significant events which they initially perceive as minor occurrences such as lateness and absence. The leader has the obligation in the early stages to model good therapeutic practice and raise these issues. It is usually possible to illustrate that the "unavoidable" lateness resulted from a reluctance to attend in the first place. Soon the group will take over this function as part of a growing identification with the leader. By encouraging discussion about such matters as seating arrangements, the group becomes attuned to some of the non-verbal aspects of their functioning. For example, at the height of one group's wish to be given more direction from the leader, the group seated itself in a cluster at some distance from the leader. Inquiry into the meaning of the choice of seats revealed that this arrangement simulated a lecture classroom and conveyed a wish for more didactic activity by the leader.

Outcomes of the training group

Group phenomena are affectively experienced by the members and are learned in vivo and not simply as abstract concepts. An important adjunct to the course is often a reading group of several sessions which follows after the unstructured group experience. The reading assignments are discussed whenever possible in terms of the recently completed group experience. Concepts like scape-goating, cohesion, role-suction, focal group conflicts, etc., are examined in the light of the real-life situations which they all have shared. The reading group shares some similarities to the Tavistock human relations conference application group in which the learning from the experiential groups is examined from the point of view of its relevance to various back-home tasks.

A training group also illustrates general clinical phenomena and therapeutic techniques that apply to both individual as well as group treatment. First, with regard to clinical modes of thinking, a lesson of paramount importance is that there are multiple levels of communication and that one should not be content with simply attending to manifest content. The question the clinician should always be asking is: Why is the patient raising this point in this way at this time? What is occurring in the here and now which is being expressed indirectly or obliquely and is perhaps just outside the ken of consciousness?

The central concept of transference in dynamic psychotherapy and its communication via metaphor is an essential lesson learned in a training group. In one of its early sessions, one group became interested in the problem of whether a psychiatrist should always perform a complete physical on a patient simply because the patient expects it despite his own conviction that the procedure, when necessary, should be performed by another physician. The minister in the group was asked if he used prayer when he counseled with a parishioner simply because the latter expected it. These preoccupations were not too far from their concern about their own wish for the leader to take over more active control of the group while at the same time fearing that he might accede to these wishes to the detriment of their learning experience. The group's reaction to the leader's translation of these metaphors is often one of great surprise. Gradually, however, they begin to acquire the attitude that all is not what it seems, and this lesson is one of the most valuable dividends of the course. As mentioned in the previous chapter, Ganzarain (1989) reached a similar conclusion in his controlled experiment in teaching psychiatry to medical students. One group received ordinary didactic instruction while the other group had a course of group psychotherapy. The latter students not only profited personally from the therapeutic aspects of the course but seemed to have a better, more vivid grasp of certain clinical concepts, particularly transference.

Another psychodynamic principle, more easily learned in the abstract than understood in a life situation, is that of the multiple and shifting meanings of a given piece of behavior. One group had an opportunity to explore the many different facets of their silences. They were able to see that silence could have multiple meanings: angry reaction to deprivation; a protest against the perceived necessity to submit to a passive, compliant role; a wish on their part to be "fed" by the leader; a defense against their own hostile impulses *as* well as their fear of possible counterattack. Or, it could sometimes indicate that the group is merely attempting to reflect about some event in the group. This kind of complexity is easily demonstrated in a group situation because the differing character structures of the members tend to elucidate the spectrum of motives underlying a single piece of behavior

In terms of clinical techniques, the participant has an opportunity to observe an experienced clinician dealing with a group of "patients". Basic to any educational and growth process is an identification with one's mentors, and the model the students perceive unquestionably helps many of them in their search for a proper professional approach in dealing with their patients. When the students in one training group were asked which of the leader's techniques they found themselves using with their own patients, each member stressed a particular facet of the leader's technique with which he identified himself. Frequent reference was made to the prodding intervention which the leader used to encourage further elaboration: "would you care to say more about that?" This intervention embodies the attitude mentioned above that behaviors are complexly motivated and that one should seek to explore beyond the face value of a comment.

Each student mentioned particular techniques designed to encourage freedom of expression, particularly of negative feelings toward the leader or toward each other. They spoke of learning to tolerate better the hostility of their patients, to refrain from retaliation, and to view the attacks usually as something to be understood rather than as personal criticism.

They saw the importance of using non-verbal expressions of interest, curiosity, and the effort to understand as a means of eliciting material from their patient. Some stressed the leader's neutrality in the face of conflicts of opinion by dissident factions and the importance of trying to elucidate feelings rather than expressing one's own biases or values. On this latter point, they were able to learn that neutrality is not synonymous with complete inhibition of one's feelings. A common misconception of the novice in doing therapy is that the treater should maintain an attitude of cool and detached interest, a caricature of the psychoanalyst who suppresses all of his affective responses. One member stated: "The group leader participated more than I thought he would. This was particularly true of his non-verbal behavior. In clinical situations I have identified particularly with the leader's openness. On the ward and in group discussions on the ward, I have participated more freely and made less effort to blunt my affect in response to patients' statements".

While the acquisition of insight into one's personality is not an objective of the course, it often turns out to be a by-product. According to the survey conducted by Gans, Rutan, and Wilcox (1995) the directors of training in those residency programs that offer T-groups maintain that such groups not only teach psychodynamic processes but are a "source of support and cohesion during the difficult years of professional training" (p. 176). Beginners in psychiatry are beset by many anxieties concerning the new field they are entering and the new professional identity they must begin to acquire. They are often eager for a therapeutic experience and are particularly intent on learning more about techniques with their patients as well as more understanding about their own personality functioning. To the extent that the group may give "feedback" to each other, share impressions and observations about their behavior in the group, there develops some degree of increased self-understanding. For the most part, the learning consists of an underlining of facets of functioning of which they already were aware. Many are surprised to observe the extent of their own hostility. Some report that what they formerly regarded as a penchant for humor turned out to be vitriolic sarcasm, particularly in the way others responded to it. Some were surprised to learn that their passive compliance was a thin defense against competitive and aggressive wishes. More often than not, such insights are based on self-observations. Occasionally, certain maladaptive character traits are pointed out which the person has not been aware of before. Sometimes the observations by peers are dismissed lightly or ignored while others may take these observations seriously and attempt to understand them more fully.

Summary

Experiential groups consisting of participation in an unstructured group as a participant-observer are an important part of the curriculum in many mental health training programs. Offered early in training, the course is viewed partly as an introduction to group psychotherapy, but also partly as a general introduction to clinical concepts and clinical techniques, taught and learned in a real-life situation as a supplement to the more abstract, didactic courses. Although the course is not advertised as psychotherapy and is not intended as such, many of the issues which arise resemble those occurring in a therapeutic group. The emphasis, however, is upon understanding group dynamic issues, and the leader confines himself largely to group-wide interventions. The extent to which the group delves into self-understanding is a matter of choice for the members, provided that the group does not lose its focus on studying the group process. Two major dimensions govern the extent of the regressive preoccupation which develops around the leader: the degree of frustration which he induces by limiting his participation and the extent to which his interpretations focus upon leader-member as opposed to member-member transference. Because of the relatively limited amount of time available to resolve regressive transference reactions, the leader strives for a more diluted and less intense relationship with himself than he would encourage in a therapeutic group.

CHAPTER EIGHTEEN

A workshop model for mental health professionals

C ertain mental health organization may wish to offer a three-day workshop designed to facilitate the development and consolidation of skills for beginning and/or experienced group therapists. When the Menninger group therapists considered the possibility of offering this type of workshop to outside professionals, we wondered whether a workshop of such short duration could provide the participants with substantive and lasting learning. However, our doubts were dispelled shortly after our initial forays in this area. In particular, the combination of experiential and didactic groups which we provided for the workshop participants proved to be an especially effective format for teaching psychodynamic group therapy. In this chapter I shall describe the rationale, design, and organization of these workshops and explain how the specific combination of the events we offer contributes to learning. The model being presented is the result of over three decades of experience which has resulted in a smoothly operating program enjoyed by the staff and participants alike.

Unfortunately, other groups who have offered comparable brief programs have not published their models. The only similar program that has been described is the two day institute of experiential groups presented over many years by the American Group Psychotherapy

Association. Articles by Coche, Dies, and Goettlemann (1991) and Tschuschke and Greene (2002) studied factors that enhance learning in the experiential groups but do not constitute the same kind of combination of didactic and experiential learning attempted in our workshops. Both studies emphasized the importance of the leader as a role model, both in terms of his or her personal involvement and technical skill. They also demonstrated the value that the participants placed on their participation in these groups.

The brief human relations training such as those sponsored by the National Training Laboratories of Bethel Maine and the A. K. Rice Institute offer training mainly in improving organizational behavior. They use models that could be applied to group therapy training even though they do not focus on group treatment per se. Thus, A. K. Rice offers both experiential and didactic units in their brief "laboratories" which can be adapted for therapy training. Their application groups, for example, help apply learning to the back-home situation that are similar to didactic discussions that may be used in group psychotherapy workshops.

Rationale of workshop

In designing a workshop with the goal of providing the optimal conditions for learning psychodynamic group psychotherapy, the following seemed essential to provide for the participants: First, members should have the experience of being a patient in a dynamically oriented group therapy. Second, they should have the opportunity to see skilled professionals taking a variety of roles, including the role of therapist. Third, and most important, members should participate in a carefully balanced program of experiential and didactic groups. Our workshop experience has reinforced our conviction that these are essential elements for an effective workshop.

The value of being a patient in a group experience

The psychoanalytic training model has given special emphasis to the importance of therapists undergoing their own personal psychotherapy. Having a training analysis, for example, is an essential aspect of preparing to become a psychoanalyst. Salvendy (1985) has expressed the view that the experiential option of choice is to become a member of a bona fide patient group without any other colleagues present.

I suspect that many teachers would agree, but for whatever reason, this option is rarely pursued. Short of the ideal, workshops for professionals which includes a brief therapy experience offers considerable promise. In designing our workshop, we felt it was essential that members have the opportunity to participate in a psychodynamically oriented group treatment. Partly it affords both the affective experience and appreciation of how patients feel in a group setting as well as the opportunity to identify oneself with a senior therapist who may become an internalized role model.

The value of seeing skilled professionals taking a variety of roles

Our staff felt that the opportunity to see skilled professionals in a variety of roles is a particularly valuable learning experience. For this reason the workshop was designed to allow participants to observe staff in multiple roles, for example, leading a therapy group, leading a didactic group, or interacting with colleagues in a staff discussion. This helps the participants appreciate the importance of "staying in role" and facilitates their learning that behavior appropriate to one role may not be appropriate for another. Many beginners confuse neutrality with putting on a mask or "playing a role" and may fail to appreciate that the activity and constraints of a particular role is an important professional task.

The value the combined experiential-didactic approach

The central organizing principle of our workshop is that a careful balance of experiential and didactic groups provides the optimal conditions for learning about psychodynamic group psychotherapy. The brief psychotherapy groups give meaningful affective content to the intellectual understanding which occurs in the didactic groups. The didactic groups provide the conceptual and cognitive framework which allows the participants to organize and make sense of their therapy group experience.

We believe that the didactic groups, in addition to their explicit teaching function, would allow the membership to make optimal use of the experiential therapy groups. Without the intellectual structure provided by the didactic groups, members may experience their own intense transference reactions in the therapy groups as being "wrong" or "sick", leading to denial or avoidance of their experience rather than to adaptive integration and learning. We conceptualized the didactic groups as having a supportive function, helping the members use intellectualization in the service of a less anxiety-arousing therapy experience.

Despite our staff's belief in the value of the opportunities outlined above, we feared initially that the workshop we were designing might be unsuccessful, or at least disappointing, based on two realities. First, the workshop was a brief one and therefore we had some early questions regarding the potential effectiveness of a therapy group that would meet only five or six times over a period of a few days. As a group of analytic therapists, we conceptualized change and learning as a slow process that occurs over time. Some of us were skeptical of intense, short-lived experiences of any kind, and the very notion of a "brief intensive psychoanalytic experience" sounded like an oxymoron at first. Could a psychoanalytically oriented psychotherapy experience actually be incorporated into a three-day workshop? Second, the membership consisted of professionals whose primary goal was to learn and not to be treated, even though we included a written notice in the catalog "being a patient in a brief therapy group" as part of the contract.

Some of us had questions about the proposed combination of experiential and didactic groups which were to comprise the backbone of the workshop experience. Would these events be mutually facilitative as we hoped, or might they be mutually interfering or disruptive? For example, a staff member who functioned as a therapist in the experiential group would also be functioning as a teacher or seminar leader (with the same members) in a discussion about the therapy group. The members would also be observing their group therapist interacting with other staff members, sharing their anxieties, counter-transference reactions, and feelings about the workshop. Might this not dilute the transference and interfere with the work of the ongoing therapy groups inasmuch as transference reactions require some deprivation of cues regarding the therapist as a real person. Our actual experience over the years has dispelled these doubts and has given us greater respect for the degree of learning psychodynamic group therapy which can be provided over a period of a few days. In the remainder of this chapter we will describe the various events of the workshop and discuss how they facilitated learning group psychotherapy concepts and skills.

Psychotherapy groups

The psychotherapy groups are the central event in the workshop, consuming more of the membership's time and psychic energy than the other events combined. Invariably, they receive the highest ratings in our membership's evaluations. There may be five or six therapy group sessions in a workshop, usually running for an hour and a half each, although no two workshops are ever identical in design and we often attempt to "fine tune" each offering. For example, in one workshop we began with a prolonged three-hour group session rather than the usual two regular one and a half-hour meetings separated by dinner. A few weeks prior to the beginning of the workshop the director selects the staff and assigns special roles. The staff is assembled for at least one organizational meeting in which the proposed structure is reviewed and suggestions for modifications are entertained. This preliminary meeting help to give the staff a sense of ownership of the workshop plan.

The psychotherapy group is always the first event after a brief introductory session in which the director welcomes the membership, introduces the staff, and restates the contract and primary task of the workshop. Though most of our staff has found that a co-therapy arrangement is more gratifying than working as a solo therapist, financial considerations often mitigate against this plan. As a compromise, we use a co-therapy arrangement only as a way of introducing new staff people into the workshop.

The membership characteristically shares highly personal material in an attempt to work on conflicts. In fact, we have been surprised to learn that many people attending our workshops are primarily motivated (often unconsciously, but sometimes explicitly) by the wish for a therapeutic experience. We have observed that mental health professionals often feel a need for a therapeutic experience, however brief, in order to help them cope with the strains of their professional work. Interestingly, we have occasionally received feedback that some members decided to seek treatment following the workshop experience. The primary task of the workshop, however, is to facilitate professional development rather than personal change, and for this reason we are focusing here on the contribution that the psychotherapy group makes toward this end. Our observations, as well as feedback from the participants, suggest that the following kinds of learning in the therapy groups take place.

Increased empathy with patients

The group psychotherapy sessions provide the membership with an opportunity to experience what it feels like to be a patient in a therapy group. Participants experience first-hand the anxiety of being in a group of strangers and feeling the contradictory pressures of wanting to hide, wanting to share, and also wishing to please the leader and one's peers by self-exposure. Members have stated that the anxiety they experience gives them greater empathy for their own patients; the staff facilitates an awareness of this by identifying and speaking to the feelings and conflicts associated with beginning a group experience.

The enhanced appreciation of the vulnerability of being a patient helps members to develop a greater sense of timing and tact in their own therapeutic work. The latter are crucial elements in good technique, helping patients to become more open rather than increasing their resistances. Thus, opportunities to learn first-hand how their own patients feel facilitates the membership's therapeutic skills.

Experience of transference

The members experience affects associated with the intensity of primitive feelings that are stirred in groups. In particular, they are impressed by the extent of their own aggression which is set off when their dependency wishes are frustrated by the therapist. The staff's willingness to acknowledge and make constructive therapeutic use of the membership's anger (rather than trying to dampen aggressive feelings or trying to create a "nice" group atmosphere) often allows the members to see another way of working. Many of the members characteristically tend to ignore or suppress expressions of anger in their own group psychotherapy work. Here, they learn how aggressive feelings in the participants can be worked with to facilitate growth and how they can, on the other hand, interfere with the work if aggression is avoided rather than brought into the open and dealt with.

Learning the psychodynamic model

There are many things that the members learn from seeing a good psychoanalytic therapist practice what he or she does. Most important, the membership learns that "neutrality" involves respect and tolerance for each person without having to offer more activity and benevolence than is necessary. Put somewhat differently, the membership learns the therapeutic value of avoiding the temptation to offer advice. The common error for beginning group therapists is to feel pressured from their own anxiety to actively intervene and solve people's problems. The staff's capacity to refrain from this and also to tolerate and make use of the resultant initial hostility is educational. Eventually it is experienced by the group as respectful of their autonomy and it allows for a greater impact of interventions when they are made. The members learn that the group process proceeds best in spite of, or because of, restraint on the therapist's part.

We have found that many participants in the workshop have little psychoanalytic training and come with considerable ignorance or skepticism about this way of working. In the therapy sessions, however, they become mindful of the forces within the group which influence both group and individual behavior. Concepts such as the common group tension, basic assumptions, spokesman phenomena, scape-goating, and projective identification—are felt as real and powerful aspects of group life rather than merely abstract intellectual psychoanalytic concepts.

Therapy discussion

The therapy discussion groups are usually given twice and are introduced relatively late in the workshop. The primary task is to change the therapy group into a seminar discussion group dealing with technical issues raised in the therapy group, with the therapist shifting to the role of a seminar leader. The topics to be discussed are the process of the therapy group and the techniques of group therapy. The secondary task is to begin reducing the group's transference by gratifying their need to be "fed" by the erstwhile frustrating therapist. The first therapy discussion group does not occur until after the third or fourth therapy session when the group's anger over the frustration of its dependency needs has been sufficiently worked on by the therapist and is hopefully beginning to subside. We have found that a therapy discussion group is especially effective when held after the "staff fish bowl" (to be described below) when the participants have had an opportunity to hear about the therapist's counter-transference and anxieties.

At the start of the therapy discussion group, the leader (ex-therapist) may begin by briefly outlining the highlights of the process of the therapy sessions up to that point. The members are then invited to ask questions or offer their own observations. The membership may inquire, for example, why the therapist said one thing and not another, what data in the group supported a particular intervention, or why an intervention was made at a certain point in time. The members may be interested in the style of the therapist and his theoretical rationale for what he did or did not do.

Although certain participants have suggested that the discussion group be conducted by a neutral staff member who is not a transference figure, such a person would obviously suffer from ignorance of the process in that particular group. Further, we have found that subsidiary goals, like transference diminution and the opportunity for the members to observe a staff person go through a role shift from therapist to seminar leader, and back to therapist again, are valuable experiences for the membership. Interestingly, our experience has been that the discussion groups help to attenuate the transference to the therapist but do not dilute it to the extent that work on transference issues is disrupted in subsequent sessions.

Didactic group

The workshop typically includes three didactic group sessions, run by staff members who are not therapy leaders, and consisting of a membership composition that differs from that of the therapy groups. We have found that early morning is the best time for the didactic groups, rather than later in the day when fatigue is setting in. While fatigue does not disrupt the process of the therapy groups (and may even facilitate the decline of defenses), it is detrimental to the intellectual activity that is demanded by the didactic groups.

The didactic groups provide an introduction to group psychotherapy as practiced at The Menninger Clinic and, in so doing, provides a theoretical framework for the ongoing experiential groups. Following a brief prepared lecture, the members are invited to raise questions from their practice or their home setting which can be discussed in the group. Members, for example, may inquire about how to deal with a problem patient in their own back-home therapy group (e.g., a monopolist or help-rejecting complainer) or may ask about the indications or contraindications for psychoanalytic group therapy. We have found that our attendees consist of individuals with a wide range of backgrounds and varied levels of experience. While this enhances the experience of the therapy groups, such heterogeneity does pose some problem for the didactic groups, where we often have to pitch the teaching at some middle level of skill which may not be completely satisfactory to either the beginning or the advanced clinician. Nonetheless, we have found that the didactic groups are usually quite effective when the members involved are practicing group psychotherapists and bring with them specific problems and questions.

The didactic and experiential groups have been mutually facilitative. The formal teaching which occurs in the didactic group comes alive since the members are experiencing in the therapy groups what is being cognitively conceptualized. And the didactic groups allow members to make better use of the therapy groups by providing an intellectual structure which has the supportive effect of making the members less anxious in their therapy sessions. With the didactic groups, the basic assumptions are modulated to some degree, aided by intellectualization.

The combined experiential-didactic approach is akin to having a patient in a supportive structure when one is trying to do expressive treatment; that is, where one of the treaters is supportive (the didactic leader) the other (the therapist) can be more expressive. Thus, despite the necessary anxieties which are engendered in the therapy groups, the didactic format offers a built-in support which helps the members avoid undue stress. We believe that our workshops are considerably less stressful compared to others such as A. K. Rice and NTL groups. For this reason, we offer our workshop to any person employed as a mental health professional, without having to rely on a careful selection procedure to screen out potential "casualties". While we occasionally do screen out people from the application material who are apparently too disturbed to profit from the experience, we have thus far found that a minimal selection procedure is adequate.

Staff fish bowl

The staff fish bowl is a single one-hour event in which the staff, led by the director, sits together in a circle surrounded by the membership and engages in a spontaneous discussion of the thoughts and feelings they experienced prior to and during the workshop—a report of personal reactions and counter-transference issues. Obviously, this goes a long way toward resolving transference reactions, particularly over-idealizations, and usually points up the value of supervision or consultation in dealing with technical and counter-transference issues. The staff fish bowl is the most controversial event among the membership and often receives lower ratings than the other workshop events. Some members complain of boredom and even depreciate this part of the program as a waste of time, sometimes because they would prefer not to learn that their idealized therapist is anything less than omniscient. Other members view it as an extremely valuable experience to learn that their revered therapist actually experienced anxiety or uncertainty in doing his or her work. Despite the occasional low ratings of this activity, we believe the self-revelations of the faculty in the fish bowl are both important and educational.

We have experimented with various formats and techniques for the staff fish bowl and have discovered that a predetermined period of time, like forty minutes of the hour, should be set aside for discussion among the staff with participants silently observing. Some of the usual topics are anxiety about one's competence, competitive feelings among the staff, and differences in the experience of co-therapy pairs versus the solo therapist. Sometimes a staff member will bring in a current dream which throws light on his or her reaction to the stress experienced in doing the workshop. Initially, we organized the fish bowl to give the director the option to open the floor to the membership whenever he or she saw fit; however, this played into staff avoidance of difficult issues. We subsequently moved in the direction of keeping the staff-membership interaction relatively brief following the initial staff discussion. Frequently the participants find it difficult to raise questions about what they have heard. If they do have reactions to observing that the staff also experiences anxieties and doubts, they may prefer to bring this to the privacy of their own therapy group.

Pictorial summary

The task of this next to last workshop event is for each therapy group to draw pictorially the experiences they have undergone in their therapy groups. Each group is supplied with magic markers of various colors and a large sheet of paper, perhaps three feet by five feet. No specific instructions are given as to how they are to proceed and groups may vary considerably in how they approach this task. They are given an hour to work and then asked to present their production, with proper explanation, to the plenary session where questions may be entertained from the audience. This exercise provides the participants with an opportunity to experience a catharsis of the feelings generated during their therapy group. Most of the participants report that the event is exciting and fun, and the group presentations are often marked by a good deal of hilarity.

Another benefit of the pictorial summary is that it provides the opportunity for members to learn about the other groups and thus broaden their perspective about the various therapy groups within the workshop. Competitive feelings among therapy groups often become conscious for the first time (who had the "best" therapy group and the "best" therapist). Also, members who have had several days of being "patients" together in a stressful situation, appreciate this role shift into a mutual collaborative effort where they are interacting as co-workers rather than patients. Unresolved tensions among the group members are typically diminished in this event.

Conference discussion

The conference discussion is a plenary session at the close of the workshop which provides participants with the opportunity to evaluate their experience and to give positive and negative feedback to the staff. Participants may have criticisms to share, many of which have been helpful to us in our ongoing work of improving the format of our workshop.

The conference discussion begins with the director's circulating a prepared evaluation form which typically takes about ten minutes to complete and is filled out anonymously. After these are completed, the director opens the floor for discussion. The participants find this closing event useful to tie up some loose ends which may still be troubling them, and the staff benefits from the helpful feedback.

In addition to the formal events of the workshop, the staff group meets during meals and coffee breaks in a group supervisory process which includes staff presentation of the therapy process and reports of the didactic groups as well. This is especially helpful to the group therapists who may have a special issue they would like to bring to the staff group, and who usually benefit from feedback, suggestions, and transference—counter-transference observations offered by the director and other staff members. Further, working together in an intensive way over a period of a few days has a positive effect on staff morale and offers a valuable opportunity for professional development and growth.

Summary

A three-day workshop in psychodynamic group psychotherapy for mental health professionals was offered for many years by the Menninger Clinic in Topeka. The backbone of the approach is the demonstration of the technique of group psychotherapy within a brief, but intense, group therapeutic experience. This process is cognitively organized with the help of a few discussion groups within the psychotherapy group and led by the therapist-turned-instructor. Learning is furthered by a few didactic groups conducted by a seminar leader who focuses on the model of group psychotherapy used at the institution, as well as specific problems brought by the participants from their back-home settings. Other events, such as the staff fish-bowl and pictorial summary, are primarily used to help attenuate the transference reactions engendered in the therapy groups. The model presented has enjoyed considerable approval by both participants and staff members alike.

CHAPTER NINETEEN

Exciting opportunities ahead: opening plenary address to AGPA institute participants

I have participated in numerous experiential training groups over the years both as a leader and as a member. I can assure you that the most vivid memories I have come from those that I experienced *as a member*. They have been among the most important learning experiences that I have had during my career. Let me try to explain why training groups are so valuable for a group therapist.

First, you will have the opportunity to understand in depth through direct experience the kind of inner struggles patients undergo as they attempt to form relationships and use a group for personal growth. I still remember vividly my fears of diving into the uncertain waters of these groups, and I knew that I either screwed my courage to the sticking post and entered into the fray or left the group feeling like I did not have the guts to risk exposing an aspect of my personal life that perhaps portrayed me in a less than favorable light.

When I thought about it, there were plenty of issues in my personal life to discuss—problems with colleagues, bosses, parents, children, spouse—but did I want to share any of them with a group of strangers? How would they react? Would I be criticized, humiliated or the worst of all, ignored? Would everyone at American Group Psychotherapy Association (AGPA) hear about it the next day? These are the very same anxieties our patients have when they enter and try to participate in a group. And there is no better way to learn about such struggles than to undergo them yourself, to feel them inside and firsthand—not from a book. It makes you more sensitive to your patients' anxieties and a great deal more tolerant of their resistances. Much as we all desire help from others, there are inevitable anxieties, inhibitions, and shameful feelings that make us want to withhold and withdraw.

Because we are all professional helpers, it is not uncommon for us to adopt the role of therapist's assistant in experiential groups, hiding behind one's persona as a clinician to deal only with the problem of others. Groups of professionals sometimes appear like 12 therapists in search of a patient.

Another favorite escape hatch, used by patients as well as therapists, is to retreat into the role of silent observer. After all, one is there to learn how groups function, how members and patients interact, and what better way than to be a fly on the wall? Let me assure you that such a role will not only make you a problem member, but you will be cheating yourself of a potentially rich experience of being as full a participant as possible.

So far I have described only the advantage of learning better how our patients feel. But there is also the possibility, nay the probability, that you will learn something important about yourself: if you tend to monopolize or conversely, if you are too silent, you are likely to hear about it from your fellow members. If you are too self-absorbed and don't attend sufficiently to others, you will probably be told about it. If you don't reflect about what others tell you, let it bounce off your back or ignore it, the group will tell you. Most often these reminders will be relatively gentle and given in a constructive manner. In any case this personal feedback about how you come across in a group, how you behave as a group member, can be extremely helpful in expanding your self-awareness.

Another way of learning more about oneself is also by silent self-observation. I began to observe in more than one group that I was constantly evaluating leaders' interventions, giving them grades for their performance. More often than not they felt short of my expectations, and I often persuaded myself silently that I could do a better job. One leader didn't take well to negative transference and discouraged its expression, another talked in strange metaphoric language, whereas still another made weak eye contact with members. Although some of these criticisms may have been warranted, the more important lesson I began to learn was about my own competitiveness with authority figures.

This brings me to another rich source of learning, that is, the opportunity to observe an experienced group therapist in action. If you are not intent on criticizing the group leader, as I was, you will be able to learn about a skilled clinician's approach to a group, how he or she thinks, what gets observed, interpreted, or confronted. When is the therapist silent and when interpretive? When is the intervention addressed to the whole group and when to an individual? What interventions seemed to work and move the process forward and which were ineffective? In individual psychotherapy training, we rarely see our supervisors and mentors in action. Groups are unique in providing clinicians an opportunity to watch, evaluate, and learn from an experienced therapist.

Still another learning experience is the opportunity to become knowledgeable about group dynamics. I have learned more about these matters as a participant than as a therapist, probably because the role of observer without the responsibility of managing the group permits more relaxed opportunities to study what is transpiring. I was a member of an experiential group some years ago, where I observed a striking combination of group dynamics that was instructive and memorable. This was a group in which it was difficult for members to express hostility, mainly to the leader. Some tentative jibes at him resulted in certain non-verbal reactions, like tightening of his facial muscles, which convinced the group that this was a leader who was not exactly welcoming of such behavior. As a result the group found a spokesperson, Dan, whose disposition to freely express negative feelings made him a likely candidate to fill that role for them. They subtly encouraged Dan to speak up and he was more than happy to vent his spleen at the leader. Does this sound like projective identification? Indeed it does. It is also the basis for role suction. But when Dan began to freely express his criticisms of the leader, the group gave him little support and, in fact, began to ostracize him for his unwelcome ideas, which in turn made his devaluations of the leader even more extravagant. This scape-goating made it necessary eventually for him to leave the group. I remember his departure quite vividly because he left with some fanfare in which he went around the room describing the Achilles' heel of each member and then nominated me to carry on the good fight, an invitation that I wisely declined. The whole episode was a memorable experience, which I have put to good use in my understanding and teaching about group phenomena.

I would like to mention one last potential benefit from experiential groups. It has the possibility of throwing light on problems of authority, leadership, and followership in organizations. Some years ago the Menninger Clinic was undergoing a radical change in leadership, and the torch was being passed from the founder, Dr. Karl Menninger, to the next generation, led by Dr. Roy Menninger. The staff needed to give up its dependency on a strong charismatic father figure and begin taking more responsibility for decision making. At that time the organization turned to the A. K. Rice Institute's group-relations conferences, an experiential method for studying organizations, and most of the staff attended at least one week-long conference. We did a follow-up study some ten years later and most of the participants still spoke enthusiastically about the important learning they had gained from the experience. There was little doubt that the organization had become better able to negotiate the needed shift from a dependency culture to one in which greater autonomy was called for.

I have often tried to understand the various factors that have led to making the AGPA as successful an organization as it has become. Most of us who have been associated with AGPA have a sense of closeness and bonding with the organization and with our peers that makes membership highly valued. Over and above the professional and scientific benefits, we form close friendships that enrich us. I believe that the Institute experience contributes in no small measure to the personal relationships that develop. Friendships made in these groups often continue and endure.

What you are about to enter is a two-day intensive personal experience in which you have the opportunity to learn about yourself, to learn about group leadership, and to learn about group dynamics—all in a way that you can't possibly learn from reading. You may even get a new perspective about a problem in your personal life. Each of you will make unique observations and will carry away different facets of the experience, depending on where you are in your own development as a clinician and as a person. If you are especially motivated to learn more about yourself, you will probably come away with new personal insights. If you are interested in focusing on techniques of leadership, those concepts will be paramount.

This will be a challenging and exciting adventure in personal growth. I am certain that the experience will stay with you forever. My recommendation: Seize the opportunity.

The value of group-as-a-whole models

M any models of group psychotherapy abound in private offices, outpatient clinics, hospitals, and day hospitals. Very often the particular model is determined by the nature of the population being treated and by the objectives of the treatment, where dimensions of supportive vs expressive or socialization *vs.* insight govern the choice of the model. When the therapist is well trained, the particular method used is likely to be appropriately chosen and effective regardless of the particular orientation that is applied. This observation harks back to an early classic study done by Fiedler (1950) which found that outcome in individual psychotherapy is more influenced by the therapist's length of experience than by the particular model of treatment he was using. Also, most research in individual psychotherapy has failed to show significant differences between a variety of approaches, leading Luborsky, Singer, and Luborsky (1975, 2002), after these colleagues examined a wide variety of studies, to proclaim like the Dodo bird in Alice in Wonderland, "Everyone has won and all shall have prizes". This conclusion makes sense insofar as all of the major psychotherapy models probably have more commonalities than they do differences.

A classic survey of the field of psychoanalytic group psychotherapy was done many years ago by Morris Parloff (1968) in which he categorized three major approaches: intrapersonal, interpersonal, and integralist (group-as-a-whole). The intrapersonal method associated with Slavson (1964) and Wolf and Schwartz (1962) in which anything smacking of the use of the dynamics of the whole group was considered anathema, has now largely faded from the group scene among trained group therapists. On the other hand, as Parloff predicted, the group-as-a-whole method, in all its variations, would begin to gain acceptance by many professionals. In a survey by Dies (1992) of over 100 clinicians, the largest number described their predominant approach as psychodynamic and among that group the leading methods were group-as-a-whole (GAW) and Interpersonal (IP).

This concluding chapter will be devoted to a comparison of two models: First, the interpersonal model which emphasizes working with the relationship between members while relying on feedback by the group as the main vehicle of insight and change and downplaying the transference to the therapist. Second, the GAW approach which emphasizes both attention to peer interactions as well as the dynamics of the whole group. There is no doubt in my mind that each of them are effective in helping patients achieve good outcomes but I believe it is useful to compare the two methods as a way of clarifying the special merits that each offers to prospective patients.

The many usages of "group-as-a-whole"

Before embarking on this comparison, it is important to recognize that GAW is used in a variety of ways by authors engaging in very different methods. I believe there is a continuum of usage of the term that I would like to spell out in order to avoid confusion.

First, there are models that attend to characteristics of the whole group but do not necessarily include interventions addressed to the entire group. For example, a system that only values characteristics such as cohesion, a valuable property of a group, is a minimal type of GAW. The therapist may attempt to foster cohesion by transparency, self-disclosure, empathy, etc. but one would have to make a distinction between the therapist recognizing and keeping in mind cohesion building and actually making GAW interventions. Similarly, for a model that formulates its curative power based on what develops in the whole group, such as the concept of universalization. This refers to the positive generalized effect when one member shares her anxieties and thus serves as a catalyst to other patients. Certainly it is an important mechanism that stimulates self disclosure and interaction but quite different from those therapies that explicitly address the thematic content occurring in the GAW.

Next on the continuum are the approaches that mainly address the whole group when a group-wide resistance has set in. Such a reaction may be manifested by significant lateness, low level of self-disclosure, or other restraints on participation that deserve attention by the therapist. These interventions are important and necessary and provide the possibility of constructive forward movement in the group and may elicit significant content.

Another level of GAW work occurs when the therapist observes group-wide reactions in relation to boundary alterations. The entry of a new member, the departure of an old member, a therapist's planned or unplanned absence often result in shared group responses. These interventions represent a further step in addressing the content of the group's shared reactions to various group events. For the most part, those approaches that largely restrict themselves to these developments represent what I have earlier referred to as intermittent GAW models.

My view of the most comprehensive type of GAW methodology is one which is based on what I refer to as the group centered hypothesis, the view that the group is to a greater or lesser extent always under the influence of a "common group tension". In other words there is a commonly shared group reaction, or group-wide conflict, continuously influencing the group members. Sometimes this reaction is quietly evolving, not fully developed, and not clearly observable, while other times it is clearly visible and ready for interpretation. It is important to emphasize that the common group tension does not mean that the group is reacting with similar or identical behaviors.

Each member reacts to this group development in their own unique way which means that there is no uniformity of response despite the fact that each member shares in the same underlying tension or affect. This type of work by the therapist is what I consider the most useful form of GAW work. It occurs when the treater is "listening with the fourth ear", using his third ear for the dynamics of the individual patient and his fourth ear to listen for the underlying commonality occurring in the group.

Comparing modern Tavistock and interpersonal models

In undertaking this study, I decided to compare two well-known models representing each of the two approaches: the interpersonal (IP) and group-as-a-whole (GAW) methods. First, the most widely known and clearly articulated of the interpersonal models, particularly in the United States, is that of Yalom and Leszcz (2005) and now recently expanded in a detailed article by Leczsz and Malat (2012). It is well accepted in the American group therapy scene and taught in numerous training centers. In terms of GAW models, there are two models to choose from. One widely used method, particularly in Europe, is the group analytic approach first introduced by Michael Foulkes (1964) and further elaborated by Malcolm Pines and his associates (Pines & Schlapobersky, 2010). I am aware that group analytic covers a wide range of practices and some therapists use a "common group tension" approach while others tend to downplay this type of intervention. On the other hand, there is another GAW model practiced at the Tavistock Clinic, considerably revised from the now defunct Ezriel model, and this current contemporary model is clearly articulated in the recent book by Garland (2010) and her colleagues.

While both GA and Tavi possess similarities, they differ in how they conceptualize GAW: First, Tavi is quite clear about the importance of the common group tension concept and how it influences the therapist's interventions; GA emphasizes the communication matrix, the sum total of all of the contributions of members and conductor, which influences all of the reactions of the patients. In my view, they are not averse to using the idea of a shared common theme but many do not make it a guiding principle. A second difference is in how they formulate the role of the therapist. GA describes the conductor as a dynamic administrator who gradually moves as much as possible into a member-like role while Tavi tends to emphasize a clear boundary that the therapist maintains between himself and the members. This difference is consistent with the GA view that transference to the therapist should be downplayed inasmuch as it detracts from the importance of peer interaction. Tavi views the interpretation of the transference to the therapist as a major element of their model.

Hence, I shall focus on the contrast between the Yalom/Leszcz interpersonal approach as opposed to the contemporary model used at the Tavistock clinic, inasmuch as the latter contains the "common group tension" concept of GAW which clearly seeks out and interprets the shared conflicts of the group.

While I am aware that there is some overlap between the IP and Tavi models, I shall seek to emphasize their differences. For example, the IP model pays attention to what is transpiring in the whole group and is not averse to presenting GAW interventions at certain times, to be discussed below. And of course Tavi practitioners pay attention to peer interaction and peer transferences, and like IP, use feedback as a method of mirroring for patients their impact upon others, but this method has less primacy and in fact is probably secondary to the Tavi uncovering approach using common group tension interventions.

I am keenly aware that models are only guidelines for the therapist and that the personal qualities of the therapist inevitably play a role in how the treatment is conducted. As mentioned in Chapter Sixteen on narcissistic group leadership, such characteristics may place limitations on what transpires, for example, where the therapist may have a neurotic need to be affirmed and has difficulty in tolerating negative reactions. In the early days of psychoanalysis the effect of the personality of the analyst was minimized by referring to the "average expectable analyst" but this view has been supplanted by recent theoretical and technical advances, emphasized by the relational and inter-subjective schools, which emphasize that in addition to counter-transference, there are such qualities as empathy, attunement, and sensitivity as well as specific personality complexes possessed by the therapist which play a role in the patient-therapist relationship. These characteristics have a significant impact on the process regardless of the specific model the therapist espouses.

The interpersonal model of Yalom and Leszcz

This model is spelled out with increasing clarity in a number of different writings by Yalom and Leszcz. Like all other group therapies they emphasize the importance of the group as a microcosm of the patients' behavioral patterns so that their here-and-now interactions within the group are typical of their ways of interacting in the external world. They emphasize the use of Kiesler's concept (1996) of the Maladaptive Transaction Cycle (MTC) as a guiding principle of their work combined with Weiss's control-mastery theory (1993). The MTC consist of "an unbroken causal loop in which the patient continues to elicit responses by others that confirm her pathogenic beliefs while failing to integrate readily schema that disconfirm those ingrained beliefs" (Leszcz & Malat, 2012, p. 36). The authors describe four elements of the MTC: (1) identify the overt behavior of the initiator; (2) the overt response of the respondent/therapist; (3) exploration of the less conscious response of the respondent/therapist; and (4) finally the examination and exploration of the deeper, covert experience and covert self-representation of the patient. The main thrust of this thinking is that the patient is unknowingly eliciting negative responses based on her distorted view of self in relation to other and IP therapy is an attempt to interrupt this vicious circle.

The method of achieving this kind of therapeutic change is mainly via the encouragement of peer interactions in which the maladaptive behavior becomes manifest to members of the group but to a much lesser extent to the patient who is enmeshed in a series of unconscious actions and reactions. The primary vehicle for helping the patient become aware of her maladaptive behavior is through the use of personal feedback, primarily by peers who have been able to observe, and be affected by, the patient's neurotically based behavior. The therapist is transparent in presenting his observation in the feedback process and attempts to present himself as a model of helpful and empathic communication.

One of the strengths of the article by Leszcz and Malat is the large number of excellent clinical vignettes to demonstrate their views. For example, one persuasive illustration of the effectiveness of the method was that of a college professor who sought individual treatment to help with a lingering depression after the death of his wife of thirty-eight years. He developed a good relationship with his individual therapist but he continued to be quite isolated and this therapist recommended a group to help with his reclusiveness. The group was initially supportive of his efforts to overcome his reaction to his loss but within a short time his arrogant, haughty, know-it-all attitude emerged, while berating other group members for their poor judgment and foolishness. Quite rapidly he became marginalized in the group and eventually he received the important feedback from his peers that his isolation, both within the group and in his life outside, was due to his devaluing, demeaning attitude toward others. "He was stunned to learn about his impact in the group, and to his credit, welcomed the feedback"

(p. 46). Unquestionably a favorable and encouraging development for this man.

The authors describe the group therapist's role as "disciplined personal therapeutic involvement" (p. 53). As mentioned above, the therapist ideally models the most effective way of presenting empathic and judicious feedback in order to maximize the possibility of the messages being heard and used by the patient receiving these communications. The therapist takes the role of "special member", not reluctant to be transparent about his reactions, and, to the extent possible, not encouraging of transference reactions to himself. He avoids the role of the distant, anonymous, and omniscient leader who encourages the patients to project fantasies upon him. He is active in attempting to stimulate the group to interact with each other.

The attitude of the authors toward the use of group-wide interventions is mainly that his focus should be on member-to-member transference rather than on the group-wide transference to the therapist. Their attention to group-wide developments should be on the avoidance of anxiety laden issues or the development of anti-therapeutic norms. They also attend to such group-wide events as boundary alterations like the entry of new members, terminations, and vacation interruptions. The presence of positive group developments, like group cohesion, which facilitates the work of the group, should be silently observed by the leader but need not be addressed.

The revised contemporary Tavistock model

It is most important again to emphasize that the current Tavistock model is quite different from the widely criticized Bion/Ezriel models that were associated with Tavistock decades ago. Many anachronistic critiques continue to regard the current Tavistock model as stuck in the old, outmoded method. First, the Bion model of confining interventions solely to the group-as-a-whole never really took hold, even at the Tavistock Clinic. The early model that was indeed adopted and used during the post-war years was the Ezriel approach which eventually faded out, to a large extent because of the Malan study (1976) which found that patients were largely dissatisfied with their group therapy experience because their personal issues were ignored in favor of the therapist's attention to the group-as-a-whole.

The recent Garland book (2010) describing the new and revised model in use at the Tavistock clearly labels the attribution of the old methods to them as "mythology". Francesca Hume (2010), director of training in adult psychotherapy at Tavistock, characterizes their approach as a flexible integration of Bion's understanding of group process with a "clinical style that owes more to Foulkes" (p. 126). In other words, they still adhere to the "common group tension" idea propounded by their predecessors while adopting a method that emphasizes flexibly moving back and forth between individual and GAW interventions. They emphatically disagree with the Bion technique of focussing solely upon the dynamics of the group.

Hume describes the role of the therapist as often silent until she becomes aware of a unifying theme and making her interventions, individual and group-wide, when the group theme has become clear. She emphasizes the necessity of directly addressing individuals in order to avoid conveying that you may be abandoning or neglecting them. Such individual interventions may relate to their personal issues, either inside or outside the group. Garland further amplifies this idea by stating that there are long passages of time when the dynamics of the group are somewhat in the background and do not need to be interpreted since individual members are engaged with and cooperating in addressing their problems of personal growth. They also are cognizant of the fact that individual interventions at the same time have an effect upon the entire membership, acknowledging Hopper's observation (1985) that talking to an individual is also talking to the whole group.

While the therapist attends to both the GAW as well as to each individual, Garland tends to put a greater emphasis upon a rough division of labor between therapist and group members. The therapist's main function is to listen for and interpret the unconscious functioning of the whole group, and offering GAW interpretations (listening with the fourth ear), while she leaves peer transference feedback largely to the members. "Transferences within the group are responded to and commented on by group members far more often than they are by the therapist" (p. 43).

Although they give primacy to uncovering interpretations of the transferences in the group, they also recognize that therapeutic effects are often generated simply out of being a member of the group. First, insofar as each member is contributing to the therapy process of her peers, she experiences a rise in self-esteem. Second, the pressure in the group to move from a narcissistic self-preoccupation to caring and concern for others is "work that one has to do on a daily basis" (p. 36).

A comparison and contrast of two methods

Theoretical foundations and process

Both the interpersonal (IP) and the contemporaneous Tavistock (Tavi) models share a number of underlying similarities. They both subscribe to the notion that the behavior manifested by the patient in a group is a microcosm of the patterns she demonstrates in her interpersonal relations of her everyday life. They both believe that the here-and-now behavior manifested in the group should be the major data used by the therapist and the group as the source of what is learned by the patient. They both use a feedback/interpretive method coming primarily from peers attempting to provide helpful observations to each other of the impact a patient is having upon them. In both models, there is recognition of the helpful aspect of being a member of a group insofar as one is playing a helpful role in the lives of other people. And of course, the pressure to be attentive to others in the group also adds to one's shift from "narcissism to social-ism".

However, they differ in how they conceptualize some aspects of the change process. The IP model relies largely on the formulations of numerous theorists, both analytic and cognitive, but primarily on Kiesler (1996) and Weiss (1993). They attempt to emphasize how the patient's behavior elicits certain responses from others and how this pattern tends to reinforce the patient's conviction about how others behave toward her. Weiss's control mastery theory amplifies this view in the sense that much of the patient's behavior with others is a test that will either confirm or disconfirm the patient's hopes or fears about how she will be treated by others. The feedback offered by the patient's peers and therapist is an effort to interrupt the maladaptive cycle and disconfirm the patient's feared expectations.

In contrast, a major emphasis in Tavi is on the uncovering of unconscious wishes and fears via interpretation of the various transferences manifesting themselves in the group. The Tavi theory of change is partly based on personal insight which may be gained through interpretations to individuals, similar to the feedback process used in IP, but is also based on group-wide interventions concerning the group-wide transferences primarily made by the therapist. In Tavi, the therapist flexibly moves between attending to individuals and to the group-as-a-whole, depending on which aspect of the group that presents the main "point of urgency". Although IP therapists may also shift in this way, they prefer to emphasize individual interactions and the feedback process.

Role of therapist

There is a distinct difference between the two models in the way they conceive of the therapist's role insofar as the IP therapist attempts as much as possible to assume a member-role. Since the focus of the IP therapist is on each individual's neurotic pattern of behavior and stresses an effort to provide feedback, the dynamics of the GAW, particularly as it applies to the group's relationship to the therapist is downplayed. In fact, the IP proponents state that attending to such dynamics, which they acknowledge is usually present, would interfere with the work of observing individual patterns that need the primary attention of the group. Thus the therapist attempts to assume a member-like role and tries as much as possible to minimize attention to the member-therapist transference that ensues when the therapist is restrained in his participation.

In contrast, the Tavi therapist maintains a distinct boundary between herself and her patients with the rationale that transference to the therapist constitutes a significant dimension of the treatment and becoming like another member in terms of transparency could interfere with the transference developments. For example, while members address each other by first names, the therapist is addressed with her professional title. As mentioned earlier, the Tavi therapist is happy to permit much of the feedback of a personal nature to be given by other patients, while she also recognizes the importance of the therapist clearly conveying attention to the personal needs and issues of individual members.

Insofar as the IP therapist recognizes the existence of group-wide reactions, he will address such developments mainly when they constitute a resistance or interference in the functioning of the group. For example, when the therapist notes the development of anti-therapeutic norms (like members tolerating lateness and absence) or a generalized avoidance of anxiety-laden topics, he will address the entire group.

Similarly, when group boundaries are being altered or breached, such as the admission of a new member or the termination of an old member, the therapist is likely to deal with a group-wide reaction. But unlike Tavi, the IP therapist does not usually seek out and interpret commonly shared themes.

The IP therapist attempts to model ideal member behavior for his patients. He tries to be as open and transparent as possible in providing feedback, readily revealing his personal, affective reactions to the behavior of members. He attempts to maintain the focus on peer interactions and mostly views attention to the GAW themes as a distraction from his primary objective.

Undoubtedly, the therapist's membership status in IP enhances his human qualities and contributes to the cohesion and attractiveness of the group. It avoids the pitfalls of Bion's tendency to produce iatrogenic behavior and also counteracts the tendency to endow the therapist with omniscience found in the now discarded classical Tavistock model. Another virtue of IP is that there is a sense of excitement and engagement that occurs in the whole group when a member becomes the object of interpersonal work. "It demands that all of the members of the group be alive to the moment and to the immediacy of the engagement" (Leczsz & Malat, 1012, p. 47).

Furthermore, the technique of using the IP model is that it is simpler and more straightforward inasmuch as the focus of the work is narrower. The Tavi therapist must maintain binocular vision in the sense of paying attention both to the individual as well as the GAW, while the IP therapist focuses mainly on the individual's interpersonal and interactional behavior that is the source of his relational problems.

Depth of transference

I believe that attention by the Tavi therapist to the GAW leads to uncovering greater depth of unconscious conflict. It appears that group mechanisms such as Foulkes' resonance, mirroring, contagion, and projective identification produce an enhanced affective reaction in its members and this shared, group-wide reaction will lead to an intensification of the transference. In my view (Chapter Eight), transference in groups may be either diluted or intensified, with GAW interpretations tending to intensify the transference, particularly the group's transference to the therapist.

An example of a GAW intervention is given by Schlapobersky (2000), a prominent group analyst, in which a group showed a pattern of the members ignoring reports of other patients' success. One woman happily announced that after a long struggle to conceive, a long-sought pregnancy had occurred, but the news was greeted with a muted response. Later a male member was pleased to announce that he had finally reached a financial target in a business he had established. His announcement also elicited little enthusiasm from the group. The group analyst noted this unusual reaction and uncovered the fact that the group's awkwardness and resistance to exploring these important events was based on envy of the successes of their fellow members. The interpretation opened a "wide-ranging exploration of envy and jealousy in intimate relations" (p. 222).

The above is a good example of the therapist attending to the group's common group tension and produces a depth result that is less likely to appear in the interpersonal model. Envy and jealousy is part of the human condition and affects every person to some extent. Uncovering its presence as a commonly shared reaction in the entire group helps each individual to become aware of unconscious and unacceptable affects.

A further example of therapist transference is that offered in the previous chapter in which the leader was averse to dealing with the negative transference to himself. He showed facial reactions which demonstrated displeasure with any criticism directed to him and he certainly did not ask any of the members to elaborate on their negative reactions. The group found a spokesman in one patient who was relatively comfortable with his hostility and encouraged him to speak for them. There is little doubt that this was a GAW transference reaction to the therapist and could not be attributed solely to the member who was willing to offer himself as the spokesman. Since the IP writers make it clear that their method tends to deemphasize therapist transference, it would be more difficult to uncover attitudes toward authority figures and the host of issues associated with that complex.

Garland (2010) presents several vignettes of GAW interventions. The briefest one, given without context but situationally obvious is the therapist's interpretation: "Mary's silence is tolerated by the rest of you because it represents that bit of each of you that you want to withhold, and not be seen" (p. 22).

A more extended example is that of two co-therapists who arrive at a session not more than two minutes late. The group is already engaged in animated conversation and continues for the next twenty minutes, ostensibly without taking note of the therapists' arrival. The girlfriend of one of the members had recently discovered that her father was engaged in a bigamous relationship and he had let it be known that she and her boyfriend were not welcome to visit his home over the Christmas holidays. The group was quite absorbed in trying to help the member with this disturbing development. One of the therapists tried to break in with an announcement about the exact dates of the upcoming Christmas break but she was clearly ignored. The therapist finally got their attention when she noted that the group was shutting the therapists out, "making them feel unwanted and unnecessary out of anger at their lateness". She said they were expressing their anger indirectly because they were afraid the therapists might get angry back. This intervention led to a discussion of how the therapists felt about the group members and their fantasies of how the therapists would be enjoying the Christmas holiday together.

The therapist was picking up the metaphor of the member under discussion not being welcome for the holidays at the home of his in-laws as well as the obvious exclusion of the therapists. Among other things, the intervention struck deep into the members' psyches regarding the anger the infant feels when mother is late attending to his needs since he expects immediate caretaking. It is an excellent illustration of how the therapist transference can uncover important psychological issues that are universal but do not easily surface.

While various GAW methods differ with regard to therapist activity, openness, and transparency, they generally tend to encourage the development of transference. Most modern GAW models emphasize three types of transference: member to member, member to therapist, and member to GAW. Probably the greater the boundary set up by the leader between him and her patients, the more will she elicit therapist transference. Although this pattern can be carried to an extreme (as seen in Bion's groups), not working with the group-wide therapist transference may deemphasize a wide variety of important issues: competition with authority figures, excessive dependence on the therapist, readiness to feel frustrated or excluded, struggles to become the therapist's favorite, and tendency to idealize the therapist, to name just a few.

The Tavi method is probably more attuned than IP to a whole variety of group dynamics. For example, the well-known dynamic of role suction is usually considered a GAW phenomenon and might be more easily ignored in the IP format. As the group seeks out a spokesperson for certain anxiety laden feelings, they encourage the member who is most comfortable with those feelings to take the initiative in speaking up. There is a real question whether the focus on peer interaction would tend to miss the GAW pressure involved in role suction.

The binocular vision involved in seeking out shared group themes can contribute to the development of group cohesion, often viewed as comparable to the therapeutic alliance in a dyadic process. Interventions addressed to the entire group about a shared anxiety, conflict, or unacceptable fantasy, provides each patient with what I have called "the protection of the group theme". Such interventions reduce the shame, guilt, and threat to self-esteem to group members and thus facilitates openness.

The Tavi model moves back and forth flexibly between working with individuals and attending to the GAW. This approach tends to avoid the hazard in the now defunct Ezriel method which left the patient feeling that her needs were being sacrificed on the altar of the therapist's interest in what is transpiring at the group-wide level.

Slavson's intrapersonal model, also now outmoded, eschewed the use of group dynamics and was criticized for failing to harness the power of the whole group's energy. While IP is quite different and does occasionally attend to whole group phenomena, a major question about the method is the decision to focus on interpersonal interactions, largely to the exclusion of what is transpiring at the group level. I believe that group-wide reactions carry the group to a deeper, more intense transferential level and hence the question must be posed whether IP misses an opportunity to uncover the commonly shared and deeper conflicts and transferences.

The method used by the contemporary clinicians of the Tavistock Clinic (Garland, 2010) is very close to my inductive group centered model (Chapter Six). The current Tavistock clinicians refer to the Bion/Ezriel method as a mythology of the past. In fact they describe their current model having a clinical style that owes much to Foulkes. They emphasize the necessity to maintain a "double vision" in which attention is paid to both the dynamics of the individual as well as the dynamics of the whole group. "Too great a focus on the individual (doing individual therapy in public) stirs envy and rivalry and will damage the potential of the group for becoming the therapeutic medium. Yet too insistent a focus on the group-as-a-whole can leave individuals feeling overlooked and sometimes abandoned" (Garland, p. 35).

A research study

Piper (1995) has observed that most psychodynamic group therapists subscribe to the view that a group-as-a-whole orientation is useful in illuminating group process but many are ambivalent about using group-wide interventions. He speculates that this is due to two factors, both associated with the Tavistock model, obviously the older model rather than the contemporary one. First, the research by Malan, Balfour, Hood, and Shooter (1976) on Tavistock group therapy demonstrated a poor outcome for most of the patients who reported frustration with the therapist's emphasis on the whole group to the neglect of individual members. Second, many clinicians have been exposed to Tavistock group relation workshops and experienced "powerful, regressive, and at times frightening reactions to the persistent group-as-a-whole interpretations" (p. 158).

On the other hand, Piper and his group report that their study of types of interventions in a clinical trial with twelve short-term groups of psychiatric patients struggling with issues of loss, produced a favorable impression of the efficacy of group-wide intervention. He stated: "It is our clinical impression that the group interpretations have contributed to the favorable outcomes associated with treatment as evidenced in our controlled clinical trial" (p. 188).

Conclusion

Both the interpersonal and the modern contemporary Tavistock models may produce good therapeutic outcomes, but their differences in theory and technique could produce varied results. My own background and experience inclines me toward the new Tavistock model, particularly with patients who are candidates for a more expressive, uncovering treatment, such as the person struggling with a personality disorder with deeply buried neurotic roots. The tendency of the IP therapist to confine GAW interventions to group-wide resistances or to the development of anti-therapeutic norms and to minimize transference to the therapist will probably limit the reach of the therapy to a lesser level of depth and intensity of transference. This was nicely illustrated in the session in which the group ignored the presence of their co-therapists based on their lateness as well as their fantasy of being excluded by the therapists during the upcoming holiday.

I do not wish to minimize the importance of easily observed, overt levels of behavior that are emphasized in IP which the targeted patient tends to be oblivious to. However, many patients can profit by a more expressive, uncovering approach which also reaches more deeply buried affects. Also less likely to be observed in the IP treatment are such group dynamics as role suction and scapegoating. Inasmuch as these occurrences are generally embedded in group-as-a-whole reactions.

On the other hand, the IP model, provides the advantage of emphasizing the importance of feedback to members which enhances a heightened sense of engagement resulting in increased cohesion among members. Also their view that the therapist should adopt as much of a membership role as possible adds to the patients' perception of the therapist's human qualities and enhances their comfort in relating to the therapist. Additionally, insofar as the IP therapist does not focus on what is transpiring in the whole group, the IP therapist's task is made somewhat easier.

* * *

Group psychotherapy has established itself over the last half century as an important modality in helping people with problems in living and with their personal relationships in particular. Most group therapists subscribe to the idea that group treatment makes a unique contribution to how people manage their personal interactions, oftentimes teaching them how they elicit unwelcome responses from others. Many individuals who have been treated in a long-term individual process as well as a course of group psychotherapy often comment that, despite the helpfulness of their individual treatment, their group experience brought out new facets of their behavior never uncovered in their dyadic therapy.

Both individual and group are significant and helpful modalities and frequently they overlap in what they contribute. At the same time each has unique features not possessed by the other. Although definitive conclusions of these differences has yet to be reached, most therapists with experience in both modalities believe the individual treatment excels at uncovering and resolving unconscious neurotic conflict while group treatment has the special virtue of focusing on maladaptive narcissistic and self-defeating behaviors. Perhaps the ideal treatment of the future will be a combination of the two, either simultaneously or successively. One caveat, however, is that group treatment is not necessarily indicated for everyone seeking help.

In these days of fiscal strain world-wide and an ongoing necessity to contain medical costs, group modalities should become a frequent choice, provided there are no special contraindications. I have often mentioned throughout this book that many models of group psychotherapy have merit and have proved useful to multitudes of patients. In my view an approach which emphasizes working with the group-as-a-whole, and in particular makes use of the shared group theme or common group tension, has much to offer in resolving personal conflicts as well as maladaptive interpersonal behaviors.

REFERENCES

Abend, S. & Nersessian, E. (1989). Changing psychic structure through treatment. *J. American Psychoanalytic Association, 37*: 173–185.

Agazarian, Y. M. (1997). *Systems Centered Therapy for Groups*. New York: Guilford.

Agazarian, Y. M. (2008). Introduction to a theory of living human systems. In: G. M. Saiger, S. Rubenfeld, M. D. Dluhy (Eds.), *Windows into Today's Group Therapy* (pp. 23–30). New York: Routledge.

Agazarian, Y. & Gantt, S. (2005). The systems centered approach to the group-as-a-whole. *Group, 29*: 163–185.

Aledort, S. L. (2008). Model for the development of intensive multi-weekly group psychoanalysis. In M. Dluhy, S. Rubenfeld, M. Saiger (Eds). *Windows into Today's Group Therapy* (pp. 177–189). New York: Routledge.

Alford, C. F. (1995). Response to Horwitz, Debbane, & Piper. *International J. Group Psychotherapy, 45*: 163–167.

Allen, J. G. (2012). *Restoring Mentalizing in Attachment Relationships: Treating Trauma with Plain Old Therapy*. Washington, D.C.: American Psychiatric Publishing.

Allen, J. G., Fonagy, P., & Bateman, A. W. (2008). *Mentalizing in Clinical Practice*. Arlington, VA: American Psychiatric Publishing.

Anthony, E. J. (1971). The history of group psychotherapy. In: H. I. Kaplan & B. J. Sadock (Eds.), *Comprehensive Group Psychotherapy* (pp. 4–31). Baltimore: Williams & Wilkins.

Anzieu, D. (1975). *The Group and the Unconscious*. London: Routledge & Regan Paul.

Appelbaum, S. A. (1963). The pleasure and reality principles in group process teaching. *British Journal of Medical Psychology, 36*: 1–7.

Arsenian, J., Semrad, E. V., & Shapiro, D. (1962). An analysis of integral functions in small groups. *International Journal of Group Psychotherapy, 12*: 421–434.

Ashbach, C. & Schermer, V. L. (1987). *Object Relation, the Self, & the Group*. New York: Routledge & Kegan Paul.

Aveline, M. O. (1993). Principles of leadership in brief training groups for mental health professionals. *International Journal of Group Psychotherapy, 43*: 107–129.

Bacal, H. A. (1975). A therapist, peer, and group transference: Transference structuring as a guide to intervention in group psychotherapy. Unpublished.

Bacal, H. A. (1991). Reactiveness and responsiveness in the group therapeutic process. In: S. Tuttman (Ed.), *Psychoanalytic Group Theory and Therapy* (pp. 309–318). Madison, CT: International University Press.

Baker, H. & Baker, M. (1993). Self-psychological contributions to the theory and practice of group psychotherapy. In: A. Alonso & H. Swiller (Eds.), *Group Therapy in Clinical Practice* (pp. 49–68). Washington, D.C.: American Psychiatric Press.

Bateman, A. W. (1998). Thick and thin-skinned organization and enactment in borderline and narcissistic disorders. *International Journal Psychoanalysis, 79*: 13–25.

Bateman, A. W. & Fonagy, P. (2001). Treatment of borderline personality with psychoanalytically oriented partial hospitalization: An 18 month follow-up. *American Journal Psychiatry, 158*: 36–42.

Bateman, A. W. & Fonagy, P. (2004). *Psychotherapy for Borderline Personality Disorders: Mentalization Based Treatment*. Oxford: Oxford University Press.

Bateman, A. W. & Fonagy, P. (2006). *Mentalization-Based Treatment for Borderline Personality Disorder: A Practical Guide*. New York: Oxford University Press.

Battegay, R. (1991). The Hunger Diseases. Toronto: Hogrefe & Huber.

Bennis, W. G. & Shepard, F. (1956). A theory of group development. *Human Relations, 9*: 415–437.

Billow, R. M. (2003). *Relational Group Psychotherapy: From Basic Assumptions to Passion*. New York: Jessica Kingsley.

Bion, W. R. (1961). *Experiences in Groups*. New York: Basic Books.

Brown, D. (2006). Foulkes' basic law of group dynamics 50 years on: Abnormality, injustice, and the renewal of ethics. In: J. Maratos (Ed.), *Resonance and Reciprocity* (pp. 167–186). London: Jessica Kingsley.

Burstein, E. & Beale, E. (1976). Group Psychotherapy: A Treatment for Narcissistic Disturbances? Unpublished manuscript.

Caligor, E., Diamond, D., Yeomans, F. E., & Kernberg, O. F. (2009). The interpretive process in the psychoanalytic psychotherapy of borderline personality pathology. *Journal of the American Psychoanalytic Association, 57*: 271–301.

Chiere, M. & Fonagy, P. (2003). Psychosocial treatment for severe personality disorder: 36 month follow-up. *British Journal of Psychiatry, 183*: 356–362.

Clarkin, J. F. & Levy, K. N. (2003). A psychodynamic treatment for severe personality disorder. *Psychoanalytic Inquiry, 23*: 248–267.

Clarkin, J. F., Marziali, E., & Munroe-Blum, H. (Eds.) (1992). *Borderline Personality Disorder: Clinical and Empirical Perspectives*. New York: Guilford.

Coche, E., Dies, R. R., & Goettelmann, K. (1991). Process variables mediating change in intensive group therapy training. *International Journal Group Psychotherapy, 41*: 379–398.

Colman, A. D. & Geller, M. H. (1985). *Group Relations Reader 2*. Washington, D.C.: A. K. Rice Institute.

Colson, D. (1974). Behavior of borderline patients in groups. Interviews with therapists. (Unpublished manuscipt)

Cooke, A. L., Braazel, M., Craig, A. S., & Greig, B. (Eds.) (1999). *Reading Book for Human Relations Training, 8th ed.* Alexandria, VA: NTL Institute for Applied Behavioral Science.

Day, M. (1981). Process in classical psychodynamic groups. *International Journal of Group Psychotherapy, 31*: 153–174.

Day, M. & Semrad, E. (1971). Group therapy with neurotics and psychotics. In: H. I. Kaplan & B. J. Sadock (Eds.), *Comprehensive Group Psychotherapy* (pp. 566–580). Baltimore: Williams & Wilkins.

Dicks, H. V. (1977). *Marital Tensions*. London: Routledge and Kegan Paul.

Dies, R. R. (1992). Models of group psychotherapy: Sifting through confusion. *International Journal of Group Psychotherapy, 42*: 1–17.

Dimeff, L. A., Koerner, K., & Linehan, M. M. (2007). *Dialectical Behavior Therapy in Clinical Practice: Applications Across Disorders and Settings*. New York: Guilford.

Durkin, H. E. (1964). *The Group in Depth*. New York: International Universities.

Durkin, H. E. (1982). Change in group psychotherapy: Theory and practice: A systems perspective. *International Journal of Group Psychotherapy, 32*: 431–439.

Eagle, M. N. (2011). *From Classical to Contemporary Psychoanalysis: A Critique and Integration.* New York: Routledge.

Edelson, M. (1967). The sociotherapeutic function in a psychiatric hospital. *Journal of the Fort Logan Mental Health Center, 4:* 1–45.

Eisold, K. (1985). Recovering Bion's contribution to group analysis. *American Journal of Psychoanalysis, 45:* 327–340.

Erikson, E. H. (1975). *Childhood and Society.* New York: Norton.

Ethan, S. (1978). The question of the dilution of transference in therapy. *The Psychoanalytic Review, 65:* 569–578.

Ettin, M. F. (1992). *Foundations and Applications of Group Psychotherapy: A Sphere of Influence.* Boston: Allyn & Bacon.

Ezriel, H. (1950). A psychoanalytic approach to the treatment of patients in groups. *Journal of Mental Science, 96:* 774–779.

Ezriel, H. (1973). Psychoanalytic Group Therapy. In L. Wolberg & E. K. Schwartz (Eds.) *Group Therapy: 1973: An overview* (pp. 183–210). New York: Intercontinental Medical.

Fairbairn, W. R. D. (1952). *An Object Relations Theory of Personality.* New York: Basic Books.

Feiner, S. E. (1998). Course design: An integration of didactic and experiential approaches to graduate training of group therapy. *International Journal of Group Psychotherapy, 48:* 39–60.

Feldberg, T. M. (1958). Treatment of "borderline" psychotics in groups of neurotic patients. *International Journal of Group Psychotherapy, 8:* 76–84.

Fiedler, F. (1950). The concept of an ideal relationship. *Journal of Consulting Psychology, 14:* 436–445.

Finnell, J. S. (1985). Narcissistic problems in analysts. *International Journal of Psychoanalysis, 66:* 433–445.

Forer, B. R. (1961). Group psychotherapy with outpatient schizophrenics. *International Journal of Group Psychotherapy, 11:* 188–195.

Foulkes, S. H. & Anthony, E. J. (1973). *Group Psychotherapy: The Psychoanalytic Approach. 2nd Edition.* Baltimore: Penguin.

Foulkes, S. H. (1975). *Group-Analytic Psychotherapy: Method and Principles.* London: Gordon and Breach.

Frank, J. D. (1964). Training and therapy. In: Bradford, L. P., Gibb, J. R., & Benne, K. D. (Eds.), *T Group Theory and Laboratory Method* (pp. 442–451). New York: Wiley.

Frieswyk, S. H., Allen, J. G., Colson, D. B., Coyne, L., Gabbard, G. O., Horwitz, L., Newsom, G. (1986). Therapeutic alliance: its place as a process and outcome variable in dynamic psychotherapy research. *Journal of Consulting and Clinical Psychology, 54:* 32–38.

Freedman, M. B. & Sweet, B. S. (1954). Some specific features of group psychotherapy and their implications for selection of patients. *International Journal of Group Psychotherapy, 4:* 355–368.

Freud, S. (1921c). Group Psychology and the Analysis of the Ego. *S. E., 18*: 69–144. London: Hogarth.

Fried, E. (1975). The narcissistic cocoon: How it curbs and can be curbed. Unpublished manuscript.

Friedman, L. (1978). Trends in psychoanalytic theory of treatment. *Psychoanalytic Quarterly, 47*: 524–567.

Gabbard, G. O. (1989). Two subtypes of narcissistic personality disorder. *Bulletin of the Menninger Clinic, 53*: 527–532.

Gans, J. & Alonso, A. (1998). Difficult patients: their construction in group therapy. *International Journal of Group Psychotherapy, 48*: 311–326.

Gans, J. S., Rutan, J. S., & Wilcox, N. (1995). T-groups (training groups) in psychiatric residency programs: facts and possible implications. *International Journal of Group Psychotherapy, 5*: 169–183.

Ganzarain, R. (1958). Group Psychotherapy in the Psychiatric Training of Medical Students. *International Journal of Group Psychotherapy, 8*: 137–153.

Ganzarain, R. (1960). "Psychotic" anxieties in group analytic psychotherapy. *International Mental Health Research News, 2*: 15.

Ganzarain, R. (1977). General systems and object relations theories: their usefulness in group psychotherapy. *International Journal of Group Psychotherapy, 27*: 441–456.

Ganzarain, R. (1989). Object *Relations Group Psychotherapy: The Group as an Object, a Tool, and a Training Base.* Madison, CT: International Universities Press.

Ganzarain, R. (1992). Effect of projective identification on therapists and groupmates. *Group Analysis, 25*: 15–18.

Ganzarain, R. (1995). Psychology and psychotherapy groups. In: B. Morse & B. Fine (Eds.), *Psychoanalysis and Major Concepts* (pp. 61–78). New Haven: Yale University Press.

Ganzarain, R. (2008). Introduction to object relations group psychotherapy. In: G. M. Saiger, G. M., Rubenfeld, S., & M. D. Dluhy (Eds.), *Windows into Today's Group Therapy* (pp. 97–111). New York: Routledge.

Garland, C. (Ed.) (2010). *The Groups Book.* London: Karnac.

Glatzer, H. T. (1969). Working through in group psychotherapy. *International Journal of Group Psychotherapy, 19*: 292–306.

Glatzer, H. T. (1972). Treatment of oral character neurosis in group psychotherapy. In: C. J. Sager & H. S. Kaplan (Eds.), *Progress in group and family therapy* (pp. 54–65). New York: Brunner/Mazel.

Glatzer, H. T. (1978). The working alliance in analytic group psychotherapy. *International Journal of Group Psychothherapy, 28*: 147–161.

Glatzer, H. T. (1978). Working alliance in analytic group psychotherapy. *International Journal of Group Psychotherapy, 28*: 147–161.

Goldstein, W. (1991). Clarification of projective identification. *American Journal Psychiatry, 148*: 153–161.

Golembiewski, R. T. (1999). Perspectives on the T-group and laboratory training. In: A. L. Cooke, M. Braazel, A. S. Craig, & B. Greig (Eds.), *Reading Book for Human Relations Training, 8th edition*. Alexandria, VA: NTL Institute.

Greenbaum, H. (1957). Combined Psychoanalytic Therapy with Negative Therapeutic Reactions. In: A. H. Rifkin (Ed.), *Schizophrenia in Psychoanalytic Office and Practice* (pp. 56–65). New York: Grune & Stratton.

Greene, L. R., Rosenkrantz, J., & Muth, D. Y. (1985). Splitting dynamics, self-representations and boundary phenomena in the group psychotherapy of borderline personality disorders. *Psychiatry, 48*: 234–245.

Grinberg, L. (1973). Projective identification and projective counter-identification in the dynamics of groups. In: L. Wolberg & E. Schwartz (Eds.), *Group Therapy 1973* (pp. 145–153). New York: International Medical Book Corporation.

Grinberg, L. (1979). Countertransference and projective counter-identification. *Contemporary Psychoanalysis, 15*: 226–247.

Grinberg, L., Gear, M. C., & Liendo, M. C. (1976). Group dynamics according to a semiotic model based on projective identification and counter-identification. In: L. Wolberg & M. Aronson (Eds.), *Group Therapy 1976* (pp. 167–179). New York: Stratton Intercontinental Medical Book.

Grinker, R. R., Werble, B., & Drye, R. C. (1968). *The Borderline Syndrome: A Behavioral Study of Ego-Function*. New York: Basic Books.

Grobman, J. (1980). The borderline patient in group psychotherapy: A case report. *International Journal of Group Psychotherapy, 30*: 299–318.

Grossmark, R. (2007). The edge of chaos. *Psychoanalytic Dialogues, 17*: 566–580.

Grotjahn, M. (1984). The narcissistic person in analytic group therapy. *International Journal of Group Psychotherapy, 34*: 243–256.

Grunebaum, H. & Solomon, L. (1980). Towards a peer theory of group psychotherapy. *International Journal of Group Psychotherapy, 30*: 22–49.

Harwood, I. H. (1983). The application of self-psychology concepts to group psychotherapy *International Journal of Group Psychotherapy, 33*: 469–487.

Harwood, I. H. (1989). Advances in group psychotherapy and self psychology: An intersubjective approach. In: I. N. H. Harwood & M. Pines (Eds.), *Self Experience in Group: Intersubjective and Self Psychological Pathways to Human Identity* (pp. 30–46). London: Jessica Kingsley.

Harwood, I. H. (1992). Group psychotherapy and disorders of the self. *Group Analysis, 25*: 19–26.

Harwood, I. H. (1992b). Advances in group psychotherapy and self psychology. *Group, 16*: 220–232.

Harwood, I. H. (2003). Distinguishing between the facilitating and self-serving charismatic leader. *Group, 27*: 121–129.

Harwood, I. H. (2008). Toward the optimum group placement from the perspective of the self or self-experience. In G. M. Saiger, S. Rubenfeld, & M. D. Dluhy, (Eds.), *Windows into Today's Group Therapy* (pp. 221–224). New York: Routledge.

Harwood, I. H. & Pines, M. (Eds.) (1998). *Self Experiences in Group: Intersubjective and Self-Psychological Pathways to Human Understanding*. London: Kingsley.

Hinshelwood, R. D. (2008). Bion and Foulkes: The group-as-a-whole. *Group Analysis, 40*: 344–356.

Hoffman, I. Z. (1998). *Ritual and Spontaneity in the Psychoanalytic Process: A Dialectical-Constructivist View*. Hillside, N. J: Analytic Press.

Holden, M. A. (1966). Group therapy of women with severe character disorders: The middle and final phases. *International Journal of Group Psychotherapy, 16*: 174–189.

Hopper, E. (1985). The problem of context in group-analytic psychotherapy: A clinical illustration and a brief theoretical discussion. In: M. Pines (Ed.), *Bion and Group Psychotherapy* (pp. 330–353). London: Routledge.

Hopper, E. (2003). *Traumatic Experience in the Unconscious Life of Groups: The Fourth Basic Assumption: Incohesion: Aggregation/Massification or (ba) I:A/M*. London: Jessica Kingsley.

Horwitz, L. (1968). Group psychotherapy training for psychiatric residents. *Current Psychiatric Therapies, 8*: 223–232.

Horwitz, L. (1971). Group-centered interventions in therapy groups. *Comparative Group Studies, 2*: 311–331.

Horwitz, L. (1974). *Clinical Prediction in Psychotherapy*. New York: Jason Aronson.

Horwitz, L. (1976). Indications and contraindications for group psychotherapy. *Bulletin of the Menninger Clinic, 40*: 505–507.

Horwitz, L. (1977a). A Group-Centered Approach to Group Psychotherapy. *International Journal of Group Psychotherapy, 27*: 423–439.

Horwitz, L. (1977b). Group Psychotherapy of the Borderline Patient. In: P. Hartocollis, (Ed.), *Borderline Personality Disorders* (pp. 399–422). New York: International Universities Press.

Horwitz, L. (1983). Projective identification in dyads and groups. *International Journal of Group Psychotherapy, 33*: 259–279.

Horwitz, L. (1984). Group psychotherapy for borderline and narcissistic patients. In: F. Shectman & W. Smith (Eds.), *Diagnostic understanding and treatment planning: The elusive connection* (pp. 338–354). New York: Wiley.

Horwitz, L. (1985). Therapist's personality and levels of competence. Unpublished manuscript.

Horwitz, L. (1986). An integrated, group-centered approach. In: I. L. Kutash & A. Wolf (Eds.), *Psychotherapist's casebook: Theory and technique in practice* (pp. 353–363). San Francisco: Jossey-Bass.

Horwitz, L. (1992). A group centered approach to group psychotherapy. In R. K. Mackenzie (Ed.). *Classics in Group Psychotherapy* (pp. 317–328). New York: Guilford.

Horwitz, L. (1994). Depth of transference in groups. *International Journal of Group Psychotherapy, 44*: 271–290.

Horwitz, L., Gabbard, G. O., Allen, J. G., Frieswyk, S. F., Colson, D. C., Newsom, G. E., & Coyne, L. (1996). Borderline *Personality Disorder: Tailoring the Therapy to the Patient.* Washington, D.C.: American Psychiatric Press.

Hulse W. C. (1958). Psychotherapy with ambulatory schizophrenic patients in mixed analytic groups. *Archives of Neurology & Psychiatry, 79*: 681–687.

Hulse, W. C. (1956). Private practice. In: S. R. Simon (Ed.), *The Fields of Group Psychotherapy* (pp. 260–272). New York: International Universities Press.

Hutten, J. M. (1996). The use of experiential groups in the training of counselors and psychotherapists. *Psychodynamic Counseling, 2*: 247–256.

Karterud, S. W. (1990). Bion or Kohut: Two paradigms of group dynamics. In: B. Roth, W. Stone, & H. Kibel (Eds.), *The Difficult Patient in Group: Group Psychotherapy with Borderline and Narcissistic Disorders* (pp. 45–65). AGPA Monograph Series, Madison, CT: International Universities Press.

Karterud, S. & Stone, W. N. (2003). The group self: A neglected aspect of group psychotherapy. *Group Analysis, 36*: 7–22.

Kauff, P. F. (1979). Diversity in analytic group psychotherapy. *International Journal of Group Psychotherapy, 29*: 51–65.

Kauff, P. F. (1991). The unique contribution of analytic group therapy to the treatment of preoedipal character pathology. In: S. Tuttman, *Psychoanalytic Group Theory and Therapy* (pp. 175–190). Madison, CT: International Universities Press.

Kauff, P. F. (1993). The contribution of analytic group therapy to the psychoanalytic process. In A. Alonso & H. I. Swiller (Eds.), *Group Therapy in Clinical Practice* (pp. 3–28). Washington, D.C.: American Psychiatric Press.

Kennard, D., Roberts, J., & Winter, D. A. (2000). *A Workbook of Group-Analytic Interventions.* London: Jessica Kingsley.

Kernberg, O. F. (1967). Borderline personality organization. *Journal of the American Psychoanalytic Association, 15*: 641–685.

Kernberg, O. F. (1975). *Borderline Conditions and Pathological Narcissism*. New York: Aronson.

Kernberg, O. F. (1980). Regression in groups: Some clinical findings and theoretic implications. *Journal of A. K. Rice Institute, 2*: 51–75.

Kernberg, O. F. (1982). Self, ego, affects and drive. *Journal of the American Psychoanalytic Association, 30*: 893–918.

Kernberg, O. F. (1984). *Severe Personality Disorders*. New Haven: Yale University Press.

Kernberg, O. F. (1989). The narcissistic personality disorder and the differential diagnosis of antisocial behavior. In: O. F. Kernberg, (Ed.), *The Psychiatric Clinics of North America* (pp. 553–557). Philadelphia: Saunders.

Kernberg, O. F. (2004). *Contemporary Controversies in Psychoanalytic Theory, Technique, and their Application*. New Haven: Yale University Press.

Kernberg, O. F. (2006). Identity: Recent findings and clinical implications. *Psychoanalytic Quarterly, 75*: 969–1003.

Kernberg, O. F., Yeomans, F. E., Clarkin, J. F., & Levy, K. N. (2008). Transference focused psychotherapy: Overview and update. *International Journal Psychoanalysis, 89*: 601–620.

Kibel, H. D. (1978). The rationale for the use of group psychotherapy for borderline patients on a short-term unit. *International Journal of Group Psychotherapy, 28*: 339–358.

Kibel, H. D. (1987). Contributions of the group therapist to education on the psychiatric unit: Teaching through group dynamics. Presidential Address. *International Journal of Group Psychotherapy, 37*: 3–29.

Kibel, H. D. (1991). The therapeutic use of splitting: The role of the mother-group in therapeutic differentiation and practicing. In: S. Tuttman (Ed.), *Psychoanalytic Group Theory and Therapy* (pp. 113–132). New York: International Universities Press.

Kibel, H. D. (1992). Clinical application of object relations theory. In R. H. Klein, H. S. Bernard, D. L. Singer (Eds.) *Handbook of Contemporary Group Psychotherapy: Contributions from Object Relations, Self Psychology, and Social Systems Theories* (pp. 141–176). Madison, CT: International Universities

Kibel, H. D. (2005). The evolution of group-as-a-whole and object relations theory: from projection to introjection. *Group, 29*: 139–162.

Kibel, H. D. & Stein, A. (1981). The group-as-a-whole approach: An appraisal. *International Journal of Group Psychotherapy, 31*: 409–427.

Kiesler, D. J. (1996). *Contemporary Interpersonal Theory and Research*. New York: Wiley.

Kipling, R. (1946). *Rudyard Kipling's Verse*. New York: Doubleday.

Klein, G. S. (1973). Two theories or one? *Bulletin of the Menninger Clinic, 37*: 102–132.

Klein, M. (1946). Notes on some schizoid mechanisms. *International Journal of Psycho-Analysis*, 27: 99–110.

Klein, M. (1952). Some theoretical conclusions regarding the emotional life of the infant. In: J. Riviere (Ed.), *Developments in psycho-analysis* (pp. 198–236). London: Hogarth Press.

Kohut, H. (1977). *The Restoration of the Self*. New York: International Universities Press.

Kohut, H. (1984). *How Does Psychoanalysis Cure?* Chicago: University of Chicago.

Konig, K. (1991). Group-analytic interpretations: individual and group, descriptive and metaphoric. *Group Analysis*, 24: 111–115.

Kosseff, J. (1975). The leader using object-relations theory. In: Z. A. Liff (Ed.), *The Leader in the Group* (pp. 212–242). New York: Aronson.

Kosseff, J. (1980). The unanchored self: clinical vignettes of change in narcissistic and borderline patients in groups. *International Journal of Group Psychotherapy*, 30: 387–388.

Lenzenweger, M. F. (2010). Current status of the personality disorders: An overview of epidemiological, longitudinal, experimental psychopathology, & neurobehavioral perspectives. *Journal of the American Psychoanalytic Association*, 58: 741–778.

Leszcz, M. (1989). Group psychotherapy of the characterologically difficult patient. International Journal Group Psychotherapy, 39: 147–171.

Leszcz, M. (1992). The interpersonal approach to group psychotherapy. *International Journal of Group Psychotherapy*, 42: 37–62.

Leszcz, M. (2008). The interpersonal approach to group psychotherapy. In: G. M. Saiger, S. Rosenfeld, & M. D. Dluhy (Eds.), *Windows into Today's Group Therapy* (pp. 129–149). New York: Routledge.

Lichtenberg, J. D. (1998). Experience as a guide to psychoanalytic thory and practice. *Journal of the American Psychoanalytic Association*, 46: 16–36.

Lichtenstein, H. (1965). Towards a metapsychological definition of the concept of self. *International Journal of Psycho-Analysis*, 46: 117–128.

Lichtenstein, H. (1977). *The Dilemma of Human Identity*. New York: Aronson.

Lieberman, M. A., Yalom, I. D. & Miles, M. B. (1973). *Encounter Groups: First Facts*. New York: Basic Books.

Liff, Z. (1978). Group psychotherapy for the 1980's: Psychoanalysis of pathological boundary structuring. *Group*, 2: 184–192.

Linehan, M. M. (1987). Dialectical behavior therapy for borderline personality disorder: theory and method. *Bulletin of the Menninger Clinic*, 51: 261–276.

Livingston, M. (2005). After the storm: further thoughts on working with dyadic conflict within the group. *Group*, 29: 373–389.

Livingston, M. S. & Livingston, L. R. (2006). Sustained empathic focus and the clinical application of self-psychological theory in group psychotherapy. *International Journal of Group Psychotherapy, 56*: 67–85.

Loewald, H. W. (1960). On the therapeutic action of psycho-analysis. *International Journal of Psychoanalysis, 41*: 16–33.

Lorentzen, S., Bogwald, K. P. & Hoglund, P. (2002). Change during and after long-term analytic group therapy. *International Journal of Group Psychotherapy, 52*: 419–429.

Luborsky, L., Singer, B. & Luborsky, L. (1975). Comparative studies of psychotherapy: Is it true that "Everybody has won and all must have prizes"? *Archives of General Psychiatry, 32*: 995–1008.

Luborsky, L., Rosenthal, R., Diguer, L., Andrusyna, T. P., Berman, J. T., Seligman, D. A., & Krause, E. D. (2002). The Dodo bird verdict is alive and well—mostly. *Clinical Psychology: Science and Practice, 9*: 2–12.

Macaskill, N. D. (1980). The narcissistic core as a focus in the group therapy of the borderline patient. *British Journal of Medical Psychology, 53*: 137–143.

Macaskill, N. D. (1982). Therapeutic factors in group therapy with borderline patients. *International Journal of Group Psychotherapy, 32*: 61–73.

Malan, D. H., Balfour, F. H. G., Hood, V. G., & Shooter, M. N. (1976). Group psychotherapy: A long term follow-up study. *Archives of General Psychiatry, 33*: 1303–1315.

Malcus, L. (1995). Indirect scapegoating via projective identification and the mother group. *International Journal of Group Psychotherapy, 45*: 55–71.

Malin, A. & Grotstein, J. S. (1966). Projective identification in the therapeutic process. *International Journal of Psychoanalysis, 47*: 26–31.

Mandelbaum, A. (1977). A family centered approach to residential treatment. *Bulletin of Menninger Clinic, 41*: 27–39.

Marziali, E. & Munroe-Blum, H. (1994). *Interpersonal Group Psychotherapy for Borderline Personality Disorder*. New York: Basic Books.

Masler, E. G. (1969). The interpretation of projective identification in group psychotherapy. *International Journal of Group Psychotherapy, 19*: 441–447.

Masterson, J. (1976). *Psychotherapy of the Borderline Adult*. New York: Brunner Mazel.

Masterson, J. F. (1983). *The Emerging Self: A Developmental, Self, and Object Relations Approach to the Treatment of the Closet Narcissistic Disorder of the Self*. New York: Brunner/Mazel.

Masterson, J. F. & Rinsley, D. B. (1975). The borderline syndrome: The role of the mother in the genesis and structure of the borderline personality. *International Journal of Psycho-Analysis, 56*: 163–177.

McCallum, M. & Piper, W. E. (1999). Personality disorders and response to group oriented evening treatment. *Group Dynamics: Theory, Research, and Practice, 3*: 3–14.

McCarley, T. (1975). The Psychotherapist's Search for Self-Renewal. *American Journal of Psychiatry, 132*: 221–224.

Meissner, W. W. (1980). A note on projective identification. *Journal of the American Psychoanalytic Association, 28*: 43–68.

Meissner, W. W. (1984). *The Borderline Spectrum: Differential Diagnosis and Developmental Issues.* New York: Aronson.

Menninger, R. W. (1972). The impact of group relations conferences on organizational growth. *International Journal of Group Psychotherapy, 22*: 415–432.

Menninger, R. W. (1985). A retrospective view of a hospital-wide group relations training program: costs, consequences, and conclusions. In A. D. Colman & Geller, M. H. (Eds.) *Group Relations Reader 2* (pp. 285–298). Washington, D.C: A. K. Rice Institute.

Miller, A. (1979). The drama of the gifted child and the psychoanalyst's narcissistic disturbance. *International Journal of Psycho-analysis, 60*: 47–58.

Modell, A. H. (1971). The origin of certain forms of pre-oedipal guilt and the implications for a psychoanalytic theory of affects. *International Journal of Psycho-analysis, 52*: 337–346.

Modell, A. H. (1978). The conceptualization of the therapeutic action of psychoanalysis: The action of the holding environment. *Bulletin of the Menninger Clinic, 42*: 493–504.

Morrison, A. P. (1986). On projective identification in couples' groups. *International Journal of Group Psychotherapy, 36*: 55–73.

Munich, R. L. (1993). Varieties of learning in an experiential group. *International Journal of Group Psychotherapy, 3*: 345–361.

Murphy, L., Leszcz, M., Collings, A. K. & Salvendy, J. T. (1996). Some observations on the subjective experience of the neophyte group psychotherapy trainees. *International Journal Group Psychotherapy, 46*: 543–552.

Nathan, V. & Poulsen, S. (2004). Group-analytic training groups for psychology students: A qualitative study. *Group Analysis, 37*: 163–177.

Nemiah, J. C. (1978). Alexithymia and psychosomatic illness. *Journal of Continuing Education in Psychiatry, 39*: 25–37.

Nitsun, M. (1996). The *Anti-Group: Destructive Forces in Group and their Creative Potential.* London: Routledge.

Nitsun, M. (2005). Destructive forces in group therapy. In: L. Motherwell & J. J. Shay (Eds.), *Complex Dilemmas in Group Therapy: Pathways to Resolution.* New York: Brunner-Routledge.

Ogden, T. H. (1979). On projective identification. *International Journal of Psycho-Analysis, 60*: 357–373.

Ogden, T. H. (1994). The analytic third: working with intersubjective clinical facts. *International Journal Psychoanalysis, 75*: 3–19.

O'Leary, J. D. & Wright, F. (2005). Social constructivism and the group-as-a-whole. *Group, 29*: 257–276.

Papparo, F. & Nebbiose, G. (1988). How does group psychotherapy cure? A reconceptualization of the group process: From self-psychology to the intersubjective process. In: I. N. H. Harwood & M. Pines (Eds.), *Self Perspectives in Group. Intersubjective and Self Psychological Pathways to Human Understanding* (pp. 70–82). London: Karnac.

Parloff, M. B. (1968). Analytic group psychotherapy. In: J. Marmor, (Ed.), *Modern Psychoanalysis* (pp. 492–531). New York: Basic Books.

Pines, M. (1978). Group analytic psychotherapy of the borderline patient. *Group Analysis, 11*: 115–126.

Pines, M. (1982). Reflections on mirroring. *Group Analysis, 15*: 2–26.

Pines, M. (1990). Group analytic psychotherapy with the borderline patient. In: B. E. Roth, W. N. Stone & H. D. Kibel (Eds.), *The Difficult Patient in Group*. Madison, CT: International Universities Press.

Pines, M. (1993). Group analysis. In: A. Alonso & H. I. Swiller (Eds.) *Group Therapy in Clinical Practice* (pp. 29–47). Washington, D.C.: American Psychiatric Press.

Pines, M. (2008). The group-as-a-whole approach in Foulkesian group analytic psychotherapy. In: G. M. Saiger, S. Rubenfeld, & M. D. Dluhy. *Windows into Today's Group Therapy* (pp. 73–84). New York: Routledge.

Pines, M. & Schlapobersky, J. (2010). Gruppenanlyse und analytische Gruppenpsychotherapie. In V. Tschuschke (Ed.) Gruppenpsychotherapie: Von der Indication bis zu Leitungstechniken (pp. 264–268). Stuttgart & New York: Thieme.

Piper, W. E. (1994). Client variables. In: A. Fuhriman, & G. M. Burlinghame (Eds.), *Handbook of Group Psychotherapy: An Empirical and Clinical Synthesis* (pp. 83–113). New York: Wiley.

Piper, W. E. & Rosie, J. (1998). Group treatment of personality disorders: the power of the group in the intensive treatment of personality disorders. *Session: Psychotherapy in Practice, 4*: 19–34.

Post, J. M. (1993). Current concepts of the narcissistic personality: Implications for political psychology. *Political Psychology, 14*: 99–121.

Pyrke, M. (1961). Group therapy of women with severe dependency problems. *American Journal of Orthopsychiatry, 31*: 776–785.

Racker, H. (1968). *Transference and Countertransference*. New York: International Universities Press.

Rangell, L. (1982). The Self in psychoanalytic theory. *Journal of the American Psychoanalytic Association, 30*: 863–892.

Redl, F. (1949). The phenomenon of contagion and "shock effect" in group therapy. In: K. R. Eissler (Ed.), *Searchlights on Delinquency* (pp. 315–328). New York: International Universities Press.

Redl, F. (1963). Psychoanalysis and Group Therapy: A Developmental Point of View. *American Journal of Orthopsychiary, 35*: 135–147.

Renik, O. (2006). *Practical Psychoanalysis for Therapists and Patients.* New York: Other Press.

Richards, A. (1982). The superordinate self in psychoanalytic theory and in the self psychologies. *Journal of the American Psychoanalytic Association, 30*: 939–957.

Rinsley, D. B. (1962). A contribution to the theory of ego and self. *Psychiatric Quarterly, 36*: 96–120.

Rioch, M. J. (1970). Group Relations: Rationale and Technique. *International Journal of Group Psychotherapy, 20*: 340–355.

Rockland, L. H. (1992). *Supportive Therapy for Borderline Patients: A Psychodynamic Approach.* New York: Guilford.

Rosenfeld, H. (1963). Notes on the psychopathology and psychoanalytic treatment of schizophrenia. In: *H. Rosenfeld (1965), Psychotic States: A Psychoanalytic Approach* (pp. 155–168). New York: International Universities Press.

Rosenfeld, H. (1975). Notes on the psychopathology and psychoanalytic treatment of some borderline patients. *International Journal of Psychoanalysis, 59*: 215–221.

Rosenfeld, H. (1987). *Impasse and Interpretation: Therapeutic and Anti-Therapeutic Factors in the Psychoanalytic Treatment of Psychotic, Borderline, and Neurotic Patients.* London: Tavistock.

Roth, B. E. (1980). Understanding the development of a homogeneous, identity-impaired group through countertransference phenomena. *International Journal of Group Psychotherapy, 30*: 405–426.

Roth, B. E. (1982). Six types of borderline and narcissistic patients: An initial typology. *International Journal of Group Psychotherapy, 32*: 9–27.

Roth, B. E. (1990). Countertransference and the group therapist's state of mind. In: B. E. Roth, W. Stone, & H. D. Kibel (Eds.), *The Difficult Patient in Group (pp. 287–294).* New York: International Universities Press.

Rutan, J. S. (2000). Growth through shame and humiliation. *International Journal Group Psychotherapy, 50*: 511–516.

Rutan, J. S. (2005). Treating difficult patients in group. In: L. Motherwell & J. J. Shay (Eds.), *Complex Dilemmas in Group Therapy: Pathways to Resolution* (pp. 41–50). New York: Brunner-Routledge.

Rutan, J. S. & Alonso, A. (1982). Group therapy, individual, or both? *International Journal of Group Psychotherapy, 32*: 267–282.

Rutan, J. S., Stone, W. N., & Shay, J. J. (2007). *Psychodynamic Group Psychotherapy, 4th edition*. New York: Guilford Press.

Sadock, B. J. (1968). Integrated Group Psychotherapy Training and Psychiatric Residency. *Archives of General Psychiatry, 18*: 276–279.

Saiger, G. M., Rubenfeld, S., & Dluhy, M. D. (Eds.) (2006). *Windows into Today's Group Therapy*. New York: Routledge.

Saperstein, J. & Gaines, J. (1973). Metapsychological considerations on the Self. *International Journal of Psycho-Analysis, 54*: 415–424.

Saretsky, T. (1980). The analyst's narcissistic vulnerability. *Contemporary Psychoanalysis, 16*: 82–89.

Schafer, R. (1976). *A New Language for Psychoanalysis*. New Haven: Yale University Press.

Scharff, J. S. (1992). *Projective and Introjective Identification and the Use of the Therapeutic Self*. Nothvale, N. J: Aronson.

Scheidlinger, S. (1964). Identification, the sense of belonging, and identity in small groups. *International Journal of Group Psychotherapy, 14*: 291–306.

Scheidlinger, S. (1968). The concept of regression in group psychotherapy. *International Journal of Group Psychotherapy, 18*: 3–20.

Scheidlinger, S. (1974). On the concept of the "mother-group." *International Journal of Group Psychotherapy, 24*: 417–428.

Scheidlinger, S. (1980). Identification, the sense of belonging, and of identity in small groups. In: S. Scheidlinger, *Psychoanalytic Group Dynamics* (pp. 213–231). New York: International Universities Press.

Scheidlinger, S. (1982a). On scapegoating in group psychotherapy. *International Journal of Group Psychotherapy, 32*: 131–143.

Scheidlinger, S. (1982b). Group process in group psychotherapy: trends in the integration of individual and group psychotherapy. In: S. Scheidlinger (Ed.), *Focus on Group Psychotherapy: Clinical Essays* (pp. 25–60). New York: International Universities Press.

Scheidlinger, S. (1994). Individual and group psychology—are they opposed? *Group 8*: 3–11.

Scheidlinger, S. (2004). Group psychotherapy and related helping groups today: an overview. *American Journal of Psychotherapy, 58*: 265–280.

Scheidlinger, S. & Holden, M. A. (1966). Group therapy of women with severe character disorders: The middle and final phases. *International Journal of Group Psychotherapy, 16*: 174–189.

Scheidlinger, S. & Pyrke, M. (1961). Problems in group therapy of women with severe dependency. *American Journal of Orthopsychiatry, 31*: 776–785.

Schermer, V. L. (1994). Between theory and practice, light and heat. In: V. L. Schermer & M. Pines (Eds.), *Ring of Fire*. New York: Routledge.

Schermer, V. L. (2005). An orientation to volume two of the special edition: the group-as-a-whole: An update. *Group*, *29*: 213–237.

Schlapobersky, J. (2000). The language of the group: Monologue, dialogue, and discourse in group analysis. In: D. Brown and L. Zinkin (Eds.), *The Psyche and the Social World*. (pp. 211–231). London: Jessica Kingsley.

Schlapobersky, J. & Pines, M. (2009). Group methods in adult psychiatry. In: M. Gelder, (Ed.) *New Oxford Textbook of Psychiatry*, (pp. 1350–1369). Oxford: Oxford University Press.

Schwartz, E. K. & Wolf, A. (1961). Psychoanalysis in groups. *Journal of General Psychology*, *64*: 153–191.

Searles, H. (1963). Transference psychosis in the psychotherapy of chronic schizophrenia. *International Journal of Psychoanalysis*, *44*: 249–281.

Segal, H. (1973). *Introduction to the Work of Melanie Klein*. New York: Basic Books.

Segalla, R. A. (1998). Motivational systems and group object theory. In I. H. Harwood & M. Pines (Eds.), *Self Experiences in Group: Intersubjective and Self-Psychological Pathways to Human Understanding* (pp. 141–153). London: Kingsley.

Segalla, R. A. (2008). Beyond the dyad. In: G. M. Saiger, S. Rosenfeld, & M. D. Dluhy (Eds.), *Windows into Today's Group Therapy* (pp. 203–219). New York: Routledge.

Semrad, E. V. & Arsenian, J. (1951). The use of group processes in teaching group dynamics. *American Journal of Psychiatry*, *108*: 358–363.

Shaskan, D. A. (1957). Treatment of a borderline case with group analytically oriented psychotherapy. *Journal of Forensic Science*, *2*: 195–201.

Shaskan, D. A. (1971). Management and group psychotherapy of borderline patients. Presented to Fifth World Congress of Psychiatry, Mexico City.

Shields, W. (2000). Hope and the inclination to be troublesome: Winnicott and the treatment of character disorders in group therapy. *International Journal Group Psychotherapy*, *50*: 87–103.

Slavinska-Holy, N. (1982). Theory and practice in group psychotherapy with borderline and narcissistic psychopathologies. In M. Pines & L. Rafaelsen (Eds.), *The individual and the group: Boundaries and interrelations: V. 2: Practice* (pp. 221–223). New York: Plenum.

Slavson, S. R. (1957). "Are there 'group dynamics' in therapy groups?" *International Journal of Group Psychotherapy*, *7*: 131–154.

Slavson, S. R. (1961). Group psychotherapy and the nature of schizophrenia. *International Journal of Group Psychotherapy*, *11*: 3–32.

Slavson, S. R. (1964). *A Textbook in Analytic Group Psychotherapy*. New York: International Universities Press.

Spanjaard, J. (1959). Transference neurosis and psychoanalytic group psychotherapy. *International Journal of Group Psychotherapy, 9*: 31–42.

Spotnitz, H. (1957). The borderline schizophrenic in group psychotherapy. *International Journal of Group Psychotherapy, 7*: 155–174.

Stein, A. (1963). Indications for group psychotherapy and the selection of patients. *Journal of the Hillside Hospital, 12*: 145–155.

Stein, A. (1964). The nature of transference in combined therapy. *International Journal of Group Psychotherapy, 4*: 413–423.

Stone, W. N. (1985). Discussion. In: B. E. Roth (Chair). The severely disturbed patient: Perspectives from object relations theories and self psychology. Symposium conducted at the annual meeting of the American Group Psychotherapy Association, New York City.

Stone, W. N. (1990). On affects in group psychotherapy. In: B. P. Roth, W. N. Stone, & H. D. Kibel (Eds.), *The Difficult Patient in Group Psychotherapy* (pp. 191–214). New York: International Universities Press.

Stone, W. N. (2005). The group-as-a-whole: a self psychological perspective. *Group, 29*: 239–255.

Stone, W. N. (2009). *Contributions of Self-Psychology to Group Psychotherapy: Selected Papers*. London: Karnac.

Stone, W. N. & Gustafson, J. P. (1982). Technique in group psychotherapy of narcissistic and borderline patients. *International Journal of Group Psychotherapy, 32*: 29–47.

Stone, W. N. & Whitman, R. M. (1977). Contributions of the psychology of the self to group process and group therapy. *International Journal of Group Psychotherapy, 27*: 343–359.

Sutherland, J. D. (1952). Notes on Psychoanalytic Group Therapy. I. Therapy and Training. *Psychiatry, 15*: 111–117.

Sutherland, J. D. (1980). The British object relations theorists: a prolegomena to the metapsychology of the self. *Journal of the American Psychoanalytic Association, 28*: 829–860.

Sutherland, J. D. (1982). Bion Revisited: Group Dynamics and Group Psychotherapy. In: M. Pines (Ed.), *Bion and Group Psychotherapy* (pp. 47–86). London: Tavisock/Routledge.

Swiller, H., Lang, E. A., Halperin, D. A. (1993). Process groups for training psychiatric residents. In: A. Alonso & H. I. Swiller (Eds.), *Group Therapy in Clinical Practice* (pp. 533–546). Washington, D.C.: American Psychiatric Press.

Ticho, E. A. (1972). The effects of the psychoanalyst's personality on psychoanalytic treatment. In: J. A. Lindon (Ed.), *Psychoanalytic Forum, 4*: 135–172.

Ticho, E. A. (1982). The alternate schools of the self. *Journal of the American Psychoanalytic. Association, 30*: 849–862.

Trist, E. (1985). Working with Bion in the 1940s: The group decade. In: M. Pines (Ed.), *Bion and Group Psychotherapy* (pp. 1–46). London: Routledge & Keegan Paul.

Tschuschke, V. & Greene, L. (2002). Group therapists' training: what predicts change? *International Journal Group Psychotherapy, 52*: 463–482.

Tuttman, S. (1990). Principles of psychoanalytic group psychotherapy applied to the treatment of borderline and narcissistic disorders. In: B. E. Roth, W. N. Stone, & H. D. Kibel (Eds.), *The Difficult Patient in Group* (pp. 7–29). Madison, CT: International Universities Press.

Van Schoor, E. P. (2000). A sociohistorical view of group psychotherapy in the United States. *International Journal of Group Psychotherapy, 50*: 437–454.

Volkan, V. (1980). Narcissistic personality organization and reparative leadership. *International Journal of Group Psychotherapy, 30*: 131–152.

Wachtel, P. (2008). *Relational Theory and the Practice of Psychotherapy.* New York: Guilford Press.

Wallerstein, R. S. (1986). *Forty Two Lives in Treatment.* New York: Guilford.

Weber, R. (2005). Unravelling projective identification and enactment. In: L. Motherwell & J. J. Shay (Eds.), *Complex Dilemmas in Group Therapy: Pathways to Resolution* (pp. 75–86). New York: Brunner-Routledge.

Weiss, J. (1993). *How Psychotherapy Works: Process and Technique.* New York: Guilford.

Welt, S. R. & Herron, W. G. (1990). *Narcissism and the Psychotherapist.* New York: Guilford.

Whitaker, D. (1987). Some connections between a group analytic and a group focal conflict perspective. *International Journal of Group Psychotherapy, 37*: 201–218.

Whitaker, D. (1989). Group focal conflict theory: description, illustration, evaluation. *Group, 13*: 225–251.

Whitaker, D. S. & Lieberman, M. A. (1964). *Psychotherapy through the Group Process.* New York: Atherton.

Whitman, R. & Stock, D. (1958). The group focal conflict. *Psychiatry, 21*: 269–276.

Wilberg, T. et al. (2003). Outpatient group psychotherapy following day treatment for patients with personality disorders. *Journal of Personality Disorders, 17*: 510–521.

Winnicott, D. W. (1965). Ego distortion in terms of true and false self. In: D. W. Winnicott, *The Maturational Processes and the Facilitating Environment* (pp. 140–152). London: Hogarth.

Wolf, A. & Schwartz, E. K. (1962). *Psychoanalysis in Groups*. New York: Grune & Stratton.

Wolman, B. B. (1960). Group psychotherapy with latent schizophrenics. *International Journal of. Group Psychotherapy, 10*: 301–312.

Wong, N. (1979). Clinical considerations in the group treatment of narcissistic disorders. *International Journal of Group Psychotherapy, 29*: 325–345.

Wong, N. (1980). Combined group and individual treatment of borderline and narcissistic patients: Heterogeneous versus homogeneous groups. *International Journal of Group Psychotherapy, 30*: 399–404.

Yalom, I. & Leszcz, M. (2005). *The Theory and Practice of Group Psychotherapy*, 4th Edition. New York: Basic Books.

Zender, J. F. (1991). Projective identification in group psychotherapy. *Group Analysis, 24*: 117–132.

Zetzel, E. R. (1971). A developmental approach to the borderline patient. *American Journal of Psychiatry, 127*: 867–871.

Zinner, J. & Shapiro, R. (1972). Projective identification as a mode of perception and behavior in families of adolescents. *International Journal of Psychoanalysis, 53*: 523–530.

INDEX